Facets of Corporate Identity, Communication and Reputation

Corporate branding and communication is big business. Companies throughout the world invest millions in strategies which aim to reinvent their profile in subtle yet important ways. The investment must be working, but what is it being spent on, and how do these rebranding exercises work?

Including contributions from academics and practitioners, this important collection unravels the complexities of this growing field of study. The text is split into three coherent parts, focusing in turn on identity, communication, and reputation. Case studies are used throughout the book to illustrate important issues, such as the basic principles of visual communication, the importance of reaching both internal and external stakeholders, and the challenges faced by companies working in multi-cultural environments.

This book brings clarity and new theoretical insights to an important aspect of modern business. It is an invaluable companion for all students, researchers, and practitioners with an interest in marketing, communications, and international business.

Professor T. C. Melewar is Professor of Marketing and Strategy at Brunel Business School, Brunel University, London. He teaches on a range of undergraduate, MBA, and executive courses with companies such as Nestlé, Safeway, Corus, and Sony, and is a Visiting Professor at Groupe ECS Grenoble, France, and Humboldt University, Berlin, Germany.

He is also the Joint Editor-in-Chief for the *Journal of Brand Management*, and on the Editorial Advisory Board for the *Journal of Marketing Communications, Corporate Reputation Review*, the *Journal of International Consumer Marketing, Corporate Communications: An International Journal*, and the *Journal of Euro-Marketing*.

Facets of Corporate Identity, Communication and Reputation

Edited by

T. C. Melewar

Routledge
Taylor & Francis Group

LONDON AND NEW YORK

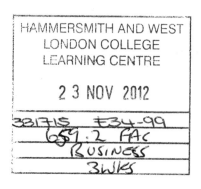
First published 2008 by Routledge
2 Park Square, Milton Park, Abingdon, Oxon OX14 4RN

Simultaneously published in the USA and Canada
by Routledge
270 Madison Ave, New York, NY 10016

Routledge is an imprint of the Taylor & Francis Group, an informa business

Typeset in Perpetua by
RefineCatch Limited, Bungay, Suffolk
Printed and bound in Great Britain by
Antony Rowe Ltd, Chippenham, Wiltshire

British Library Cataloguing in Publication Data
Facets of corporate identity, communication, and reputation / edited by T. C. Melewar.
    p. cm.
    ISBN 978–0–415–40527–0 (hardback)—ISBN 978–0–415–40528–7 (pbk)
    1. Corporate identity.   2, Corporate image.   3. Communication in marketing.
4. Industrial publicity.   5. Corporations—Public relations.   I. Melewar, T. C.   II. Title.
    HD59.2.F33 2007
    659.2—dc22

                                                                    2007032018

Library of Congress Cataloging in Publication Data
A catalog record for this book has been requested

ISBN13: 978–0–415–40527–0 (hbk)
ISBN13: 978–0–415–40528–7 (pbk)
ISBN13: 978–0–203–93194–3 (ebk)

Contents

CONTENTS

Illustrations

FIGURES

TABLES

Contributors

Sue Westcott Alessandri (Ph.D., University of North Carolina at Chapel Hill) is an Assistant Professor at the S. I. Newhouse School of Public Communications at Syracuse University. She holds a joint appointment with the advertising and public relations departments. Dr. Alessandri's research has been published in a variety of books and journals.

John M.T. Balmer (BA, MBA (Dunelm), Ph.D.) is Professor of Corporate Marketing at Brunel University, London. Previously, he was Professor of Corporate Identity at Bradford University School of Management and then Professor of Corporate Brand/Identity Management at the same school. Earlier on he was Director of the International Centre for Corporate Identity Studies at Strathclyde Business School, Glasgow. His work has appeared in the *California Management Review*, *European Journal of Marketing*, *Long Range Planning*, and the *British Journal of Management*, among others. He is the founder/chairman of the International Corporate Identity Group (ICIG) which regularly holds conferences on identity as well as co-founder of the International Centre for Corporate and Organisational Marketing Studies.

Guido Berens is Assistant Professor of Corporate Communication at the department of Business-Society Management at RSM Erasmus University, Rotterdam, the Netherlands. His research interests include corporate branding, corporate social responsibility, and reputation management

Albert Caruana is Professor of Marketing at the University of Malta. His research interests include marketing communications and services marketing. He was Fulbright Scholar at San Diego State University, in the U.S.A., in 2004. He sits on the editorial board of several journals and has published in numerous refereed journals.

Rosa Chun is Professor of Business and Ethics and Corporate Social Responsibility at Manchester Business School, England. Her work on testing the link between corporate reputation, stakeholder satisfaction, and performance; aligning image and identity; and virtue ethics, appears in over thirty publications including the *Journal of Academy of Marketing Science (JAMS)*, *Harvard Business Review*, and a co-authored book, *Corporate Reputation and Competitiveness*. She serves on the editorial boards of *Corporate Reputation Review* and *Creativity and Innovation Management*.

Joep P. Cornelissen is Professor in Corporate Communication at Leeds University Business School, University of Leeds. He is the author of *Corporate Communication: Theory and Practice*.

Gary Davies is Professor of Corporate Reputation at Manchester Business School, England. He has published inter alia in the *Journal of the Academy of Marketing Science*, *Journal of International Business Studies*, *Journal of Advertising Research*, and *Industrial Marketing Management*. His books include *What Price Reputation?*, a study of how companies manage their corporate reputations and *Corporate Reputation and Competitiveness*, the latter covering much of the work of the Corporate Reputation Group at MBS.

Sally Dibb is Professor of Marketing at the Open University Business School, UK. She graduated in Management Science and has a research master's from the University of Manchester and a Ph.D. in marketing from Warwick University. She has published widely in U.S. and European marketing journals on the marketing of services, marketing planning, market segmentation, and corporate identity, as well as textbooks and practitioner-oriented workbooks on these themes.

Grahame Dowling is a Professor in the Australian School of Business at the University of New South Wales and the Australian representative of the U.S. and European think tank, the Reputation Institute. He has published over fifty academic papers and two books: *Creating Corporate Reputations* and *The Art & Science of Marketing*.

Ali M. Kanso (Ph.D., Ohio University) is a Professor in the Department of Communication at the University of Texas at San Antonio. Kanso's research focuses on international advertising, marketing, and public relations strategies. His work has appeared in the *Journal of Advertising Research*, *International Journal of Advertising*, *International Marketing Review*, *Journal of Marketing Communication*, *Journal of Promotion Management*, and elsewhere.

Philip J. Kitchen (Ph.D.) is Professor of Strategic Marketing at Hull University Business School, Hull, UK. He is editor of the *Journal of Marketing Communications*. He has published 11 books and over 100 articles in leading journals around the world. He was listed in "The Top 50 Gurus who have influenced the Future of Marketing," *Marketing Business*, December 2003, pp. 12–16. He is a Fellow of CIM, the RSA, and Member of the Institute of Directors. A recent report for the CIPR, UK, was *A Marketing Communications Scenario for 2010*. Recent co-authored books which relate to the topic of public relations and marketing are: *Raising the Corporate Umbrella: Corporate Communications in the 21st Century* and *Integrated Marketing Communications: A Primer*.

T. C. Melewar is Professor of Marketing and Strategy at Brunel University London. He has previous experience at Warwick Business School, University of Warwick, MARA Institute of Technology in Malaysia, Loughborough University, UK, and De Montfort University, UK. T. C. teaches Marketing Management, Marketing Communications, and International Marketing on a range of undergraduate, MBA, and executive courses with companies such as Nestlé, Safeway, Corus, and Sony. He is a Visiting Professor at Groupe ECS Grenoble, France, and Humboldt University, Berlin, Germany. His research interests are global corporate identity, corporate branding, corporate reputation, marketing communications, and international marketing strategy.

Richard Alan Nelson (Ph.D., Florida State University) is a Professor in the Manship School of Mass Communication at Louisiana State University and editor of the *Journal of Promotion Management* and *Journal of Website Promotion*. His public relations and integrated marketing communications research appears in the *Journal of Advertising Research*, *International Marketing Review*, *Journal of Marketing*, *Journal of Marketing Communications*, *Public Relations Review*, and other leading journals.

Cláudia Simões is an Assistant Professor in the Department of Management at the University of Minho, Portugal. She holds a Ph.D. in Business and Industrial Studies from Warwick Business School. Her research interests and publications are in corporate identity, image, brand, and reputation, as applied to service organizations.

Nopporn Srivoravilai is a Lecturer in Marketing and Strategic Management at the Faculty of Business Administration, Dhurakij Pundit University, Thailand. He received his doctorate in industrial and business administration from Warwick Business School, the University of Warwick, UK. His research interests include corporate reputation and identity, brand management, entrepreneurship, and the social dimension of strategic management. He also has ten years of industry experience in the banking sector and is currently a consultant to various Thai SMEs.

Tibor van Bekkum (M.Sc.) is a senior consultant for the Positioning Group (www.positioneringsgroep.org): a European brand strategy consultancy based in the Netherlands. His main focus is on positioning strategy issues for corporate brands. In 2005 he published a booklet on the development of positioning strategy: "Analyze This!"

Johan van Rekom is Assistant Professor at the Department of Marketing Management at RSM Erasmus University in Rotterdam, the Netherlands, where he received his Ph.D. His research interests include organizational identity, its effects on employee motivation, cognitive structures at the individual and at the organizational level, and brand essence.

Betteke van Ruler is full Professor of Communication and Organization at the University of Amsterdam and member of the Amsterdam School of Communications Research (ASCoR). Her research focuses on the influence of public relations on journalism and the mediatization of organizations, on the practice of communication management, and on the organization of the communication of the organization. She has published in *Public Relations Review*, *Journal of Communication Management*, *Journal of Public Relations Research*, and in many Dutch scientific and professional journals. Recent books include *Communication Management: A Communication Scientific Approach* and *Career in Communication* (both in Dutch).

Kevin James Vella has an extensive track record in international sales and marketing for several IT blue-chip brands, and is presently VP Sales and Operations for Acunetix, a global web-security vendor. Kevin graduated in Business Management with Honours from the University of Malta and read an MBA in e-business from the Grenoble Graduate School of Business (France).

Tom Watson is Deputy Dean (Education) and Reader in Communications at Bournemouth University's Media School. Before becoming a full-time academic, he was managing director of a public relations consultancy and chaired the U.K.'s Public Relations Consultants Association from 2000 to 2002.

Acknowledgements

INTRODUCTION

The facets of corporate identity, corporate communications, and reputation management have become increasingly important in theory and practice.

In theory, the volume of literature contributing to corporate identity, corporate communications, and reputation through academic journals and conferences is increasing exponentially. There is now a rise in the number of academics researching these concepts at some well-reputed business schools since the 1980s. Many research-led institutions, notably Brunel Business School, Birmingham Business School, RSM Erasmus, Manchester Business School, Copenhagen Business School, Queens School of Business, McIntire School of Commerce, Corporate Communications Institute, William S. Spears School of Business, Leeds University Business School, Australian Graduate School of Management (just to mention a few) have now become the hub of world-class research in these disciplines.

In practice, these facets are now recognized as strategic tools driving and enhancing the achievement of competitive advantage. It is now certain that the presentation of corporate identity through corporate communications is influential and bears on corporate reputation. Thus, many national, multinational, and even SMEs that are smart enough to quickly recognize the benefits and importance of the management of these tools, are devoting millions of dollars to them. The rising importance of these tools reflects the enormous amount of resources devoted to them. For instance, after a consolidation exercise in 2000 with Amoco and ARCO, BP committed a whopping sum of $US7m on researching and preparing its new corporate identity and corporate communications and protecting its corporate reputation around the world. The sum of $US25m was further proposed to support the changes in BP's retail signage. In 2003, BT (British Telecom) dedicated about £5m to the development of a new visual identity (i.e. connected world) to represent its incursion into a wide range of business activities, project its multimedia capabilities and express its internationalization.

Increasingly, firms have realized that the management of these tools can increase return on investment, motivate employees, attract the most intelligent and talented executives, and serve as a means of differentiating their products and services. Many firms that would never have included the management of these tools within the corporate strategy framework are now taking greater interest in them. Consequently, the facets of corporate identity, corporate communications, and reputation, have attracted the interest of many senior managers—and these facets are increasingly becoming one of the key responsibilities of the CEO.

In spite of the rising prominence of the facets of corporate identity, corporate communications, and reputation, many issues surround them remains ambiguous. For instance, it is not clear how corporate identity functions within the context of organizational culture; neither is theoretical literature clear on the quintessential nature of corporate identity, corporate branding, and corporate marketing and these have not been fully explored. In another vein, there is limited understanding of how integrated marketing communications (IMC) frames non-traditional expressions of identity; neither are we clear on how corporate internalities can be deployed to enhance the effective management of a firm's visual identity.

This book bridges these gaps and attempts to fill several other vacuums in literature by providing readers with insights into a range of exciting dialogues taking place across the facets of corporate identity, corporate communications, and corporate reputation management. Contributions to this book are momentous in implication, reflecting the currency of thought, ideas, analysis, and practices taking place within these disciplines. The debate in this book does not only unsettle the conceptual landscape within the disciplines of corporate marketing but it also complements existing theory, offering unparallel opportunities for further academic deliberation in the future. This book invites readers to view new theories from which a greater understanding of the management of these disciplines can emerge.

The first part of this book contains four chapters, which squarely addresses the facet of corporate identity. Chapter 1 provides a focus on the understanding of corporate identity within the context of organizational culture. It fertilizes corporate identity literature within cultural theory perspectives in order to amplify present understanding of the concept of identity. The chapter attempts to achieve these objectives by proposing a conceptual model, which explains identity formation, maturation, and dissemination at the cultural level of analysis. Chapter 2 explores the quintessential natures of corporate identity, corporate branding and corporate marketing. The chapter explains the importance and practical utility of adopting an identity-based view of the corporation and identity-based view of corporate branding. It addresses the paradigm shift that has led to the introduction and adaptation of the marketing orientation and corporate marketing philosophy in business organizations. The chapter draws attention to the six elements of corporate marketing mix, namely, character, culture, constituencies, communications, conceptualization, and covenant.

Chapter 3 addresses how IMC can be deployed in the framing of non-traditional expressions of identity. Additionally, this chapter traces the historical roots of non-traditional expressions of identity in order to establish how and why organizations depend on non-traditional expressions. The chapter also attempts to explain the meaning of non-traditional expressions of visual identity and addresses how these expressions can be strategically deployed to reach customers. Specific examples are drawn to illustrate the relevance of non-traditional expressions of corporate identity and how they reinforce visual identity. Chapter 4 (the last chapter in this part) concerns the internalities of managing a corporate identity. Specifically it considers how different aspects of corporate identity (including visuals) can be internally managed by organizations. In addition, the chapter examines corporate identity together with other related concepts and gives focus to the features of corporate identity management.

The second part contains four chapters and it addresses the facet of corporate communications and the management of this discipline. The fifth chapter in this part of the book is devoted to how best practices (within corporate brand management and corporate communications framework) can be deployed to focus on describing and understanding the ways that organizations build and maintain strong corporate reputations with stakeholders. In so doing, the chapter attempts to distinguish between best practices and signature practices, highlighting why signature practices make a difference. The chapter also attempts to explain the issues and challenges facing corporate communication professionals. The main objective in Chapter 6 is to establish whether factual information (in corporate advertisements) about an organization's corporate social responsibility (CSR) activities influences corporate reputation. More importantly, the chapter addresses the importance of providing factual information in relation to the advertisement of an organization's corporate social responsibilities. In addition, trade-offs between the persuasion of external stakeholders through factual information and the fostering of the identification of internal stakeholders through impressionistic information is comprehensively addressed.

Chapter 7 takes a look at 'reputation in action' as a key driver of corporate communication and explores case studies of reputation. The chapter aims to create a better understanding of the various notions and definition of corporate reputation by giving insight into the nature of the current debates about this concept. The chapter highlights the nature of corporate reputation management and underscores its relationship with corporate communications strategy. In addition an attempt is made in this chapter to explain the factors enhancing best practices in reputation-led corporate communication. Chapter 8 determines how corporate reputation is understood and evaluated and explores the importance and limitations of public relations in the management of business crises. The chapter also applies a case study method to corporate identity challenges as witnessed by organizations.

Part III draws together contributions towards the corporate reputation facet—and it begins with an insight into the practicalities of implementing a new direction for the corporate reputation of an organization by drawing from a study of Manchester Business School, repositioning experience and using the corporate character scale to measure an organization's corporate reputation. In addition, this chapter also provides insight into how organizations can use visual identity as part of their reputation management process together with how a visioning process can work collaboratively with market research on the reputation perceptions of internal and external stakeholders.

Chapter 10 looks at how organizations can build and restore their good names in a multicultural society like Australia. It highlights some aspects of the Australian business culture that affect the creation of corporate reputations and provides a blueprint for corporate reputation development. The chapter also discusses some of the challenges and issues facing corporate reputation managers.

Chapter 11 considers the concept of corporate reputation from an attitudinal approach drawing on Ajzen's (1991) theory of planned behavior. By drawing together an established theory with recognized questionnaire-building procedures, the chapter provides a platform for a better understanding the role of corporate reputation in relation to other corporate marketing concepts. In addition, this chapter addresses the concepts of corporate identity, corporate image, and corporate reputation, highlighting the main ways in which corporate reputation is currently measured. Importantly, the introduction and inclusion of an alternative attitudinal measure within the theory of planned behavior is advocated. The chapter maps this theory to the development of questionnaires in order to measure corporate reputation. The advantage and implications of the study are highlighted and possible limitations are discussed. This book ends with Chapter 12, which addresses the gap in understanding the development and maintenance of corporate reputation in organizations outside Europe and the United States. A qualitative research approach (including a semi-structured interview and focus group) was deployed to investigate the determinants of corporate reputation of companies in Asia. This chapter attempts to give an insight into the nature of economic and non-economic determinants of corporate reputation together with the importance of long-term corporate reputation, particularly in Asia. It highlights cultural complexities and how they impinge on the understanding of corporate reputation.

It has been a highly challenging and stimulating experience to edit this book. I have gathered a collection of refreshing views on corporate identity, emanating from a diverse spectrum of perspectives. Academics and practitioners have contributed to this collection and to this diversity through the different countries that are included in their research. Special thanks go to Francesca Heslop, senior commissioning editor, whose enthusiasm for the field and constant encouragement have contributed to the high caliber the publication has achieved. A note of thank you to Tayo Otubanjo and Suraksha Gupta for assisting in compiling the book. We hope you will find the book interesting and thought-provoking. This collection of research material aims to push the boundaries of our knowledge and understanding of corporate branding, identity, and communication, and to steer future research agendas towards newer horizons.

REFERENCES

Ajzen, I. (1991) "The theory of planned behaviour." *Organizational Behaviour and Human Decision Process,* 50: 179–211.

Part I

Corporate identity

Chapter 1

Explicating the relationship between identity and culture

A multi-perspective conceptual model

Kevin James Vella and T. C. Melewar

AT THE END OF THIS CHAPTER READERS SHOULD BE ABLE TO:

1 Understand corporate identity, related concepts, and benefits of corporate identity management to internal and external stakeholders
2 Appreciate the dire need in the present case of affairs for furthering a unified and multi-disciplinary approach within the parameters set out by leading authors in the field
3 Specify internal corporate identity management dimensions
4 Specify the role of culture within corporate identity and the interplay of related variables in the formation, maturation, and dissemination of identity at the cultural level of analysis

KEY POINTS

■ A strong identity is an avenue for achieving positive images among internal stakeholders, a favorable reputation in the labor market, and, thus, a means to secure and sustain competitive advantage
■ Practitioners and academics have shown consistency in the concepts of identity for a number of years; however, an impasse has been reached and the area requires a move towards addressing an empirical paralysis
■ Central to the identity formation, maturation, and dissemination process, are management and employees
■ Organizational culture is central to the study of identity. However, identity literature shows weakness in the treatment of the concept with regard to several aspects including the approach that culture is shared by most, if not

all, organizational members, thus disregarding aspects of conflict and ambiguity
- Organizational culture is an important frame of reference and an interpretive mechanism also used by all organizational members to translate management-transmitted identity programs into images, perceptions, cognitions, and emotions towards their organization, colleagues, and subordinates. Cultural processes are dynamic and require close attention
- Identity studies necessitate the study of meanings behind all cultural manifestations deposited by management and employees
- An identity formation, maturation, and formation process model is presented and is aimed at galvanizing empirical research

INTRODUCTION

Although not the panacea to modern corporate ills, identity provides managers with a strategic resource for building and delivering value among employees and, consequently, enhancing employee retention, recruitment and loyalty. Over time, such desirable outcomes result in strong and enduring reputations that fuel profitability, growth, and competitive advantage.

Whereas organizations may deploy similar products, marketing campaigns, business strategies, and structural configurations, there exist characteristics that are inimitable elsewhere. These characteristics emerge from the synergic conglomeration of unique individuals who come together, bringing to bear their skills, personalities, expectations, and behavior upon and within organizational life while developing corporate culture through daily interaction. Moreover, from time to time, management make statements to reflect their perceptions of and aspirations for the organization they lead. Managerial influences and frames of reference are diverse and include organizational culture. Managers must expose and present these elements effectively to all organizational members (corporate identity) while attuning themselves closely to how all members perceive, think, feel, and behave towards their organizations (organizational identity). Although formal marketing communications programs may be important, research has shown that external stakeholder images are heavily influenced by interactions with employees.

Internal identity management programs, therefore, should encompass management-initiated efforts to manifest the central characteristics of their organization to its members. Equal attention, on the other hand, should be awarded to employee images of, responses to and affinity with these and other organizational characteristics. Identity programs are developed within and driven by a contextual triumvirate, namely, strategy, structure, and culture, and are brought to life by organizational members through mediated communication and behavior and a wide range of symbolic manifestations ranging from graphic design to office décor to cultural artefacts. Failure or success of identity management programs depends entirely on the resultant perceptions, beliefs, emotions, and behaviour of organizational members. The dynamics of organizational culture are also paramount.

Identity is thus a holistic construct enveloping most salient aspects of organizations. It is strategic in nature embracing all functions and aspects of organizational life.

This chapter aims to provide an understanding of the identity concepts within the context of organizational culture and to fertilize identity studies with the rich perspectives found within cultural theory, thus amplifying present understanding. We propose a conceptual model that explains identity formation, maturation, and dissemination at the cultural level of analysis and that facilitates empirical research.

The chapter is divided into four sections with the first part briefly outlining the main issues within the area and delineating the emergent multi-disciplinary movement that seeks a unified approach to identity. The second part of the chapter applies the unified cross-disciplinary approach to extract, from extant literature, working definitions of the identity concepts sometimes used, and, often confusingly so, interchangeably. We use a functionalist lens when exploring corporate identity, image, and reputation, and an interpretivist one when analyzing organizational identity. In the third part, we explore the nature of organizational culture from a symbolic perspective to address the gaps and weaknesses of extant identity models. The chapter concludes by combining the concepts of identity into a single multi-perspective conceptual model that explains identity formation, maturation, and dissemination at the cultural level of analysis.

A UNIFIED AND MULTI-DISCIPLINARY PERSPECTIVE

Identity literature is rich with contributions from practitioners and academics and reflects unanimous agreement on the importance of identity to organizations (Balmer and Greyser 2003) and on its instrumental role as a resource of strategic import (Melewar et al. 2005, 2003; Balmer 2001, 1998). However, a set of problems has hampered theoretical growth and empirical progress (Cornelissen and Elving 2003).

Considerable debate surrounds the plethora of definitions of and the relationships between the concepts of corporate identity (Melewar and Jenkins 2002) and the related terms of corporate image, organizational identity and identification, corporate reputation, and corporate branding (Balmer 2001). Although these concepts differ in meaning, often authors use the terms interchangeably and effectively. The consequent theoretical vagueness (Cornelissen and Elving 2003) and fragmentation (Balmer 1998) have created problems in operationalizing the construct and the empirical dimension of identity studies is extremely weak (Cornelissen and Elving 2003).

A second problem relates to the contrasting perspectives and paradigms existing within identity literature (Balmer 2001). Three philosophical underpinnings inform identity scholars, namely, functionalist, interpretivist, and post-modern paradigms (Gioia 1998 as cited in Balmer 2001). Authors writing in the functionalist tradition (e.g., the marketing perspective) frequently regard identity from a management viewpoint, arguing that corporate identity is an objective phenomenon, and, therefore, may be forged and managed. A quantitative research design is preferred with an emphasis on psychometric instruments. Interpretivist studies (e.g., the organizational behaviorist perspective), on the other hand, regard identity as subjective, arguing that employees do not merely react to the cues created by identity management programs. Rather, they actively interpret the environment and their subsequent behavior is based upon these interpretations. Thus, studies focus on interpretations and on how organizational members (predominantly employees) perceive their organizations and what meanings they affix to them (organizational identity) (Balmer 2001). Studies search for "thick descriptions" (Martin 2002: 4) that are provided by ethnographies and other qualitative studies. These contrasting paradigmatic traditions and perspectives, however, should not be viewed as contradictory but rather as complementary (Balmer and Greyser 2003; Martin 2002; Balmer 1998): the individual points of view and paradigms do not provide the powerful perspective needed by academics and practitioners to understand fully the identity taxonomy (Balmer and Greyser 2003, 2002; Martin 2002). Rather, together they provide a depth of understanding that neither alone could ever reach (Martin 2002).

A third problem relates to the anthropomorphization and the indiscriminate use of metaphor (Cornelissen and Harris 2001). Through metaphor analysis, numerous authors have drawn analogies from some of the concepts used to describe humans to endow organizations with identity, character, and personality by drawing generally from psychology (Cornelissen and Harris 2001). The main use of metaphors is to describe complex ideas and abstractions in more easily understood and *common* terminology, and for conjectural reasons. However, metaphor analysis is dangerous (Balmer 1998; Cornelissen and Harris 2001; Albert and Whetten 1985). Cornelissen and Harris (2001) argue that when used figuratively and to draw similarities from human and social psychology, such terms as corporate identity and personality have been reified, thus creating distortions in our views and limiting our understanding. This has given rise to multiple perspectives and definitions. Identity theories proposed through analogies drawn from "human identities" may be "conceptually flawed and

6

empirically false" (Cornelissen and Harris 2001: 50) since there is no agreement within the source domain on the concepts of identity and personality. The main arguments in the source domain revolve around whether or not identity is an inner property, a product of the mind; whether identity is an inherent physical characteristic; or, whether identity emerges through behavior. Similarly, the authors conclude, the corporate identity metaphor may face grave difficulties when used to describe and explain company behavior and communications. To promote clarity and coherence in the field, we have abandoned the metaphorical use of such concepts as corporate personality and refer to terms in their literal meaning or as "a convenient label for a particular set of variables" (Nunnally and Bernstein 1994: 104).

This necessitates an interdisciplinary approach (for example, Balmer and Greyser 2003; Balmer 1998; Melewar et al. 2003; Hatch and Schultz 1997) harmonising and combining the various perspectives with a drive to be holistic (Melewar 2003; Melewar and Jenkins 2002) and eclectic (Balmer and Greyser 2003). Such a perspective takes stock of a variety of disciplines including market-ing, public relations, graphic design, organizational behavior studies, strategic management, and corporate communications within one area of study (Balmer and Greyser 2003, 2002; Melewar 2003; Balmer 2001). More recently, Hatch and Schultz (2000) suggest the idea of "combining the understanding offered by all contributing disciplines into a single concept of identity defined at the organizational level of analysis" (Hatch and Schultz 2000: 19). Few multi-disciplinary models of identity have been proposed, and, with the growing importance of the area, the need to have such frameworks is becoming increasingly felt (Balmer and Greyser 2002).

The remainder of this chapter is written in the spirit of a unified and cross-disciplinary approach to identity studies while a combined concept of identity is also proposed.

IDENTITY, IMAGE AND REPUTATION

A resource-based view

Sustainable competitive advantage may be built by managing how an organization is perceived (Aaker 1996 as cited in Simões and Dibb 2002) and corporate identity is an important avenue to achieve this (Melewar et al. 2005; Simões and Dibb 2002).

Through corporate identity, organizations manifest salient characteristics to all their stakeholders and develop a strong channel for differentiation (Balmer 2001; Abratt 1989), an instrument for creating enduring and reliable relation-ships (Melewar et al. 2005) and a robust mechanism for delivering value. By building, maintaining, and enhancing this value over time through a *strong*, *distinct*, *inimitable*, and *immediately recognizable* identity, firms attain their strategic objectives and gain sustainable competitive advantage over rivals.

Corporate identity is transmitted to various stakeholders who then formulate images that, in turn, form the basis of the company's reputation (Melewar 2003). Stakeholders include all organizational members (internal), customers, shareholders, and investors, financial institutions, suppliers, government, industry associations, and non-government organizations and the community at large (external). By extending the marketing concept to corporate identity, it is reasonable to conclude that corporate identity managers require the focus to be on individual stakeholder target groups at a time to deliver superior value. Hence, by focusing on transmitting corporate identity to employees, a number of key outcomes accrue. Qualitative research findings show that firms leverage their identities to motivate, recruit, and retain high-quality employees (Melewar et al. 2005). Employees derive superior value from their organization from a variety of sources including such extrinsic measures as competitive pay structures and intrinsic means such as challenging and self-actualizing jobs. Through internal corporate identity management programs, managers also communicate these extrinsic and intrinsic benefits. Such benefits form the basis of positive employee images, organizational identity and affinity. Over time, a favorable reputation is created within the labor market, for example, "one of the nation's top employers". Depending on market conditions (Balmer and Greyser 2003; Balmer 1998), reputation becomes a key differentiator (Balmer and Wilson 1998) allowing the organization access to better skills, thus offering an avenue for creating and sustaining advantage, and contributing to profitability and growth.

Kennedy (1977) found important empirical evidence as to the significance of employees in image formation and dissemination. Her findings show that images held by external stakeholders are a function and a reflection of those held by employees. She concludes that building positive images among existing employees is likely to lead to a more favorable disposition among them and, hence, is instrumental in recruitment, for example. Therefore, the way organizational members perceive, feel, and think about (organizational identity) and the extent to which they identify with their organizations becomes inextricable from corporate identity. Organizational behaviorists have long since emphasized the importance of focusing on employees,[1] arguing, in parallel, the significance of management in the formation and dissemination process of identity (Simões and Dibb 2002).

Therefore, we posit that central to any discussion of the identity formation, maturation, and dissemination process intended to lead to sustainable advantage are management *and* employees.

CORPORATE IDENTITY

A number of authors have transposed the concept of human identity to the organization (Simões and Dibb 2002). Companies, therefore, have their own personalities and character (Simões and Dibb 2002), individuality and distinctiveness, meaning and essence (Balmer and Greyser 2003), and behavior (Hatch and Schultz 1997; Albert and Whetten 1985). As argued earlier, however, the identity metaphor has come under scrutiny of late and, thus, it is more appropriate to view corporate identity as relating to a set of dimensions without drawing from the domain of human and social psychology.

Consequently, corporate identity is "the set of meanings by which a company allows itself to be known and through which it allows people to describe, remember, and relate to it" (Topalian 1984 as cited in Melewar 2003: 195). The concept is an outward-looking perspective (Simões and Dibb 2002) and relates closely to the "the ways a company chooses to identify itself to all its publics" (Zinkhan et al. 2003, as cited in Simões et al. 2005: 154).

Albert and Whetten (1985) provide an influential definition (Balmer and Greyser 2003; Hatch and Schultz 1997) and state three criteria for an organization's identity: "claimed central character" or the central characteristics of an organization, "claimed distinctiveness" or those unique characteristics in relation to other organizations, and "claimed temporal continuity" or a "sense of continuity over time" or "sameness" (Albert and Whetten 1985: 85). The concept of continuity has been challenged and is now better conceived as the "evolving" nature of corporate identity (Balmer and Greyser 2003). The notion of identity is related to such diverse components as business definition, objectives, strategies, and resource configurations, capabilities, direction, leadership, and vision, mission and central focus of the organization, management ideology, corporate culture, rituals, history, values, and organizational roles over time. Environmental forces have a bearing on identity as do such economic rationales as profitability, costs, and return on investment. Managerial and employee competence and skill, together with employee commitment and orientation towards the organization, are significant factors influencing identity (Albert and Whetten 1985). Besides, corporate identity has links to products and services and formal and informal communications of the organization (Melewar and Jenkins 2002). Corporate identity is about how an organization presents, positions and differentiates itself visually and verbally at corporate, business, and product levels (Melewar 2003).

Figure 1.1 presents Melewar's holistic and multi-disciplinary taxonomy (Melewar 2003: 198) that defines identity as "the presentation of an organization to every stakeholder. It is what makes an organization unique and it incorporates the organization's communication, design, culture, behaviour, structure, industry identity, and strategy" (Melewar and Karaosmanoglu 2005).

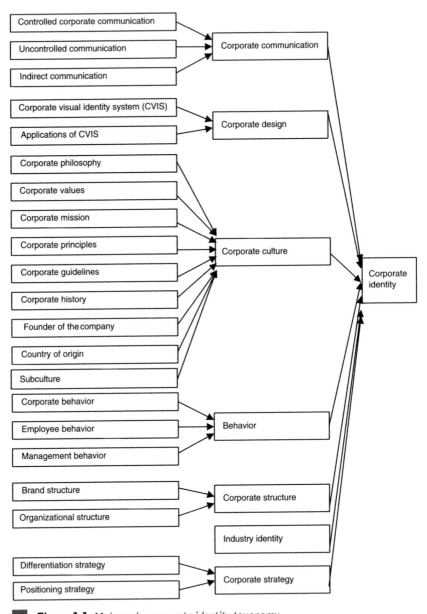

Figure 1.1 *Melewar's corporate identity taxonomy*

Source: Melewar 2003: 198.

Recent findings (Melewar et al. 2005, 2003) show a diversity of opinions among practitioners with regard to the meaning of corporate identity (Melewar et al. 2003): some perceive the concept as having solely a marketing function while others conceive identity to be more generic and all-encompassing (see

Figure 1.1). There is agreement that design, communications, behavior, and strategy are components of corporate identity. Mixed responses regarding the inclusion of culture and structure are registered.

THE BENEFITS OF CORPORATE IDENTITY

Competitive advantage accrues from a set of resources that provide superior business performance over the long term (De Wit and Meyer 2004). Research (as cited in Simões and Dibb 2002) indicates that positive correlations exist between a positive corporate image or identity of a business to superior performance. The aim of corporate identity management is to acquire a favorable corporate image among key internal and external stakeholders so that, in the long run, this image can result in the acquisition of a favorable corporate reputation, which leads to key stakeholders having a favorable disposition towards the organization. Studies have shown that reputation and image reduce risk and increase market share. Researchers have also found linkages between reputation and historical performance. Thus, the general view in literature is that effective management of corporate identity provides a potential avenue to competitive advantage (Simões et al. 2005).

Corporate identity management brings about several benefits to employees (Melewar 2003). Identity acts as a force to motivate and obtain a greater degree of support from employees. Corporate identity allows employees to adapt to the prevailing organizational culture with less difficulty and acts as an integrative force in the case of mergers or acquisition. Management's ability to recruit employees with the necessary skills is indirectly improved through corporate identity. Enhanced employee retention and morale, higher labor productivity and lower staff turnover are other benefits attributed to corporate identity management (Melewar et al. 2005). Recent researchers have found considerable agreement among respondents over such benefits (Melewar et al. 2005, 2003).

Hence, we argue, the importance of managing corporate identity for internal audiences is undisputable.

IMAGE

In general, image refers to how stakeholders perceive and interpret the ways in which an organization manifests itself (Melewar 2003; Hatch and Schultz 1997). It relates to the experiences, beliefs, feelings, knowledge, associations, and impressions that each stakeholder has about an organization. In contrast to corporate identity, image resides in the minds of audiences (Melewar 2003). Corporate identity is largely the foundation for company image (Simões and

Dibb 2002; Hatch and Schultz 2000). Culture is the cognitive instrument that translates corporate identity into image (Hatch and Schultz 1997).

Employees have a significant role in forming and disseminating image to external stakeholders (Kennedy, 1977), encompassing even "behavioural relationships" of employees with external stakeholders (Balmer and Greyser 2003). Kennedy (1977) presents empirical evidence suggesting that images held by employees are reflected among those they come into contact with. She also found that company marketing communications achieved limited success in forming images among external stakeholders (e.g., suppliers). However, top management play a key role in influencing the extent of the image formed within the minds of employees and such influence may be affected through other dimensions such as communicating policies and behaviour.

Kennedy's research uncovered five areas stakeholders (including employees) are concerned with when describing a single company:

1   physical concerns;
2   work-related concerns including work content and people's attitude towards it;
3   management style and personality concerns;
4   supervisory concerns including the atmosphere between supervisors and their subordinates; and,
5   general concerns about the company, its products and future.

Kennedy found that an image has to be enduring and based on fact. Similarly, corporate identity is concerned with organizational reality (Balmer 1998). Identity and image must be consistent in the sense that the projected image and reality must coincide (Simões and Dibb 2002). In addition, the images broadcast by managers to external stakeholders must be consistent with those broadcast by employees (Kennedy 1977).

Behavior towards an organization is regarded as a consequence of the image held of it (Balmer and Greyser 2003). Thus, in a world where the internal and external boundaries of organizations are becoming increasingly blurry and almost all organizational members have become key stakeholder touch-points,[2] employee-held images and, consequently, their behavior should take a pivotal role within any model that attempts to explain the identity formation, maturation, and dissemination processes within an organization.

REPUTATION

Whereas image reflects the more recent beliefs about the organization, reputation is the perception of an organization built over time (Balmer 1998). Reputation results from a reflection upon historical accumulated impacts of previously observed identity cues and transactional experiences (Melewar 2003). In other words, it is evaluative and is image endowed with judgment (Simões and Dibb 2002) on what the organization has done and how it has behaved (Balmer and Greyser 2003). Image may be changed relatively quickly while reputation requires consistency of image and nurturing over a relatively longer time period. Hence, reputation is an enduring perception (Balmer 2001). A consequence of identity, reputation is believed to yield distinctiveness (Balmer and Greyser 2003) and provide an organization competitive advantage (Balmer 2001); however, favorable market conditions must prevail (Balmer and Greyser 2003; Balmer 1998). Multiple reputations of a single organization may exist (Balmer and Greyser 2003).

Reputation may be seen as a standard against which decisions are evaluated (Balmer and Greyser 2003; Balmer 1998). In recruitment, executives might consider the question whether the prospective employee would maintain the organization's reputation (Balmer and Greyser 2003). Similarly, when assessing employment vacancies, an increasing number of prospective employees would consider a company's reputation in their decisions (Melewar et al. 2005). Thus, ultimately, reputation also has an influence on corporate identity management programs and, to a certain extent, organizational identity.

ORGANIZATIONAL IDENTITY

Based on Albert and Whetten's (1985) notion of identity, organizational identity largely refers to how members perceive, think, and feel about their organizations (Hatch and Schultz 1997). Thus, organizational identity is "assumed to be a collective, commonly shared understanding of the organization's distinctive values and characteristics" (Hatch and Schultz 1997: 357) and results from associations, interpretations, and understandings (Hatch and Schultz 1997). Organizational identity provides the emotional and cognitive foundation upon which employees build an attachment and a meaningful relationship with their organization. It relates to such questions as "who we are" and "what do we stand for" and is reflexive (Hatch and Schultz 2000).

Whereas corporate identity is generally a managerial viewpoint, organizational identity is its "alter-ego" (Balmer and Greyser 2003) and requires taking an employee perspective. The emphasis in corporate identity is on management's role in expressing and communicating the vision, strategy (Hatch and Schultz 1997), and mission (Hatch and Schultz 2000) through a variety of instruments including design and behavior (Melewar 2003). Similarly, Kennedy (1977) stated the importance of formulating and communicating company policies to employees in image creation. Vision, mission, strategy, and policies are all statements of organizational purpose[3] that shift the aims of corporate identity management programs to include elements of what organizational members will become and not simply what they are (Hatch and Schultz 2000). Organizational identity, on the other hand, deals with relationships, specifically those between employees and their organization. This perspective, however, recognizes management's key role in identity formation both as leaders cum builders of corporate identity, and as members of the organization.

Consensus within literature reveals that organizational identity is shaped by the degree of cohesion (Melewar et al. 2003) between the organization and its employees. In other words, organizational identity is driven by the extent of enthusiasm, commitment, and participation shown by employees towards the organization's operation, long-term survival, and development (Melewar 2003). It is reasonable to conclude that the degree of empowerment, congruent management behavior, and self-direction, for example, will have an impact on this (and consequently, on the success of corporate identity management) depending upon on such external factors as national culture and predominant workplace orientations (e.g., theory X versus theory Y: Sheldrake 2003). Organizational identity is antecedent to behaviour.

Organizational identity also concerns identification and the influence of image and reputation on members (Simões and Dibb 2002). Identification relates to affinity (Hatch and Schultz 2000) or the degree to which employees define themselves by the same characteristics they believe are attributable to their organization (Stuart 2002). Identification may increase the extent by which organizational norms and values are internalized and observed while promoting a greater degree of attitudinal and behavioral homogeneity (Simões and Dibb 2002). Organizational identification is a consequence of organizational identity (Hatch and Schultz 2000). Management have an important role to play in influencing organizational identity and identification through corporate identity management that seeks to create favorable images in the minds of their employees (Simões and Dibb 2002). Issues of credibility, trust (Simões and Dibb 2002), and managerial competence (Kennedy 1977) are, therefore, of extreme importance. Management behavior should also be consistent over time and congruent with transmitted images and corporate identity for a favorable organizational identity (and hence, a greater degree of identification) to come about. After all, everything the organization does will communicate the organization's identity in one way or another (Stuart 1999; Balmer 1998).

IDENTITY AND CULTURE

Authors writing in the interpretivist tradition conceive culture as the symbolic context within which identity is developed and maintained (Hatch and Schultz

1997). Corporate identity is a "symbolic construction" (Hatch and Schultz 1997: 358) that is communicated and enacted by management to employees. Organizational members, in turn, interpret these symbols based on organizational culture, on their work experience, on interactions with management and other employees, and on other external influences (Hatch and Schultz 1997) (professional subcultures, external relations with stakeholders). Thus, the concepts of identity, image, and culture are inextricably linked (Balmer and Wilson 1998) and mutually interdependent (Hatch and Schultz 1997). Therefore, it is reasonable to conclude that behavior, communication, and design (including such forms as logos, buildings, décor, rituals, and other symbols) are mediating influences used by management in delivering corporate identity and interpreted by organizational members to create, sustain, or change organizational identity. On the other hand, organizational identity is transmitted through interaction with others via language and behavior within the context of organizational culture (Hatch and Schultz 2000). It is assumed that employees will behave cooperatively and spontaneously in the interests of the organization if they have genuinely internalized organizational values (Balmer and Wilson 1998) and characteristics.

The symbolic construction of corporate identity becomes part of corporate identity when members of an organization start using them in everyday life. Moreover, the symbols that members use to describe themselves are resources that management use for corporate identity management programs (Hatch and Schultz 2000). This also implies the overlap between corporate and organizational identity.

Since "culture theory has much more to offer [to identity studies] than has thus far been acknowledged" (Hatch and Schultz 1997: 357), we now turn to cultural research to specify further the construct of identity at the cultural level of analysis.

ORGANIZATIONAL CULTURE

Culture is now widely recognized as a component of corporate identity (Melewar 2003). However, recent empirical research studies (Melewar et al. 2005, 2003) show that there is no unanimity among business managers regarding the inclusion of culture as a dimension of corporate identity: while some participants felt that culture was an integral part of identity, others believed that although affiliations exist between the two constructs, culture is not necessarily a component. However, most viewed corporate culture as an effective instrument used to support and reinforce corporate identity to achieve such goals as labor flexibility. All participants emphasized that one of the main benefits corporate identity could have is employee motivation, retention, and recruitment.

Other research (Melewar et al. 2005) indicates:

15

1   Corporate culture is a context that leads to behavior and strategy.
2   Those working in the same company share a similar view on the central characteristics that comprise their organization's identity.
3   Employees are instrumental in communicating these characteristics to external stakeholders. This implies that the greater the reflection of these characteristics via employees, the more positive the corporate image among external stakeholders (Melewar et al. 2005). This is similar to the findings by Kennedy (1977).
4   Corporate history, founder of the organization, country of origin (with links to national culture characteristics such as working principles and practices), and divisional and regional subcultures all have an impact on corporate culture and corporate identity (Melewar et al. 2005).

Identity literature shows weakness with respect to the definition and treatment of organizational culture. Many models do not give appropriate attention to the concept and a simplistic approach is often applied (Balmer 2001; Balmer and Wilson 1998). Balmer and Wilson (1998) argue that the dominant view within corporate identity literature emphasizes a one-dimensional corporate culture where values, beliefs, and assumptions are largely shared by all members of the organization. Martin (2002) reaches a similar conclusion. Thus, ignoring certain views on organizational culture may lead to corporate identity transmission efforts to fail. Although most organizational members may share the same values as management, others may be in conflict with and yet others may be ambivalent about them. In addition, within one organization, an individual may identify with the organization on some issues, with these values his or her sub-culture on others, and be ambiguous on others (Martin 2002; Balmer and Wilson 1998). Therefore, corporate identity management programs must address all these internal audiences to effectively achieve the desired outcomes.

Hatch and Schultz (1997), writing within the interpretivist and symbolic perspective, argue that organizational culture should be conceived as a context and as an interpretive or sense-making mechanism that can neither be measured nor controlled. On the other hand, functionalist perspectives approach culture as an observable, measurable, and controllable variable (Melewar 2003). Recent models of corporate identity have adopted the view of culture as a context (Cornelissen and Elving 2003; Stuart 1999).

The findings reported earlier (Melewar et al. 2005) seem to indicate the notion of corporate culture being an interpretive mechanism and support the argument for the need for management to deploy necessary cultural artefacts and symbols that sustain organizational development. Moreover, we argue that the functionalist perspective fails to capture the meanings behind symbols decorating, and at times, littering organizational life.[4]

We also view two other issues emerging:

1   Cultural processes are rarely, if ever, mentioned within the literature, and when they are, these processes are based on Schein's (2004) model and, hence, are implicitly assumed as static (Hatch 1993), leader-generated (Martin 2002), and linear. There is also debate with regard to the extent culture can be created by the organization's leaders in contrast to being a phenomenon that emerges from social interaction (Melewar et al. 2003).
2   Operationalization of the culture component within the context of identity is daunting.

A variety of related issues such as trade-offs rising from qualitative and quantitative approaches and depth of understanding and breadth of research focus (Martin 2002) give rise to this difficulty which will not be solved easily or quickly.

THE PREDOMINANT VIEW OF CULTURE

Schein's model of culture remains a pivotal influence within cultural research (Hatch 1993). His model has also been the basis of most conceptualizations within corporate identity models to date (e.g., Abratt 1989).

Schein (2004) suggests that culture exists on three levels each of which decreases in visibility to observers: artefacts, espoused beliefs, and values, and underlying assumptions or paradigm. At the surface of culture are cultural artefacts or visible, audible, and emotive phenomena that one encounters within an organization. Easily visible to an outsider, such artefacts include buildings, offices, products, décor, uniforms, value and mission statements, and rituals. However, outsiders cannot easily interpret the meanings behind these artefacts. Insight is possible only if investigations dig deeper into the other less visible layers of culture; otherwise, serious misinterpretations may occur. At an intermediate level of visibility, closer to the heart of corporate culture, lies the layer of beliefs and values (Schein 2004).

Over time, group-learning outcomes tend to create a shared system of conscious beliefs and values about what works and what does not, what is right and what is not. Some beliefs and values are tested while others are acquired through a socially validated and reinforced process of consensus among members. These beliefs and values eventually become part of the paradigm as long as they continue either to work reliably or to be socially reinforced. Such assumptions are supported by explicit statements (e.g., rules) that govern the behavior of existing and new members and act as a way of handling uncertainty within the organization and prevailing environmental conditions. These beliefs and values may be espoused so that they may act as predictors of what some people will say but they will not reflect what they will do. Hence, the best predictors of behavior are the

17 ■

basic underlying assumptions. When beliefs and values continually solve problems of "external adaptation and internal integration" (Schein 2004: 17), the solutions and supporting system of shared beliefs and values become assumptions about reality. Sharing results from the repeated success of these beliefs and values in solving problems to the extent that if basic assumptions become strongly held within an organization, members will find incongruent behavior inconceivable. Basic assumptions are implicit, guide behavior, and are also the ultimate predictors of values. They also "proposed to group members how to perceive, think about, and feel about things" (Schein 2004: 31).

Culture is formed by group leaders and is propagated through a process of consensus and socialization. During formation, the founder of an organization brings in his/her own visions, goals, beliefs, values, and assumptions, and selects members with whom he/she perceives commonalities. In facing decisions, he will impose solutions on the group based on his leadership position. If group action results in success, the founder's beliefs and assumptions are confirmed, reinforced, and become a shared system of beliefs and values. If success continues to hold, then such beliefs and values are fully internalized as basic assumptions and unconscious guides to "correct" behavior. Failure, on the other hand, will lead either to the disappearance of the group or to the replacement of the leader. Dissent is treated with marginalization or "excommunication" from the group and the shared culture will prevail (Schein 2004).

Schein assumes that culture (organizational and national) is largely antecedent to behavior. Hatch (1993) argues that not everything that happens within the organization can be attributed to culture. Rather, culture has *significant* effects on behavior and other sources of influence apply.

PERSPECTIVES IN CULTURAL THEORY

Three perspectives dominate cultural theory, each with its own set of definitions and conceptualizations of the phenomenon. Although several differences exist, significant intellectual debates revolve around what should be included in a cultural study and around the notion of "shared" (Martin 2002).

In contrast to Schein, Martin (2002) argues that artefacts, values, and assumptions are all cultural elements that do not necessarily reflect varying levels of depth. Rather, when the greatest understanding of the culture of an organization is required, a deep analysis of all the meanings behind each of these cultural elements should be sought. Martin identifies four cultural manifestations that together will reveal these meanings, namely, cultural forms, formal and informal practices, and content themes. All these elements represent an entire culture and studies must analyze the broad range of manifestations if they are to be said to be representative of the culture in question (Martin 2002). Therefore, it seems, conceptualizations of identity based on Schein's notion of cultural levels have failed to provide us with the understanding we require to further identity theory and empirical research. By studying the meanings behind cultural manifestations, we may realize a better understanding about how an organization manifests itself to its members and how, in turn, members represent and embed their perceptions, feelings, and emotions in their work environment. Naturally, this implies trade-offs in and consequences on research designs such as pursuing the functionalist aim of generalization through more "superficial" quantitative methods as opposed to taking a qualitative approach and developing ethnographies or case studies with a deeper content.

Again in contrast to Schein, research (as cited in Martin 2002) shows culture, is an incompletely shared system that also encompasses degrees of conflict and ambiguity (Martin 2002; Balmer and Wilson 1998). The integration perspective views culture as a monolith where everything is clear and ambiguity does not exist. Each cultural manifestation is consistent with the rest to create a system of mutually supportive and reinforcing elements. Meanings and interpretations are also consistent across the organization and hence consensus permeates at all levels of the collective. Thus, there is shared sense of commitment and loyalty towards the organization. Where deviation is acknowledged the integration perspective suggests harmony through retraining, performance appraisals or closer supervision to iron out conflict or ambiguity. The key words are consistency, harmony, pervasive consensus, and clarity of meaning. Studies taking this approach usually focus on management or professionals. Schein's work may be categorized within this perspective (Martin 2002).

The differentiation perspective views organizations as comprised of a number of subcultures that exist either in harmony, or in conflict, or in indifference to each other and to the dominant organizational culture. The sources of subcultures are multiple including divisional, functional, hierarchical, or professional subgroupings. Consensus exists only within the confines of the subculture. Studies focus on the cultural manifestations that have inconsistent meanings (Martin 2002). Extending Martin's example, top management may announce the need for curbing costs while subsequently embarking on lavishly refurbishing the management floor. Keywords here are inconsistency, subcultural consensus, and differentiation, and pockets of clarity of meaning. An individual may hold membership within several subcultures some of which may have conflicting values (Martin 2002).

The fragmentation perspective argues that neither consistency nor inconsistency is the norm. Indeed, complexity and ambiguity govern interpretations of the cultural manifestations so that consensus is fleeting and is specific to the issue at hand. Ambiguity is an integral part of organizational life. Keywords here are lack of clarity, inconsistency, confusion, paradox, and contradiction (Martin 2002).

Looking at culture only through one or two of these lenses, therefore, constitutes only a partial and simplified view. It is only through a three-perspective approach that a full understanding of corporate culture may be achieved. There is a need for field-of-identity studies that largely assume the integration perspective that looks towards the other perspectives on corporate culture in order to shed light on what really may be happening inside and outside the confines of an organization (Martin 2002).

Therefore, as do other authors (for example, Melewar 2003; Balmer and Wilson 1998), we argue the need for a broader perspective that looks at harmony within an organization as well as differentiation and ambiguity simultaneously. Once management understands the three patterns in existence within their organization, they may be able to design more effective corporate identity management programs. Moreover, they will be in a better position to understand how employees perceive, think, and feel about their organization.

CULTURAL DYNAMICS

With respect to cultural processes, Hatch (1993) proposes an alternative and more dynamic model that draws from the symbolic perspective specifically to counteract the under-specification of Schein's theories. We argue that this alternative provides a greater understanding on (1) how employees internalize the meanings behind artefacts deposited by corporate identity management programs and (2) how organizational identity comes about in a cultural context. We believe that this model will help uncover the meanings behind cultural manifestations as ideated by Martin. Hatch's model is depicted in Figure 1.2.

This model shifts the focus away from the elements of culture to the relationships that link them—manifestation, realization, symbolization, and interpretation (Hatch 1993). Thus, it answers an important question: "How is culture constituted by assumptions, values, artefacts, symbols and the process that links them?" (Hatch 1993: 660). In comparison to Schein's static model, all these processes occur simultaneously in a continual constitution and reconstitution of culture (Hatch 1993).

MANIFESTATION

Manifestation processes allow assumptions to be perceived, known, and felt, and translate intangible assumptions into conscious values. In proactive (forward along the arrow) manifestation, what employees assume to be true will shape what they value (Hatch 1993). For example, if a manager assumes a theory Y orientation, he will assume that employees do not dislike work and that they are

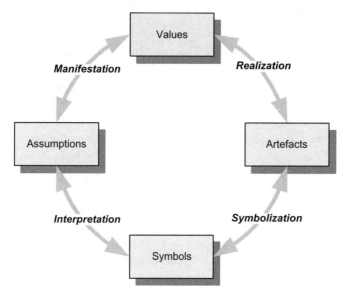

Figure 1.2 *Hatch's cultural dynamics model*

Source: Hatch 1993: 660.

internally motivated to reach the goals to which they are committed (Sheldrake 2003). Therefore, initiative will be seen in a positive light and eventually management may develop such values that reward initiative and empower employees. In parallel, if an employee assumes a theory Y orientation then he would expect and value a workplace that allows for initiative and empowerment. Such assumptions create expectations and aspirations that, in turn, influence what organizational members perceive, think, and feel about the organization. It is through such reflections that organizational members realize what they like and dislike and, hence, become conscious of what they value. These values and expectations lead to action and experience. Retroactive (backward) manifestation refers to the processes that change or keep assumptions in line with the values that are acknowledged actively within the organizational culture (Hatch 1993).

REALIZATION

Realization processes translate values and expectations into artefacts (proactive realization). Such processes also maintain or alter existing values and expectations through such artefacts (retroactive realization) (Hatch 1993). Hence, theory Y values and expectations are reified in such cultural artefacts as company policies that would allow for self-direction and schemes that reward initiative and achievement. Other examples of artefacts would include prize-giving ceremonies and "employee of the month" awards.

21

SYMBOLIZATION

Hatch argues that although all symbols are artefacts, not all artefacts become symbols. Whereas artefacts are literal, symbols are artefacts laden with interpretation and, thus, figurative meaning. Literal meaning becomes figurative and symbolic through the additional cultural process of symbolizations. Prospective symbolization processes refer to the manner by which artefacts become symbols through a series of associations that reflect both the objects that are being symbolized and the creators of the symbol. The process also includes retrospective processes that enhance the awareness of the literal meaning of the symbols (Hatch 1993).

Hence, a scheme introduced by management to motivate initiative will become a symbol when organizational members view the artefact as promoting their expectations and values and view the policy as a means of self-actualization. Some members with different values and expectations may interpret the artefact, however, as a management ploy (e.g., to weed out non-performers) that is not congruent with the reality they perceive. In both situations, the artefact becomes a symbol.

Schein's model does not specify this symbolization aspect and, therefore, fails to increase understanding of culture within identity studies.

INTERPRETATION

Organizational members use their assumptions to experience, interpret, and give meaning to symbols. In parallel, the assumptions themselves are exposed during interpretation and may be influenced by new symbols. Basic assumptions are, thus, either challenged or maintained (Hatch 1993).

By providing a framework for interpretation, organizational culture has significant effects on behavior within and expectations of the internal and external environment.

MEANINGS IN ORGANIZATIONAL LIFE

Several authors writing outside culture theory have recognized the importance of cultural manifestations and their meanings. In the strategic management field, Johnson (1992) and later Johnson and Scholes (2002) proposed a model of organizational culture based on Schein's layers of culture. They conceive the three cultural elements as overlapping and interrelated concentric layers that form the cognitive structure or the interpretive mechanism of the particular culture and that mould the view the organization has of itself and its environment.

Assumptions lie at the core of an organization's culture and are shared widely among culture members. "Cultural webs" of the organization represent these assumptions and are the physical displays of corporate culture by way of symbols (logos, titles, cars), stories (history, anecdotes, founder of the company), routines of behaviour (the way things are done here), rituals (special events, meetings, training programs), power structures (position and expert power), control systems (rewards, measurements), and organizational structure. To uncover and understand an organization's culture requires studying these physical manifestations (Johnson and Scholes 2002; Johnson 1992). This is in contrast to Schein's arguments and similar to the position taken by Martin and several other cultural researchers.

Although the concept of cultural webs as applied by Johnson (Johnson 1998, 1992), and Heracleous (1995) assumes a managerial perspective and an integrationist approach, we believe that this framework is an elaborate and appropriate instrument that may help in uncovering hidden meanings and in moving us further towards operationalizing the identity construct. If applied at all levels of the organization, cultural webs become maps that reveal shared elements, aspects of conflict as well as areas of ambiguity. When taking a functionalist perspective the cultural webs may uncover cultural inventories and commonalities of cultural manifestations across a large sample of organizations and their members. Such studies may reveal typologies of cultural artefacts deployed by management through corporate identity programs. They may also highlight typologies of artefacts and symbols deposited by organizational members to reveal organizational identity. From a symbolic perspective, cultural webs may be used to dig deeper and map sediments of meanings and interpretations within a single organization.

The items of the cultural web are regrouped according to the four cultural manifestation types envisaged by Martin.

CULTURAL FORMS

Cultural forms are recognized as providing fundamental clues to the thoughts, beliefs, and actions of employees and thus require study. Examples of cultural forms include rituals, ceremonies, organizational stories, humor and jokes, language and jargon, physical layout including architectural and office arrangements, décor, dress codes, and uniforms (Martin 2002). Cultural forms justify behaviour and become instruments for telling organizational members what is valued within the organization. They highlight what is important within the organization and support "the way we do things around here" (Johnson and Scholes 2002). A thorough analysis of meanings yields vital information on the extent of consistency, differentiation, and fragmentation within a single culture (Martin 2002).

FORMAL PRACTICES

Formal practices have been frequently studied since they are usually written and thus more controllable by management. These include routines of behaviour, pay and reward structures, organizational structure and related lines of power, authority and reporting, rules, procedures, and control systems (Martin 2002). Logos, offices, cars, and titles (Johnson and Scholes 2002) are also included here and usually reflect management-initiated efforts. Again, the symbolic interpretation is also important: titles may be literal in some national cultures, while in other they denote status with a variety of associated connotations.

INFORMAL PRACTICES

Informal practices are not written and come about through social interaction. These may include social rules and norms, informal routines of behavior, rites, and informal power structures that are not attached to hierarchical structures. Inconsistencies with formal practices are often enacted here (Martin 2002).

CONTENT THEMES

Content themes may be espoused or inferred and refer to beliefs, assumptions, and values that underlie interpretations of the various cultural manifestations. Espoused themes may be superficially embraced to make impressions whereas inferred themes would reveal what is really occurring. Hence, mission and value statements may not be enough to yield the true values of top management and deeper investigation should be sought. Examples of content themes include employee well-being, improved productivity, profitability, social responsibility, and quality (Martin 2002)

A DEFINITION OF ORGANIZATIONAL CULTURE

Thus, the view on culture being presented here is best reflected through Martin's own informal definition: "when organizations are examined from a cultural viewpoint, attention is drawn to aspects of organizational life . . . such as stories people tell to newcomers to explain 'how things are done around here', the ways in which offices are arranged and personal items are or are not displayed, jokes people tell, the working atmosphere (hushed and luxurious or dirty and noisy), the relations among people (affectionate in some areas of an office and obviously angry and perhaps competitive in another place) . . . organization's official policies, the amounts of money different employees earn, reporting relationships, and, so on. A cultural observer is interested in the surfaces of these cultural manifestations because details can be informative, but . . . also seeks an in-depth understanding of the patterns of meanings that link these manifestations together, sometimes in harmony, sometimes in bitter conflicts between groups, and some-times in webs of ambiguity, paradox and contradiction" (Martin 2002: 3).

THE IFMD MODEL: A UNIFIED FRAMEWORK

Within the conceptual framework described above, it is now appropriate to explain the identity formation, maturation, and dissemination (IFMD) process model that combines the understanding of identity into a single concept at the cultural level of analysis.

Based on Melewar's taxonomy (Melewar 2003), the model is depicted below and shows the focus on management and employees as the main sources of identity formation, maturation, and dissemination. Organizational members have direct influence on and cause such desirable outcomes as favorable images and durable reputations among external stakeholders. Strategy, structure, and culture are important moderating influences and represent fundamental frames of reference for identity to be formed, nurtured, and disseminated. Mediating influences include management and employee behaviour, official communications programs, formal and informal practices, communications, language, corporate design, cultural forms, artefacts and symbols, and content themes. Other frames of reference and influences exist and these include national culture and industry identity.

We envisage that the IFMD model (Figure 1.3) will smooth the progress of research since:

1   The model facilititates interaction among those disciplines emphasizing cor-porate identity and those accentuating organizational identity. The model is also intended to bridge the differences between functionalist and interpre-tivist approaches.
2   It is parsimonious by emphasizing a single stakeholder grouping (organiza-tional members) rather than the blanket term "stakeholders" generally used in literature and by studying identity within a single context, that of culture.
3   It identifies specific measurable consequences such as productivity and turnover.
4   It explicates the main relationships between the variables at play.
5   It is an eclectic combination of disciplines including marketing, communica-tions, public relations, strategic management, culture, and organizational behaviour.

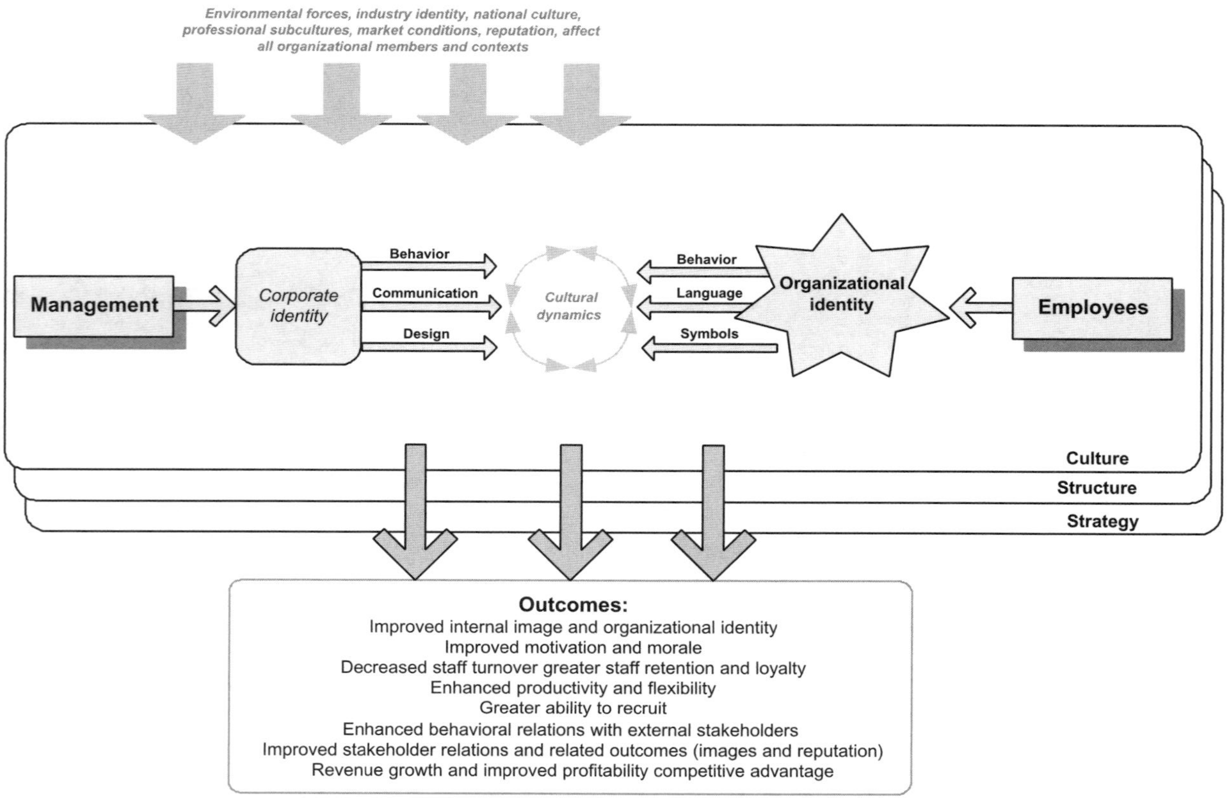

Environmental forces, industry identity, national culture, professional subcultures, market conditions, reputation, affect all organizational members and contexts

Management

Corporate identity

Behavior
Communication
Design

Cultural dynamics

Employees

Behavior
Language
Symbols

Organizational identity

Culture
Structure
Strategy

Outcomes:
Improved internal image and organizational identity
Improved motivation and morale
Decreased staff turnover greater staff retention and loyalty
Enhanced productivity and flexibility
Greater ability to recruit
Enhanced behavioral relations with external stakeholders
Improved stakeholder relations and related outcomes (images and reputation)
Revenue growth and improved profitability competitive advantage

Figure 1.3 *The IFMD model: identity formation, maturation, and dissemination at the cultural level of analysis*

6   It addresses weaknesses in identity theory by drawing heavily from cultural research and organizational theory to explain the phenomenon of culture and its inextricable link to identity.

The focal points of the IFMD process are management and their corporate identity management programs and organizational members who interpret and translate these programs into images, organizational identity, and affinity.

In defining corporate identity, management makes general statements about the central characteristics of the organization. These characteristics are the set of meanings that management wants employees to use in viewing, describing, and relating to the organization. For example, on such dimensions as "treatment of employees," three distinct sub-attributes may be "transformational management style," "work environment that awards initiative" and "enthusiasm and commitment." Such reflections are based on several facets of the organization including mission, strategy, organizational purpose, structure, products, and organizational culture. These reflections may also be intentions or aspirations for the future. For example, desirable attributes that management have gleaned from an examination of labor market opportunities and threats and identification of organizational strengths and weaknesses. Other organizations may want to be known by the same characteristics; it is commonsense to assume that most if not all companies want to be known as good employers. The key differentiators, however, lie not in the general statements per se but in such tangible factors as the effectiveness in transmitting the chosen corporate identity through behavior, communication, and design. Furthermore, the degree of management commitment to the values they want to portray lies in how congruent their behavior is to the same, and in the extent to which they will deploy the necessary supporting strategic and structural frameworks (e.g., flat hierarchy that facilitates the desired management style and work environment). In addition, as leaders of corporate identity programs, management deploy such cultural artefacts and symbols to reflect these characteristics such as competitive pay structures, flat hierarchies, delegation and employee empowerment policies, theory Y orientations, and, in general, work settings that instil trust, that provide employees with opportunities to flourish and that encourage initiative and self-direction. It is assumed that for the organization to function, a large majority of employees accepts the values chosen by management: for example, such transformational style may not function in cultures that would prefer transactional and autocratic leadership. Conflict and ambiguity will occur and management might have to address these problems through specific and special attention to the subcultures in conflict and the individuals who are ambivalent. As argued by Martin, these may be important signals and predictors of the future.

The objective of corporate identity management is to acquire a favorable corporate image and consequently organizational identity among employees so that, in the long run, it can result in the acquisition of a favorable corporate reputation, which leads to employees having a favorable disposition towards their organization. Such a favorable disposition should also result in employees transmitting a favorable image to external stakeholders through their everyday contact with them.

Corporate identity, management behavior, communications, and corporate design become grist for the cultural mill as managers interact, socialize and work with and relate to other organizational members. Within a cultural context, all these management cues and interactions are interpreted and laden with meaning to build, validate, and/or alter beliefs, values, and existing assumptions. This results in favorable images, affinity towards the organization and a positive organizational identity. After all, organizational identity and images come about largely through cultural processes (Hatch 1993). Employees deposit symbols to be interpreted by management within the existing cultural context through dynamic cultural processes as a reflection of organizational identity by way of behavior, artefacts, and language.

In designing effective corporate identity management programs, therefore, management should themselves heed such cultural artefacts to understand the prevailing climate. Moreover, viewing culture from the three-perspective approach suggested by Martin allows for the possibility of conceiving differentiation and ambiguity. Thinking in integrationist terms may lead management to marginalize or disregard employees or initiate training programs that may create further dissention or ambiguity. The degree of cohesiveness, differentiation, and/or fragmentation is also a function of the strength of corporate identity programs and the mediating influences of management behavior, communications, and design. Other influences may also come to fruition (e.g., the strength of professional subcultures).

Meanings are crucial to the study of organizational culture and, thus, require full management attention in designing successful corporate identity programs. If an artefact is introduced by management to sediment its theory Y values into the culture and produce a favorable image, how organizational members symbolize the artefact and what meanings they associate with it become paramount and critical in realizing whether the program is successful. The reasons for failure may not lie with corporate identity management per se, but with a lack of understanding of the meanings associated with, and the interpretations of each, cultural manifestation deployed.

In this light, the cultural dynamics process model is a useful predictor of the success of corporate identity management programs. It is also an important gauge for organizational identity at the cultural level of analysis. The model allows answering such questions as "are the assumptions, values, artefacts deposited by management appropriately symbolised within the organization?," "are the artefacts interpreted to reflect the associated assumptions and values?," and "are the symbols deposited by organizational members in line with assumptions, values and artefacts deposited by management?"

The desired outcomes of the IFMD process include increased employee motivation and morale, decreased staff turnover (greater staff retention and loyalty), enhanced labor flexibility and productivity, and the ability to recruit the necessary and the best skills within the marketplace. Other consequences include improved images among external stakeholders with more favorable dispositions for purchasing the organization's products and services, better access to financing and investment, improved and enduring customer and supplier relationships, durable relationships with government and non-government bodies and the community at large. These, in turn, affect revenues, profitability, growth, and survival. If such consequences are sustainable over time, competitive advantage comes about. Such consequences are influenced by and dependent on a number of environmental forces including prevailing market conditions of demand and supply, industry identity, national, regional, and professional cultures, and reputation among target stakeholders.

CONCLUSION

In this chapter, we have examined literature in order to apply an interdisciplinary approach that combines the concepts of identity into a single cogent conceptual model to explain identity formation, maturation, and dissemination at the cultural level of analysis. The model responds to the calls of several academics to fertilize the identity construct with views from cultural research. Organizational culture was explored from a symbolic perspective to attend to gaps and weaknesses in existing conceptualizations. We addressed the existing paucity of empirical research by drawing on a number of existing studies and theories to further specify and configure an existing holistic and eclectic taxonomy in terms of specific relationships and consequences and by enunciating the linkages between the identity concepts through the processes of cultural dynamics.

The main protagonists of organizational life are management and employees. Managers, as leaders, champion organizational purpose, marshal human and other resources into specific configurations, and strategize for success. Managers envision a set of characteristics they want their organization to be associated with and these characteristics formulate a corporate identity that is transmitted to employees through a complex and congruent system of communication, behavior, and design. Employees implement strategies and call upon their skills and competences to perform them. In so doing, they draw images, interpretations, and meanings from the transmitted corporate identity and from a nexus of cultural and other frames of reference and express what they perceive, think, and feel about their organization through behavior, symbols, and language.

29

Consequences of aligned corporate and organizational identity include positive internal and external images that lead to enhanced employee retention and to recruitment through favorable reputations respectively. These, it is argued, will lead to competitive advantage. Culture is one of the three contextual elements that serve as interpretive mechanisms for all organizational members. Traditional viewpoints of culture within identity studies do not allow a wider scope of analysis and management should realize that differentiation and fragmentation are also prevalent within organizations and may lead to the failure of corporate identity programs in the same way as incongruent behaviour and managerial incompetence. Studies of identity at the cultural level of analysis should include cultural artefacts, formal and informal practices, as well as espoused and inferred content themes. Moreover, cultural processes, are not static but dynamic and help explain how corporate identity is translated into favorable images and organizational identity that, in turn, should form primary inputs to any formal corporate identity program.

For an academic audience, this model lays important groundwork for a theory of identity and calls into motion the need for a combined multi-disciplinary effort towards further empirical research. The theory bridges, not blurs, existing paradigmatic underpinnings that are considered as complementary. Functionalist approaches reveal important elements, typologies, relationships, and commonalities. On the other hand, symbolic approaches uncover interpretations and meanings, ingredients essential to corporate identity strategies and programs. Future contributions to identity theory might be made to operationalize the components and empirically test the relationships presented. Further empirical research is also needed on the consequences of managed corporate identity programs including the effect on organizational identity.

For a managerial audience, we have highlighted the consensus within literature as to the definitions and components of identity. We have also presented an alternative view to the mainstream cultural literature that presents corporate culture as a monolith of consistency, clarity, and harmony. Our framework shifts the focus away from the more tangible aspects of corporate identity management such as graphic design and looks at the more abstract and subconscious forces that influence, in part, all behavior within organizations.

CASE VIGNETTE: NHS

The Cultural Webs of the NHS produced by managers in the 1990s

Routines and rituals

This took form, for example, in routines of consultation and of prescribing drugs. Rituals had to do with what managers termed "infantilizing," which "put patients in their place"—making them wait, putting them to bed, waking them up and so on. The subservience of patients was further emphasized by the elevation of clinicians with ritual consultation ceremonies and ward rounds. These are routines and rituals which emphasize that it is the professionals who are in control.

Stories

Most of the stories within health services concern developments in curing—particularly terminal illnesses. The heroes of the health services are in curing not so much in caring. There are also stories about villainous politicians trying to change the system, the failure of those who try to make changes and of heroic acts by those defending the systems (often well-known medical figures).

Symbols

Symbols reflected the various institutions within the organization, with uniforms for clinical and nursing staff, distinct symbols for clinicians, such as their staff retinues, and status symbols such as mobile phones and dining rooms. The importance of size and status of hospitals was reflected, not least, in the designation of "Royal" in the name, seen as a key means of ensuring that it might withstand closure.

Power structures

The power structure was fragmented between clinicians, nurses and managers. However historically, senior clinicians were the most powerful and managers had hitherto been seen as "administration." As with many other organizations, there was also a strong informal network of individuals and groups that coalesced around specific issues to promote or resist a particular view.

Organizational structures

Structures were hierarchical and mechanistic. There was a clear pecking order between services, with the "caring" services low down the list—for example, mental health. At the informal level there was lots of "tribalism" between functions and professional groups.

Control systems

In hospitals the key measure has been "complete clinical episodes," i.e., activity rather than results. Control over staff is exerted by senior professionals. Patronage is a key feature in this professional culture.

The paradigm

The assumptions which constitute the paradigm reflect the common public perception in the UK that the NHS is a "good thing"; a public service which should be provided equally, free of charge at the point of delivery. However, it is medical values that are central and the view that "medics know best." This is an organization concerned with curing illness rather than preventing illness in the first place. For example, pregnancy is not an illness, but pregnant women often argue that hospitals treat them as though they are ill. It is the acute sector within hospitals that is central to the service rather than, for example, care in the community. Overall the NHS is seen as belonging to those who provide the services.

Source: Johnson and Scholes (2002: 233).

ISSUES FOR FURTHER DISCUSSION

1   Does organizational culture really effect how employees perceive themselves and their role within an organization?
2   What other cultural influences are brought to bear in organizational life and how do these effect the success of the organization?
3   Is management able to influence organizational culture to the extent of modifying behavior and perpetuating its own goals?
4   Is there such thing as a unified corporate culture and can an organization function successfully in the absence of one?

NOTES

1   For example, Hatch, M. J. and Schultz, M. (1997), "Relations between organizational culture, identity and image," *European Journal of Marketing,* 31 (5/5): 356–65.
2   For example, Hatch, M. J. and Schultz, M. (1997), "Relations between organizational culture, identity and image," *European Journal of Marketing,* 31, (5/5): 356–65.
3   Organizational purpose forms part of a set of *enduring, fundamental,* and *guiding* business *principles* that allow strategic decisions to be made, that ensure the marshalling of resources, and that enable the firm to be steered in a certain direction. These principles make up the "corporate mission" with organizational purpose lying at its heart. Other components of the mission include "organizational beliefs," "organizational values," and "business definition" (De Witt and Meyer, 2004)
4   The failure by the functionalist perspective to capture meaning should not be construed as a theoretical or methodological error. Rather, it arises from the different epistemological assumptions of two contrasting paradigms within the literature.

REFERENCES

Aaker, D. (1996) *Building Strong Brands*. New York: Free Press.

Abratt, R. (1989) "A new approach to the corporate image management process." *Journal of Marketing Management*, 5(1): 63–76.

Albert, S. and Whetten, D. (1985) "Organizational identity," in J. M. T. Balmer and S. A. Greyser (eds), *Revealing the Corporation: Perspectives on Identity, Image, Reputation, Corporate Branding and Corporate-level Marketing*, 1st edn. London: Routledge, 77–105.

Balmer, J. M. T. (1998) "Corporate identity and the advent of corporate marketing." *Journal of Marketing Management*, 14: 963–96.

Balmer, J. M. T. (2001) "Corporate identity, corporate branding and corporate marketing: seeing through the fog." *European Journal of Marketing*, 35(3/4): 248–91.

Balmer, J. M. T. and Greyser, S. A. (2003) "Managing the multiple identities of the corporation," in J. M. T. Balmer and S. A. Greyser (eds), *Revealing the Corporation: Perspectives on Identity, Image, Reputation, Corporate Branding and Corporate-level Marketing*, 1st edn. London: Routledge, 15–29.

Balmer, J. M. T. and Greyser, S. A. (eds) (2003) *Revealing the Corporation: Perspectives on Identity, Image, Reputation, Corporate Branding and Corporate-level Marketing*, 1st edn. London: Routledge.

Balmer, J. M. T. and Wilson, A. (1998) "Corporate identity: there is more to it than meets the eye." *International Studies of Management and Organization*, 28(3): 12 –31.

Cornelissen, J. P. and Elving, W. J. L. (2003) "Managing corporate identity: an integrative framework of dimensions and determinants." *Corporate Communications: An International Journal*, 8(3): 114–20.

Cornelissen, J. P. and Harris, P. (2001) "The corporate identity metaphor: perspectives, problems and prospects." *Journal of Marketing Management*, 17(1/2): 49–71.

De Wit, B. and Meyer, R. (2004) *Strategy: Process, Content, Context; An International Perspective*, 3rd edn. Andover: Thomson Learning.

Gioia, D. A. (1998) "From individual to organizational identity," in D. A. Whetten and P. C. Godfrey (eds), *Identity in Organizations*. Thousand Oaks, CA: Sage Publications.

Hatch, M. J. (1993) "The dynamics of organizational culture." *Academy of Management Review*, 18(4): 657–93.

Hatch, M. J. and Schultz, M. (1997) "Relations between organizational culture, identity and image." *European Journal of Marketing*, 31(5/5): 356–65.

Hatch, M. J. and Schultz, M. (2000) "Scaling the tower of Babel: relational differences between identity, image and culture in organizations," in M. Schultz, M. J. Hatch, and M. H. Larsen (eds), *The Expressive Organization*. Oxford: Oxford University Press, 11–35.

Heracleous, L. (1995) "Spinning a brand new cultural web." *People Management*, 1(22): 24–27.

Johnson, G. (1992) "Managing strategic change: strategy, culture and action." *Long Range Planning*, 25(1): 28–36.

Johnson, G. (1998), "Mapping and remapping organizational culture," in V. Ambrosini, with G. Johnson and K. Scholes (eds), *Exploring Techniques of Analysis and Evaluation in Strategic Management*. New York: Prentice Hall, 137–51.

Johnson, G. and Scholes, K. (2002) *Exploring Corporate Strategy: Text and Cases*, 6th edn. Cambridge: Pearson Education.

Kennedy, S. H. (1977) "Nurturing corporate images: total communication or ego trip." *European Journal of Marketing*, 11: 120–64.

Martin, J. (2002) *Organizational Culture: Mapping the Terrain, Foundations for Organizational Science*. Thousand Oaks, CA: Sage Publications.

Melewar, T. C. (2003) "Determinants of the corporate identity construct." *Journal of Marketing Communications*, 9: 195–220.

Melewar, T. C. and Jenkins, E. (2002) "Defining the corporate construct." *Corporate Reputation Review*, 5(1): 76–90.

Melewar, T. C. and Karaosmanoglu, E. (2005) "Seven dimensions of corporate identity: a categorisation from the practitioners' perspectives." *European Journal of Marketing*, special issue.

Melewar, T. C., Karaosmanoglu, E., and Paterson, D. (2003) "Resolving the corporate identity conundrum: an exploratory study of the concept and its contribution," in C. Veloutsou (ed.), *Communicating With Customers, Athens Institute for Education and Research*. Greece, 9–32.

Melewar, T. C., Karaosmanoglu, E., and Paterson, D. (2005) "Corporate identity: concept, components and contribution." *Journal of General Management*, 31(1): 59–81.

Nunnally, J. C. and Bernstein, I. H. (1994) *Psychometric Theory*, 3rd edn. New York: McGraw-Hill.

Schein, E. H. (2004) *Organizational Culture and Leadership*, 3rd edn. New York: John Wiley and Sons.

Sheldrake, J. (2003) *Management Theory*, 2nd edn. Andover: Thomson Learning.

Simões, C. and Dibb, S. (2002) *Corporate Identity: Defining the Construct*. Warwick Business School Research Papers, Number 350, available from http://www.wbs.ac.uk/, accessed January 21, 2006.

Simões, C., Dibb, S., and Fisk, R. P. (2005) "Managing corporate identity: an internal perspective." *Journal of the Academy of Marketing Science*, 33(2): 153–68.

Stuart, H. (1999), "Towards a definitive model of the corporate identity management process." *Corporate Communications: An International Journal*, 4(4): 200–7.

Stuart, H. (2002) "Employee identification with the corporate identity: issues and implications." *International Studies of Management and Organization*, 32(3): 28–44.

Topalian, A. (1984) "Corporate identity: beyond the visual overstatements." *International Journal of Advertising*, 3: 56.

Zinkhan, G. M., Jaiskankur, G. A., and Genc, M. (2003) "Corporate image: a conceptual framework for strategic planning," in G. Marshall and S. Grove (eds), *Enhancing Knowledge Development in Marketing*. Chicago: American Marketing Association, vol. 12, 152–60.

Chapter 2

An epiphany of three

Corporate identity, corporate brand
management, and corporate marketing

John M. T. Balmer *

**AT THE END OF THIS CHAPTER READERS SHOULD BE
ABLE TO:**

1   Appreciate the utility of adopting what I call (a) an identity-based view of the
corporation and (b) an identity-based view of corporate branding

2   Comprehend the paradigm shift that has led to the introduction/adaptation of
the marketing philosophy to organizations in their totality and what I call
Corporate Marketing

3   Be cognizant with the Corporate Marketing Mix that I have simplified to
encompass six elements: Character, Culture, Constituencies, Communications,
Conceptualization, and Covenant

4   Appreciate the practical utility of adopting an identity-based view of
corporations/corporate brands as advanced by myself in this chapter

---

KEY POINTS

■   Adopting an identity-based view of organizations, institutional brand, and
corporate marketing can be revelatory in terms of our comprehension and
management of the contemporary business environment

■   There are *three*, major, schools of thought *relating to corporate identity*
scholarship as identified by the author:

1   *visual identification* (the projection of favorable institutional images
utilising corporate symbolism *and* other types of corporate
communication)

---

* The Right of Professor John M. T. Balmer to be identified as the author of this chapter has been asserted by him
in accordance with the Copyright, Designs and Patents Act (1988).

2 *stakeholder identification with the corporation* (identification with the corporation resulting from the internalization of an organization's values and activities or the opposite where non/ambivalent/negative identification occurs)

3 *corporate identity* (The distinctive and defining characteristics of an organization)

■ Balmer's *identity-based view of corporate brands* asserts that:

1 a corporate identity footprint (see above) provides the platform upon which corporate brands are built

2 corporate brands may be defined in terms of a *corporate brand covenant* (or promise) which serves as an informal, albeit powerful, contract between an institution/s and its stakeholders

3 whereas *legal ownership* of a corporate brand resides with one or more institutions, *emotional ownership* of a corporate brand resides with customers, employees, and other stakeholder groups (this is where the real worth of corporate brands resides)

■ The application of marketing concepts to institutions in their totality (rather than to services or products) has given rise to a paradigm shift in marketing and the emergence of what is known as *Corporate Marketing*. The six elements of the corporate marketing mix are: *Character, Communication, Constituencies, Covenant, Conceptualization and Culture*.

CORPORATE IDENTITY: MORE THAN MEETS THE EYE

Recently, Hilton announced that it was getting out of beds. In the People's Republic of China, Starbucks got up an explosive head of steam over café lattes, cappuccinos, and double espressos. In the USA, Intel was, in a manner of speaking, thinking rather more outside than inside the box. Finally, in a *Financial Times* retrospective, it was noted why employees of Continental Airways gave flight to airline insignia after the disembarkation of passengers.

What's going on here? And, what has this all got to do with corporate identity? Let me explain by elucidating the details of the four case vignettes outlined above.

Hilton Hotels of Great Britain publicized that it was changing its logo and name. From henceforth it would be known as Ladbrokes. In the People's Republic of China, Shanghai Xingbake was fined £36,000 (Rmb500,000) and the erstwhile company was ordered, in a landmark judgment, to issue a public apology, via a local newspaper, to Starbucks. The Chinese company had been using an almost identical name and logo to that of the US coffee chain Starbucks (Dickie 2006). What of Intel? Well, the ubiquitous global brand had startled many business commentators and branding pandjorams with its decision to alter its logo and to dump the eponymous, if not celebrated, strap line "Intel inside." As for Continental Airlines, a former CEO of the airline noted that when he took over in the 1990s employees were ashamed to be associated with such a lousy airline and ditched company uniforms as quickly as was expediently possible once they were off duty (Skapinker 2005).

Superficially, the above news items may, at first sight, appear to be quintessentially concerned with changes of company names, logos, and with trademark law. Clearly, such concerns are of importance to management and their importance is irrefutable. However, a focus on company logos and visual identification represents the trappings, rather than the substance, of corporate identity.

Again, further explanation is required and on closer scrutiny we can unearth the more substantive aspects of corporate identity that underpin my case vignettes relating to Hilton, Starbucks, Intel, and Continental Airways:

CASE VIGNETTE: Hilton

Delving deeper into the change of corporate name change from Hilton to Ladbrokes reveals a more substantive change of corporate identity. This is because the most profound aspect of identity change undertaken here relates to the adoption of a new *corporate strategy* by this British-based company. As such, this materially affected business purposes and activities. The British company, by divesting its hotel interests, and not inconsiderable brand equity, to a sister corporation in the US (confusingly, also called Hilton) was able to access considerable financial capital which was, to a large degree, passed on to shareholders: the erstwhile owners of the company. Moreover, the organization was of the view that it was in its long-term business interests to focus on another core competency: gambling. As such, the adoption of the Ladbrokes name for the corporation (Ladbrokes had existed as a stand-alone company within the British-based Hilton Group) was seen to be a most efficacious move. The name change was the consequence of real identity change and, in reality, had more to do with strategy than graphic design (important though it was in communicating the change of strategy).

CASE VIGNETTE: Starbucks

Starbucks, through its successful lawsuit in The People's Republic of China (PRC), was doing far more than ensuring it had sole control in the use of its name and logo. This is because senior managers appreciated that the Starbucks brand name was *an important strategic asset for the corporation*. Moreover, the Starbucks brand name and logo (as Starbucks and the Chinese company Xingbake fully realized) not only served as a marque of identification but also encapsulated key, corporate brand, values that were coveted by customers and others. As such, Starbucks in undertaking legal action was protecting a key, and highly lucrative, corporate asset, an asset that afforded considerable leverage in mature, as well as in new markets such as PRC. This is something that Starbucks, and, ironically Shanghai Xingbake, realised. Xingbake, by marshaling (albeit illegally) the positive associations of the Starbucks corporate brand clearly demonstrated the strategic importance of the Starbucks name, logo and, moreover, its positive brand values. As is commonly believed, imitation is the highest form of flattery: it can also be theft, of course!

CASE VIGNETTE: Intel

As for Intel, this corporation has embarked on a major strategic shift of organizational emphasis and purpose, by embracing new lines of activity such as consumer electronics, wireless communications, and healthcare. Superficially, the change was about tweaking the company's logo but, more substantively, it was fundamentally concerned with *a change in strategy*. As such, the tweaking of the company logo represented the trappings rather than the substantive aspects of the identity change. The substantive change relates to a broadening of Intel's core competences beyond the manufacture of microprocessors. As such, the change of logo and the accompanying corporate advertising had the aim of articulating this change to external audiences (both new and old) in the medium term.

CASE VIGNETTE: Continental Airlines

The discomfort of airline employees in sporting the airline's name, emblem, and corporate livery had nothing to do with the design and aesthetics of the corporate design but had everything to do with their acute embarrassment in working for a (then) lousy airline. In the early 1990s, company performance, management style, conditions of employment, and customer service, were abysmal. This case focuses on another, critically important, aspect of corporate identity: that of corporate identification or, as in the case cited here, non-identification. Identification with any organization can naturally be strong, moderate, or weak as well as positive and negative. Although employees are cited in this instance, the broad philosophy of corporate identification is equally applicable to others: customer, shareholder, and other types of corporate identity are, of course, of critical importance. This case vignette places visual identity into sharp relief. This is because a finely crafted, and aesthetically pleasing, visual identity is no surrogate for reprehensible management coupled with contemptible customer service. It is often not fully appreciated that identification has been within the purview of corporate identity (and not just organizational identity) for some considerable time and at least since the early 1980s. The work of the eminent Harvard academic Renato Taguiri is testimony to this fact (Taguiri 1982).

Of course, I have cited very major corporations but the general principles of what I discuss in this chapter is *equally apposite to organizations that are small or those that are in the public or not-for-profit sectors.*

However, what I hope to have achieved in this opening section, by making reference to the four examples cited above, is to illustrate *the strategic and multi-disciplinary* nature of corporate identity. This is quite different from its characterization (in some quarters) as an area quintessentially concerned with graphic design and organizational symbolism (important though these are). With some notable exceptions, such a perspective still informs non-marketing scholars who pigeon-hole corporate identity in terms of image projection through the utilization of corporate logos, etc.

Moreover, reference to real-life case examples also reflects an abiding concern of corporate identity scholars with *applied and managerial* aspects of corporate identity as reflected in the work of scholars from Great Britain and the old (British) Commonwealth (see: Abratt 1989; Baker and Balmer 1997; Balmer 1998; Bick, Jacobson, and Abratt 2003; Leitch and Motion 1999; Melewar and Harold 1999; Melewar 2001; Melewar and Jenkins 2002; Stuart 1999) who have long appreciated the utility of corporate identity/corporate identity management to contemporary organizations and, along with more traditional approaches to identity scholarship, have taken a practical approach in exploring the area (examining the territory in terms of real-world contexts): very much in the best traditions of leading US business schools such as Harvard: the work of Stephen Greyser and Renato Taguiri are cases in point (see: Taguiri 1982; Balmer and Greyser 2003).

Recently, within North America, there has been a welcome resurgence of interest in corporate identity-related concerns by marketing scholars and others: the work of Bhattacharya and Sen (2003), Brown, Dacin, Pratt, and Whetten (2006) and Cardador and Pratt (2006), provide indicative examples of this trend. Also, organizational behaviorists have began to recognize the provenance of (corporate) identity research by marketing and communications scholars, and that the practical and managerial implications of the identity construct *predates* that from scholars of organizational behavior (Hatch and Schultz 2004: 4). Alas, little of the aforementioned (British, Commonwealth, and European) literature surfaces in these articles/books from North America: more often than not, this occasionally generates considerable disquiet among British, Commonwealth and European scholars who, sometimes, view it as a denial of their formative contributions to the genre (no matter how slight) and are bemused as to why the principles of academic collegiality do not appear to be adhered to. However, rather than a slight, it probably (in most, but not all, instances) reflects a tradition where non-US articles are infrequently referred to, or cited, in North America and a failure on the part of non-US scholars to promote their work through books, conferences and US-focused publications. Of course, many North American scholars (rightly) have stellar reputations in these fields and their contributions have been great.

In the next section, drawing on only a little of the extensive literature on the area, I provide a short overview of the three dominant schools of thought relating to corporate identity.

THE CORPORATE IDENTITY PORTAL: THE THREE MAJOR SCHOOLS OF THOUGHT

In this section I detail the three, dominant, views of identity: *Visual Identity*, *Corporate Identification*, and *Corporate Identity*. (For an early examination of schools of thought relating to identity, see Balmer 1995.) A more recent discussion can be found in He and Balmer (2004, 2007).

VISUAL IDENTITY

Focus: The projection of a favorable institutional image utilizing corporate symbolism and other types of corporate communication.

> A desired image acquired and communicated by the company to the public through consistent visual communications.
>
> (Napoles 1988: 93)

At its essence, this school of thought is concerned with communication (especially visual communication) and with image-projection. Traditionally, the graphic design discipline underpinned this perspective. The literature relating to this school of thought includes the following, highly influential, practitioner literature, especially during the 1960s and 1970s (Henrion and Parkin 1967; Margulies 1977; Napoles 1988; Olins 1979; Pilditch 1971; Selame and Selame 1975). In addition, empirical work relating to visual identity (and its utility) has been undertaken (see: Green and Lovelock 1994; Melewar and Saunders 1999).

As I see it, there are three defining characteristics of this school of thought:

1   focuses on how an organization wishes to identify itself with its customers and stakeholders;
2   explains that management can materially influence (and control) the images held of the organization by customers and stakeholders;
3   explains that logos, names, and visual identification are effective vehicles for achieving the above.

The graphic design perspective of identity tends to be the perspective adopted by the public. It also remains a significant perspective among marketing scholars outside Britain and the old Commonwealth. This being the case, this perspective is appealing for a number of reasons: one of which is that this school of thought is readily grasped. At its essence is the notion that systems of visual identification (logos and other manifestations of graphic design) can represent, and project, the essence of an organization. Moreover, it is held that company names and logos can purposefully, if not materially, influence the perceptions held of the organization by customers and by key stakeholder groups. Many scholars find such a perspective to be a highly questionable one. Understandably, senior managers find this perspective to be especially attractive. The notion that CEOs can control and influence such external perceptions is a highly captivating one. Moreover, for some CEOs, the notion that they can, quite literally, leave their mark on the organization, is especially attractive one. Not only do newly appointed senior managers find such a proposition appealing but so do CEOs whose period of office is drawing to a close. Sometimes, such managers resort to such a change when their period of office has been lacklustre.

It should, of course, be remembered that an organization's logo/systems of corporate visual identification is one of the few aspects of corporate life that can be readily changed. Moreover, it can, unlike virtually any other aspect of corporate life, be introduced, controlled, and managed to the smallest detail. In some organizations some employees give the sobriquet of "logo cops" to those charged with such activities. The detailed graphic design manuals that are found in many organizations are testimony to the above (such manuals explain in considerable detail how the corporate logo should appear in every conceivable manifestation). While marketing scholars acknowledge the importance of visual identity in terms of the big picture relating to corporate identity, it represents the trappings rather than the substance of corporate identity, (Baker and Balmer 1997).

The next two schools of though illustrate why this might be the case. (There are, of course, other graphic design "schools" of thought: see for Balmer and Greyser (2003: 36) for a brief explanation of these.)

STAKEHOLDER IDENTIFICATION

Focus: Stakeholder identification with the corporation resulting from the internalization of an organization's values and activities or the opposite where non/ambivalent/negative identification occurs.

> Where the corporate identity is accepted and internalised by the personnel, it gives them a sense of purpose in their work and contributes to fulfil the basic human need to find meaning in life's important activities.
>
> (Taguiri 1982)

> Organizational identification . . . referring to an individual's self-definition and the inclusion of an organization in that definition.
>
> (Cardador and Pratt 2006: 175)

41

Here I have included two representative definitions relating to this school of first to which I have given the label *stakeholder identification*. The first, penned by an esteemed, senior colleague of mine, Renato Taguiri, provides a salient reminder that employee identification is a somewhat older concept than some of the contemporary literature would lead us to believe. It also shows how, in the early 1980s, corporate identification was seen to fall within the purview of corporate identity. The second definition provides a more recent explanation that, although coming from the field of organizational identity (which has focused almost exclusively on employee identification), allows for a broader application of the corporate identification construct to individuals beyond employees: customers are a case in point.

The varied and rich strands of thought relating to corporate identification require a degree of explication that is beyond the scope of this chapter.

For a more considered examination of corporate identification see: Dutton, Dukerich, and Harquail (1994) and Pratt (1998). For an examination of the relationship between marketing and managerial approaches to identity studies see He and Balmer (2004, 2007). For an examination of the various ways in which identification can occur see Cardador and Pratt (2006). For an examination of identification from a customer perspective see Bhattaracharya and Sen (2003).

The defining characteristics of this school of thought, as I see it, include (but are not limited to) the following:

1   Corporate identification relates to the internationalization by individuals (or members of a group) of the defining attributes of an organization (corporate identity).

2   Identification has, typically, been discussed in terms of employees *but is equally applicable to customers along with other stakeholder groups* (customer and stakeholder identification). To me, it also appears to be the case that *it can, crucially, also apply to inter-organizational identification as in the case of institutional identification with an industry or, indeed, a business alliance* (institutional identification).

3   Identification can occur through personal relationships with other members of the organization (identification, for instance, with other employees rather than, necessarily the organization per se), through processes of socialization, and through the use of organizational symbols (buildings, interior design, logos, etc.). The latter, it should be noted, is broader in conceptualization than visual identity as articulated earlier.

4   The benefits of *positive, rather than negative*, corporate identification (among customers, employees and others) includes increased loyalty, positive word-of-mouth recommendation and, generally speaking, positive behavior towards the corporation.

5   Corporate identification can, of course, be positive, negative or ambivalent.

In certain situations there can be a complete absence of identification – "non-identification" – where little, if anything, is known about the corporation other than, perhaps, that it exists. In many circumstances there is a lack of knowledge as to its existence.

CORPORATE IDENTITY

Focus: Actual Identity. Focuses on the distinctive and defining characteristics of an organization.

> [Corporate identity] constitutes the current attributes of the corporation. It is shaped by a number of elements, including corporate ownership, the leadership style of management, organizational structure, business activities and markets covered, the range and quality of products and services offered and overall business performance. Also encompasses the set of values held by management and employees.
>
> (Balmer and Greyser 2002)

This school focuses on the defining characteristics of an organization and those which differentiate one organization from another. Marketing scholars adopting this perspective include: Alessandri (2001), Balmer (2001, 2002), Bick, Jacobson, and Abratt (2003) and Melewar and Jenkins (2002). A good deal of this literature adopts a multi-disciplinary perspective as does the recent work of Simões, Dibb, and Fisk (2005) which concluded that corporate identity management entailed the dissemination of mission and values. Their work also mirrored the first school of thought in that it emphasizes the importance of visual identity and the communication of single image. Also of note (from a managerial rather than from a marketing perspective) is the work of Albert and Whetten (1985). They argued that the distinctive features of an organization are characterized by those organizational attributes that are *central* ("central character"), *distinctive* ("key differences"), and *enduring* ("the unchanging nature of an entity"). This bears a curious resemblance to earlier work of French scholars (who, alas, like Taguiri, are not adequately credited within the literature) who noted that corporate identity imbued an organization with *specificity, stability, and coherence* (Larcon and Reitter 1979). Balmer (2001a), taking a somewhat different perspective has argued that corporate identity is characterized by *complexity* (its multi-faceted and multi-dimensional nature: for instance the notion that corporate identities subsume other identities), *variability* (identities evolve over time and are not enduring), and *heterogeneity* (its multi-disciplinary roots and impacts).

The four defining characteristics of this school, as understood by myself, focus on, but are not necessarily limited to:

1   the organization's activities, business purpose, ownership and ethos, markets and audiences covered;
2   how the institution has been shaped by company history, heritage, and former strategies;
3   the influence of values (corporate, country, professional, and those of the founder/owners and senior management) in defining the organization's quintessence.

Clearly, this approach is fundamentally different in degree, and scale, to the other schools and is not, necessarily, easy to grasp. Even the most cursory examination of the business environment reveals that substantive change of identity is a regular and common occurrence. Such change often results in a domino-like effect in terms of the two schools of thought cited above (visual identity and corporate identification) since such change often requires the acquisition of a new name and logo, and can result in the loss of corporate identification.

Having, albeit briefly, outlined the three principal perspectives relating to corporate identity I now go on to introduce the related (but quite distinct) concept of the corporate brand. It is a concept that is enjoying increased prominence in the literature: both academic and practitioner. I articulate the nature and importance of corporate brands and how these differ from the concept of the corporate brand. I also outline how corporate brands differ from product brands (and to a lesser degree in relation to service brands). Moreover, I argue that corporate identities and corporate brands are inextricably linked. This is hardly surprising owing to the *ambient nature of corporate identity* and the fact that it provides the platform upon which other corporate-level concerns are built. It also provides the basis upon which we can comprehend corporate-level constructs, such as corporate communications and corporate image and reputation can be understood (see Balmer and Greyser 2003).

CORPORATE BRANDS

Corporate identity provides the grit around which a corporate brand is formed.

(Balmer 2001b)

Adored, venerated, and coveted by customers and organizations alike, corporate brands have become increasingly important for contemporary organizations (Balmer and Gray 2003). I have argued that corporate identity provides the platform upon which corporate brands emerge: in effect it is an institutional form of biogenesis. My identity-based perspective of corporate brands is characterized by the view that corporate identities give life to corporate brands with the latter being a distillation of core corporate identity values. *In short, the footprint of corporate identity is always to be found in a corporate brand.* Customers and stakeholders associate such values with the brand, and this, in effect, serves as an informal contract or what, in colloquial terms, is know as a "corporate brand promise." I have argued that whereas *legal ownership of a brand resides with an organization, emotional ownership of the corporate brand (and thereby its real value) resides with those who consume the corporate brand.*

Often there is often some confusion regarding the relationship between corporate brands and corporate identities. All too often (misguidedly in the opinion of the writer) some writers treat the corporate brand as a surrogate term for corporate identity. Within the practitioner literature, in particular, there is a tendency to advance the view that corporate identities and corporate brands are analogous. It is sometimes argued that the concept of the corporate brand is, in effect, nothing more than an up-to-date expression of what once was called corporate identity. There is one, palpably obvious, weakness with this approach. This is because, whereas the corporate identity concept in the two manifestations articulated earlier is applicable to every identity (for instance relating to the distinctive and defining characteristics of the organization/a distinct organizational name and visual identification system), not every organization is a corporate brand. The British Waterways Board, Yum Foods Corporation (the owners of Taco Bell, among others) are cases in point.

However, what is conspicuous is the degree to which the corporate brand concept has captured the attention of managers and practitioners. However, this had another, negative connotation. The ubiquity of its usage has meant that the corporate brand/corporate brand management has become a surrogate phrase for the organization itself (the corporate brand) and for general management (corporate brand management).

I have argued elsewhere that the concept of corporate identity, although related, is distinctive on a number of fronts for the following reasons:

1   Corporate brands have a value, portability, and longevity that corporate identities may not have (consider the Bentley corporate brand that had short life as a corporate brand in the early twentieth century but emerged as a fully fledged corporate brand in 1999 when Volkswagen resurrected the corporate brand). Until 1999 employees had worked for Rolls-Royce in a factory called Rolls-Royce and had made Rolls-Royce, as well as Bentley, cars. Even though the corporate brand (but not, admittedly as a product brand) Bentley had been dormant for much of the twentieth century its value, portability and longevity meant that it could, successfully, be resurrected.

2   Every entity has a corporate identity but may not necessarily have a corporate brand (holding companies often, but not always, fall into this category).

3   The focus of corporate brands is primarily external: customers are normally of critical importance (Sony, British Airways). Corporate identity has a more internal focus. Also, consider companies such as Nike and Dyson: both outsource a good deal of the production and activities associated with their corporate brands. Employees manufacturing trainers and vacuum cleaners in Asia will have little affinity with either brand but will have a stronger association (which may be positive, negative or indifferent) with the entity (corporate identity) producing the product. In contrast, consumers have a relationship with the corporate brand and not with the manufacturer.

4   Once established, a corporate brand can have a life, a meaning, and a set of expectations of its own and, although they are derived from an identity, over time the corporate brand can have a life of its own. It is an identity-type that is separate and divisible from the corporate identity that gave it existence. Over time the complex dimensions of a corporate brand result in a set of associations with the organization: this in the main provides the foundations for the corporate brand. Stakeholders understand, and experience, these brand attributes whereas the organization takes care to comprehend and communicate them both internally and externally.

To date, many practitioners and scholars have failed to make a clear distinction between product and corporate brands. In my writing (Balmer 1995, 2001, 2005) I have attempted to articulate some of the major differences between the two branding categories. Table 2.1 illustrates the differences I have identified between corporate and product brands and represents a slightly modified version of the model I outlined in 2001.

From the above it becomes apparent that the emergent theory on corporate branding is, for the most part, antithetical to traditional approaches to branding in that it draws on other disciplines and not just marketing. Consumers appropriate brands as a means of defining who they are, wish to be, and/or wish to be seen as, and as a means of creating individual identities. However, I argue that other groups such as employees, supplier, shareholders, etc. also marshal brands in a not-too-different way (Balmer 2005).

In the final section of this chapter I advance the view that there is an overriding logic in recognizing the interrelationships and interdependency of a number of corporate-level constructs such as corporate identity, corporate branding, corporate image and reputation, and corporate communication. I have advanced the view that this new area should go under the umbrella title of corporate marketing.

Table 2.1 *Comparing corporate with product brands*

	Corporate brands	Product brands
Disciplinary underpinnings	Multidisciplinary	Marketing
Formation	Medium/long term	Short
Source	Corporate identity	Product identity
Values	Corporate ("real values")	Synthetic ("created values")
Brand custodian	The CEO	Brand Manager
Commitment/responsibility	All personnel	Brand manager
Relevant stakeholders	All/many	Customers
Communication platform	Corporate communications	Marketing communication
Legal ownership	One or more entities	One or more entities
Emotional ownership	Stakeholder communities	Customer communities
Marshalling brands	Customers, employees	Customers
In creating a sense of self	Suppliers, shareholders Local communities etc.	

Source: Adapted from an earlier exhibit of mine dating back to 2001: see Balmer (2001)

RAISING THE UMBRELLA OF CORPORATE MARKETING

In this final section I examine the embryonic area of corporate marketing (Balmer 1998; Balmer and Greyser 2006). At present, marketing is undergoing a paradigm shift and is increasingly characterized by having an institutional-wide focus. Evidence of this can be found in the ascendancy of concepts such as corporate identity, corporate branding, corporate reputation, and corporate communications. Each of these concepts has its own intellectual roots and practice-based adherents but our discernment of the broad territory is constrained by focusing on one, rather than on many, concepts. What is exciting, however, is that when they are examined in the round a new gestalt of the corporation may be discerned and this explains the efficacy and necessity of raising the umbrella of corporate marketing. Integrative models relating to the domain are beginning to appear, such as the ACID Test (Balmer and Soenen 1999; Balmer 2001a; Balmer and Greyser 2002), the five-faceted approach outlined in Moingeon and Soenen (2002), and the troika of elements outlined in Brown, Dacin, Pratt, and Whetten (2006). A cross-disciplinary perspective also informs the work of He and Balmer (2005) in relation to management cognition *vis à vis* institutional identity.

Marketing's entrée in to the *corporate* domain has, already, become a reality. The rise of "new" areas of marketing interest such as relationship marketing, the marketing of services, internal marketing, marketing for non-profits, green marketing, and in specialized areas such as corporate brand management, corporate image, and reputation. Kotler's (1986) notion of megamarketing with its recognition of groups "beyond customers", the importance accorded to political power and public opinion by marketers, and the importance attached to marketing networks in their various guises, all resonate with my comprehension of corporate-level marketing.

A cardinal error of those who write about marketing is a failure to emphasize the point that marketing is, in its essence, about a philosophy rather than specific organizational functions. This raises the somewhat delicate (and, for some, contentious) issue as to the difference between public relations (PR) and marketing. The critical distinction being that corporate marketing goes *beyond a concern with communications* in that it embraces a wider palette of concerns as evinced by the six Cs which are elaborated later: many of these elements have a strong marketing inheritance. My first corporate marketing mix (Balmer 1998) has, subsequently, been simplified to form the six Cs as outlined here (see Balmer 2006; Balmer and Greyser 2006).

THE CORPORATE-LEVEL MARKETING MIX

What are the substantive differences between the marketing mix and the corporate-level marketing mix?

I hold there to be three:

1   The first is that *the elements are broader* than the traditional "four Ps" of the marketing mix.
2   The second is that the elements of *the traditional mix require a radical reconfiguration.*
3   The third is that *the mix elements have distinct disciplinary* traditions. They also transcend the traditional organizational boundaries.

The six dimensions of the corporate marketing mix are: *Character, Culture Constituencies, Communications, Conceptualizations,* and *Covenant.* The six elements of my corporate marketing mix are shown below in the form of six-sided star: see Figure 2.1.

The following section provides a brief description of each of the elements forming my corporate marketing mix. In illustrating each dimension I posit a question, which articulates the critical nature of each of the components of the mix. In addition, I make reference to the corporate-level concept that underpins the area.

Figure 2.1 *Balmer's corporate marketing mix*

CHARACTER

Question: "What are the distinctive and defining characteristics of our organization?"

Concept: Corporate identity

Those factors that, in their totality, make one entity distinct from another. These include key tangible and intangible assets of the organization as well as organizational activities, markets served, corporate ownership and structure, organizational type, corporate philosophy, and corporate history. In academic parlance this is often called the corporate identity (not to be confused with corporate identity as it relates to systems of visual identification).

CULTURE

Question: "What are the collective feelings of employees regarding the organization where they work?"

Concept/s: Corporate identification and corporate culture

This refers to the collective feeling of employees as to what they feel they are in the setting of the entity (their workplace entity). These beliefs are derived from the values, beliefs, and assumptions about the organization and its historical roots and heritage. Individuals may, in part, define themselves in terms of their relationship with the organization which they have internalized. Culture is important since it provides the context in which staff engage with each other and with other groups such as customers: employees represent the "frontline" of the organization.

CONSTITUENCIES

Question: "Which stakeholders are of critical importance and why?"
Concept/s: Stakeholder theory and corporate governance

The philosophy of corporate marketing is predicated upon the fact that the continuance and success of organizations entail meeting the wants and needs of a variety of stakeholder groups: customers are of course (in most instances) of primary importance. Without the support (and identification) of such groups with the entity the organization might not have a license to operate. Corporate marketing should also come with a realization that individuals can belong to several stakeholder groups (as a customer, employee, shareholder, and so on). Stakeholder management may, in broad terms, be viewed as analogous to "constituencies."

CONCEPTUALISATION

Question: "How are we seen by our key stakeholders?"
Concept: Corporate image and corporate reputation

This refers to perceptions (conceptualizations) held of the corporate brand by customers and other key stakeholder groups. The latent perception of the organization held by the above will affect their view of and their behavior towards the organization. Such conceptualizations of the organization will, of course, differ between different groups and account needs to be taken of this. Corporate image and corporate reputation scholarship inform this dimension of the corporate marketing mix.

COMMUNICATION

Question: "Who do we say we are and to whom do we say this?"
Concept: Corporate communications

Corporate communications relates to the various communication channels deployed by organizations to communicate with customers and other constituencies consisting of management and organizational communications. At its most comprehensive it also takes into account the communications effects of management, employee and product behavior, and of word-of-mouth and media/competitor commentary (see Balmer and Greyser 2003: 139–47).

COVENANT

Question: "What are the distinct components that underpin our corporate brand covenant (corporate brand promise)?"

Concept: Corporate brand

This specifically relates to the values and associations that are associated with a corporate brand. Such values may be viewed as a synthesis of the myriad of values that imbue a corporate identity. I have argued that a corporate brand is underpinned by a powerful (albeit informal) contract, which can be compared to a covenant in that customers and other stakeholder groups often have a religious-like loyalty to the corporate brand. Whereas (I hold) *legal ownership* of a corporate brand is vested in an entity its *emotional ownership* (and therein its substantial value) resides with those who have a close association with the brand (see Balmer 2001, 2001a, 2005; Balmer and Gray 2003).

CONCLUSION

In bringing this short chapter to a close, I am mindful that it has been an "epiphany of three": an attempt to reveal the quintessential natures of corporate identity, corporate branding, and corporate marketing. In providing an exegesis of these areas I have drawn on case vignettes and the literature (including, for purely practical reasons, a good deal from my own writing). Past and present marketing scholars of mine may remember the Balmerism, namely that *"the cerebral needs to be married with the practical."* Fingers crossed that I have practiced what I have preached! So it is my hope that in introducing you to these three areas your discernment is now, perhaps, just a little clearer and that you can appreciate the saliency of what I have discussed. Let us not forget that these areas are, more often than not, of *vital, strategic, importance and that they are an abiding concern of senior management.* We need to look no further for "evidence" than our opening examination of Hilton, Starbucks, Intel, and Continental. As a former supervisor of mine would have declared at this juncture: *"quod erat demonstrandum"* which fittingly, as I wrap up this chapter, translates as *"there you have it!"*

51

ISSUES FOR FURTHER DISCUSSION

1   Critically discuss the four case histories examined in the opening section of this chapter in the context of the three schools of thought relating to identity (visual identity, stakeholder identification, and corporate identity).

2   Select two organizations operating in the same sector (for instance banks, financial services, universities, supermarkets) and articulate their respective corporate brand covenants (promise) in terms of (a) what they promise and (b) what they deliver (from a customer as well as from an employee perspective).

3   Apply the corporate marketing mix to an organization with which you are familiar. To what extent do the elements of the mix (in their totality) comprise a meaningful whole?

REFERENCES

Abratt, R. (1989) "A new approach to the corporate image management process." *Journal of Marketing Management,* 5(1): 63–76.

Albert, S. and Whetten, D. (1985) "Organizational identity," in J. M. T. Balmer and S. A. Greyser (eds), *Revealing the Corporation: Perspectives on Identity, Image, Reputation, Corporate Branding and Corporate-level Marketing,* 1st edn. London: Routledge.

Alessandri, W. S. (2001) "Modeling corporate identity: a concept explication and theoretical examination." *Corporate Communications: An International Journal,* 6(2): 173–82.

Baker, M. J. and Balmer, J. M. T. (1997) "Visual identity: trappings of substance?" Special edition on Corporate Identity: *European Journal of Marketing,* 5–6(3): 366–82.

Balmer, J. M. T. (1995) "Corporate branding and connoisseurship." *Journal of General Management,* 21(1): 22–46.

Balmer, J. M. T. (1998) "Corporate identity and the advent of corporate marketing." *Journal of Marketing Management,* 14(8) 963–96.

Balmer, J. M. T. (2001) "Corporate identity, corporate branding and corporate marketing: seeing through the fog." *European Journal of Marketing* 35(3/4): 248.

Balmer, J. M. T. (2001a) "From the Pentagon: a new identity framework." *Corporate Reputation Review,* 4(1): 11–22.

Balmer, J. M. T. (2001b) "The three virtues and seven deadly sins of corporate brand management." *Journal of General Management,* 27(1): 1–17.

Balmer, J. M. T. (2002) "Of identities lost and found." *International Studies of Management and Organizations,* 32(3): 10–27.

Balmer, J. M. T. (2005) "Corporate brand cultures and communities" in J. E. Schroeder and M. Salzer-Morling (eds), *Brand Culture.* London: Routledge, 34–49.

Balmer J. M. T. (2006) *Comprehending Corporate Marketing and the Corporate*

Marketing Mix. Bradford University School of Management, Working Paper Series no. 06/08.

Balmer, J. M. T. and Greyser, S. A. (2002) "Managing the multiple identities of the corporation." *California Management Review*, 44(3): 72–86.

Balmer, J. M. T. and Gray, E. (2003) "Corporate brands: what are they? What of them?" *European Journal of Marketing*, 37(7–8): 972–97.

Balmer, J. M. T. and Greyser, S. A. (2003a) *Revealing the Corporation: Perspectives on Identity, Image, Reputation, Corporate Branding and Corporate-level Marketing*. London: Routledge.

Balmer, J. M. T. and Greyser, S. A. (2006) "Corporate marketing: integrating corporate identity, corporate branding, corporate communications, corporate image and corporate reputation." *European Journal of Marketing*, 40(7–8): 730–41.

Balmer, J. M. T. and Soenen, G. (1999) "The ACID test of corporate identity management." *Journal of Marketing Management*, 15(1–3): 69–92.

Bhattacharya, C. B. and Sen, S. (2003) "Consumer–company identification: a framework for understanding consumers' relationships with companies." *Journal of Marketing*, 67: 76–88.

Bick, G., Jacobson, M. C., and Abratt, R. (2003) "The corporate identity management process revisited." *Journal of Marketing Management*, 19: 835–55.

Brown, T. J., Dacin, P. A., Pratt, M. G., and Whetten, D. A. (2006) "Identity, intended image, construed image and reputation: an interdisciplinary framework and suggested terminology." *Journal of the Academy of Marketing Science*, 34(2): 99–106.

Cardador, M. T. and Pratt, M. G. (2006) "Identification management and its bases: bridging management and marketing perspectives through a focus on affiliation dimensions." *Journal of the Academy of Marketing Science*, 34(2): 174–84.

Dickie, M. (2006) "Starbucks wins key Chinese lawsuit over brand." *Financial Times*, January 3: 24.

Dutton, J. E., Dukerich, J. M., and Harquail, C. V. (1994) "Organizational images and member identification." *Administrative Science Quarterly*, 39(2): 239–63.

Green, D. and Lovelock, V. (1994) "Understanding a corporate symbol." *Applied Cognitive Psychology*, 8: 37–47.

Hatch, M.-J, and Schultz, M. (eds) (2004) *Organizational Identity*. Oxford: Oxford University Press.

He, H.-W. and Balmer, J.M.T. (2004) "Identity studies: multiple perspectives and implications for corporate level marketing." Bradford University School of Management Working Paper Series 05/04.

He, H.-W. and Balmer, J. M. T. (2005) "Managerial perceived identity/strategy dissonance." Bradford University School of Management Working Paper Series 05/07.

He, H.-W. and Balmer, J. M. T. (2007) "Identity studies: multiple perspectives and implications for corporate level marketing." *European Journal of Marketing*, 41(7–8): 765–85.

Henrion, F. and Parkin, A. (1967) *Design Co-ordination and Corporate Image*. London: Studio Vista.

Kotler, P. (1986) "Megamarketing." *Harvard Business Review* (March–April): 117–24.

Larcon, J. P. and Reitter, R. (1979) *Structures de Pouvoir et Identité de l'Entreprise*. Paris: Nathan.

Leitch, S. and Motion, J. (1999) "Multiplicity in corporate identity strategy," Special Edition on Corporate Identity. *Corporate Communications: An International Journal*, 4(4): 193–9.

Margulies, W. (1977) "Make the most of your corporate image." *Harvard Business Review* (July–August): 66–77.

Melewar, T. C. (2001) "Measuring visual identity: multi-construct study." *Corporate Communications: An International Journal,* 5(1): 36–41.

Melewar, T. C. and Harold, J. (1999) "The role of corporate identity in merger and acquisition activity." *Journal of General Management,* 26(2): 17–31.

Melewar, T. C. and Jenkins, E. (2002) "Defining the corporate identity construct." *Corporate Reputation Review,* 5(1): 76–91.

Melewar, T. C. and Saunders, J. (1999) "International global visual identity: standardisation or localisation?" *Journal of International Business Studies,* 31(3): 583–98.

Melewar, T. C., Saunders, J., and Balmer, J. M. T. (2002) "Cause, effect and benefits of a standardised corporate visual identity system of UK companies operating in Malaysia," Special Edition on Corporate Identity. *European Journal of Marketing,* 35(3/4): 414–27.

Moingeon, B. and Soenen, G. (eds) (2002) *Corporate and Organizational Identities.* London: Routledge.

Napoles, V. (1988) *Corporate Identity Design.* New York: John Wiley.

Olins, W. (1978) *The Corporate Personality: An Inquiry into the Nature of Corporate Identity.* London: Design Council.

Olins, W. (1979) "Corporate identity: the myth and the reality." *Journal of the Royal Society of Arts,* 127: 209–18.

Pilditch, J. (1971) *Communication by Design: A Study in Corporate Identity.* Maidenhead: McGraw-Hill.

Pratt, M. G. (1998) "'To Be or Not to Be?' Central Questions in Organizational Identification," in D. Whetten and P. Godfrey (eds), *Identity in Organizations: Developing Theory Through Conversations.* Thousand Oaks, CA: Sage: 171–207.

Selame, E. and Selame, J. (1975) *The Company Image.* New York: John Wiley.

Simões, C., Dibb, S., and Fisk, R. P. (2005) "Managing Corporate Identity: An Internal Perspective." *Journal of the Academy of Marketing Science,* 33(2): 153–68.

Skapinker, M. (2005) "How to hit the target in five easy steps." *Financial Times,* May 23: 8.

Stuart, H. (1999) "Towards a definitive model of the corporate identity management process," Special Edition on Corporate Identity. *Corporate Communications: An International Journal,* 4(4): 200–7.

Taguiri, R. (1982) "Managing corporate identity: the role of top management," International Seminar on Corporate Identity Building, CERAM, Sophia Antipolis, France.

Chapter 3

Non-traditional expressions of organizational visual identity

Reaching consumers through alternative means

Sue Westcott Alessandri

AT THE END OF THIS CHAPTER READERS SHOULD BE ABLE TO:

1   Understand the meaning of non-traditional expressions of visual identity
2   Appreciate a non-traditional expression of visual identity as a strategic way to reach consumers
3   Name specific examples of when non-traditional expressions of identity are relevant for reinforcing an existing visual identity

---

KEY POINTS

- **Organizational Identity** is the strategically planned and purposeful presentation of an organization. This includes all of the observable and measurable elements of an organization's identity manifest in its comprehensive visual presentation, including—but not limited to—its name, logo, tagline, color palette, and architecture (Alessandri 2001)
- **Organizational Image** is the totality of a stakeholder's perceptions of the way an organization presents itself, either deliberately or accidentally. Organizations have several images, since perceptions vary widely among stakeholders. An organization manages its image by managing its identity (Markwick and Fill 1997)
- **Non-traditional Expressions of Organizational Identity** occur when an organization explicitly uses one or more of the traditional identity elements (name, logo, tagline or colors from its palette) in a unique way. This enables the organization to extend its traditional identity while reinforcing one or more of its individual identity elements

INTRODUCTION

On the face of it, a European cycling race, a southern university's golf course and a quaint Florida town wouldn't seem to have anything in common, least of all commonality concerning an organization's visual identity. In the pioneering world of integrated marketing communications, however, where every consumer touch point is an opportunity—an imperative, even—to reinforce an organization's identity, all three of these examples represent innovative ways to communicate with stakeholders and the public—and ultimately build brand equity.

For the purposes of this chapter, an organization is any group that shares a common mission—be it a for-profit firm, a non-profit group, a college or university, or even a loosely organized ad hoc group. Each of these organizations has an identity, which is its unique way of communicating with stakeholders inside and outside the organization: from employees to vendors to shareholders or trustees. When an organization has a distinctive identity, it not only differentiates itself from its competition, but it also communicates specific messages about the organization. But what is an organization's identity? Conceptually, an organization's identity is its strategically planned and purposeful presentation of itself. Operationally, however, this definition provides limited flexibility for measuring an ever-expanding construct. How does the organization actually present itself? The answer comes in the form of the following measurable definition: an organization's identity includes all of the observable and measurable elements manifest in the organization's comprehensive visual presentation of itself, including—but not limited to—its name, logo, tagline, color palette, and architecture. An organization's identity also includes its public behavior, including—but not limited to— its reception of employees, customers, shareholders, and suppliers (Alessandri 2001).

Of course, an organization's identity does not exist in a vacuum. Rather, it exists solely to serve a higher function: to help an organization achieve a positive image in the minds of the public. Today there is a generally accepted distinction between identity (what the organization is) and image (what the organization is perceived to be). Over time, positive impressions of the organization's image can serve to promote a positive reputation. How that happens is through a relatively simple—although lengthy—process of association formation that begins with the firm's mission.

The organization's mission represents its philosophy (Abratt 1989; Leuthesser and Kohli 1997), its raison d'être. The assumption here is that every organization has a philosophy, whether tacit or codified, and whether it consciously projects it or lets it evolve naturally. Under the best circumstances, an organization will carefully develop and then nurture its identity, but even firms that pay little attention to their identities are sending a message about their philosophy. Typically, a philosophy is personified through the behavior of the organization as well as in its visual presentation; these two complementary elements make up the organization's identity. The most important reality of the organization's identity is that it is completely within the control of the organization: it can choose how to present itself visually, or through its behavior (Leitch and Motion 1999; Topalian 1984). As a result, this control gives the organization the power to manipulate or alter its identity at its discretion.

What the organization is not in control of, however, is its image, which results from interactions or experiences—any type of association—with an organization's identity (Gray and Balmer 1998; Gregory and Wiechmann 1999; Topalian 1984). While organizations do not retain any direct control over their images, how they are perceived by the public, these organizations can work diligently to project an identity that is both appropriate and pleasing.

In summary, an identity is the organization's projection of itself, while the image is the way the public perceives the organization. Over time, the identity and the image work hand-in-hand by helping the public to form a reputation of the organization, either positive or negative, through repeated impressions of the image (Gray and Balmer 1997, 1998; Markwick and Fill 1997). In this respect, an organization's identity is the first step towards reputation formation, and the identity remains an integral part of its marketing strategy since it remains within the control of the organization itself.

In theory, it sounds quite simple for an organization to develop a pleasing identity, garner a positive image, and then go on to reap the benefits of a stellar reputation. In reality, however, consumers are inundated with "pleasing identities," which are woven throughout the innumerable messages that compete for their attention everyday. The average American consumer might see anywhere from hundreds to three thousand commercial messages per day, so the challenge is upon marketers to make their messages memorable. But marketing to today's sophisticated audiences means getting under the radar of many who are savvy enough to immediately spot a commercial message—and then perhaps turn away from it. When it is not immediately evident that a message is commercial, however, it may have the power to communicate more directly with consumers.

This indirect communication comes in the form of non-traditional expressions of identity. While the traditional elements of an identity might include the organization's name, logo, tagline, color palette, and architecture, non-traditional expressions of identity might include a stuffed animal prize that represents the organization (such as the Crédit Lyonnais stuffed lion handed out each day to the leading cyclist in the Tour de France), a university golf course with a signature hole designed in the shape of the university's athletics logo (such as the tiger paw seventeenth hole at Clemson University's Walker Course), or even an entire town developed according to the philosophy of a for-profit corporation (such as Celebration, Florida, USA).

The deployment of these alternative forms of identity stems from an organization's overwhelming need to compete with more traditional messages, but organizations might also recognize the need to project a consistent identity that reaches consumers in a memorable manner. In this way, these organizations have embraced the ideals of integrated marketing: using multiple media to project a unified message.

The chapter will provide background on the concept of integrated marketing communications (IMC) to frame the relevance of non-traditional expressions of identity. It will also trace the historical roots of several non-traditional expressions of identity as a way of exploring how and why organizations have begun to depend on these non-traditional expressions as an integral component of their overall identity strategy.

INTEGRATED MARKETING COMMUNICATIONS

Since the 1980s, there has been a tremendous amount of discussion focused on "cutting through the clutter" and competing more successfully for the attention of an increasingly savvy—and skeptical—consuming public. Early in the debate over how best to reach the appropriate audiences, the concept of integrated marketing communications began to garner attention after the publication of *Integrated Marketing Communications* (Schultz et al. 1993). The promise of an IMC approach to promotion is that integrated communication—individual communications that share a common message—will separate the brand from its competition by associating it with value in the minds of the public.

Schultz et al. (1993) wrote that IMC is more efficient than more traditional models of marketing based on the way consumers process the information they receive. The authors' contention is based on advances in thinking about processing. Early information processing models, namely the replacement model, held that new marketing messages can literally replace the messages already stored in memory.

However, the more credible accumulation model, on which the concept of IMC is based, asserts that information is not replaced, but is combined with existing messages stored in memory. Therefore, marketers who send non-integrated messages risk not having their messages processed sufficiently to allow recall. In addition, many consumers may not be sophisticated enough from a marketing perspective to differentiate between the various forms of communication: advertising, public relations, promotions, etc. Rather, consumers tend to view all of a firm's communication as one flow of indistinguishable media.

While the concept of having a unified message communicated through multiple media may seem elementary, even obvious, to identity scholars, IMC has its detractors. For myriad reasons, Cornelissen and Lock (2000) have argued that

IMC is a management fashion. They contend that IMC is not academically rigorous, that the concept itself is oversimplified, that managers employ IMC because it is the "rational norm," and finally, that managers embrace IMC because it is novel. In addition, the authors model IMC on a product lifecycle and go so far as to conclude that IMC is on the decline.

In response to Cornelissen and Lock (2000), Schultz and Kitchen (2000) state that they never conceived of IMC as a theory, but as a concept that is evolving along with the research being conducted on it. The authors refute the idea that IMC is simply a management fashion, referring skeptics to other marketing concepts that are also difficult to measure. Debate notwithstanding, the concept of IMC dovetails nicely with the concept of promoting identity. In fact, Markwick and Fill (1997) assert that the rise of IMC was one of a number of factors spurring increased interest in identity.

Before the introduction of IMC, an organization's identity was typically promoted using relatively traditional media. After professionals and scholars began to embrace IMC, however, scholars began adding to the body of literature on identity by providing structure to the concept. Melewar (2001) introduced a helpful international corporate visual identity (ICVI) scale that can be applied both to firms and other types of organizations. It includes 10 traditional media used to promote their identity: product packaging, building interiors/exteriors, signs, clothing, stationery, forms, publications, vehicles, advertising and promotions/ give-away items. To round out this scale, Alessandri and Alessandri (2004) added three additional items—public relations, websites, and event sponsorship. With thirteen items, this scale is comprehensive—but certainly not exhaustive—in its ability to help scholars measure all of the new and evolving ways organizations might express their identities. To help account for more alternative, and less traditional, ways of promoting an organization's identity, it is necessary to define the concept of a non-traditional expression of identity. A non-traditional expression occurs when the organization explicitly uses one or more of the elements of its traditional identity (such as, but not limited to, its name, logo, tagline, or one or more colors of its palette) in a unique and perhaps unexpected manner. In this way, the organization is able to extend its identity while also reinforcing one or more of its elements.

Because a non-traditional expression of an identity can play a key role in reinforcement of a message, it also plays an important role in helping consumers process information about the organization. Keller (1996) suggests using visual or verbal retrieval cues within integrated campaigns to ensure more effective processing of the overall message. This reinforcement supports the cue compatibility principle, which states that successful recall of communication effects from memory is most likely to occur when the type of information contained in the cues is compatible or congruent with the type of information already stored in memory.

Because it is widely accepted that repetition of campaign elements—logos, taglines, or even colors—aids in the process of linking associations to a brand (Aaker 1991; Aaker and Joachimsthaler 2000; Keller 1996), the concept of non-traditional expressions of identity is a preferable alternative to simply repeating a simple advertising or public relations message.

EXAMPLES OF NON-TRADITIONAL EXPRESSIONS OF IDENTITY

On a strategic level, the concept of alternative expressions of identity fits nicely within the realm of IMC because it allows organizations to project their identities in creative ways while still reinforcing the message with consumers. However, on a more tactical level, non-traditional expressions of identity that are truly unique will help an organization cut through the proverbial message clutter—and perhaps spur positive word-of-mouth about the organization.

There are several examples of non-traditional expressions of identity around the world, and in such varied organizations as corporations, non-profit organizations, and educational institutions. Detailed here are the backgrounds of three different types of non-traditional expressions of identity: a European example of a firm promoting its signature color while anthropomorphizing its corporate name, an American university expressing its athletics logo on a public golf course, and an American firm that transported its corporate ethos from the boardroom to a new town.

CASE VIGNETTE: Crédit Lyonnais

Each July, the best cyclists in the world gather in France to compete in the largest and most important race of the cycling season, a 2,000-mile plus ride over three weeks known as the Tour de France. Crédit Lyonnais, a French bank, is a major sponsor of the tour, and two different elements of the bank's corporate identity are manifest in the tour in very interesting ways. Specifically, Crédit Lyonnais is able to insert itself into the actual media coverage of the event by creatively working its signature color and mascot into the daily award presentation on the podium.

Each day immediately following the race, the rider with the overall best time is awarded the *maillot jaune*, or the yellow jersey. The yellow jersey is adorned with several logos, none of which are more prominent than those of its main sponsor, Crédit Lyonnais. The bank's logotype adorns both front and back of the jersey (in a prominent space on the front left chest). Most importantly, however, the yellow jersey itself is a reflection of the bank's signature color. In addition to the jersey, the race's leader is awarded a large stuffed lion, the mascot of the bank and a trademark of the Tour de France.

As might be expected, the awards ceremony following each day's ride is a highly popular event, and one that is always included in the daily international coverage of the race. In this way, Crédit Lyonnais is able to reinforce its sponsorship of the Tour de France without explicitly advertising that sponsorship during coverage of the race. In addition, Crédit Lyonnais is also able to associate itself with some of the world's most popular athletes. For the past several years, the Tour de France has attracted unusually widespread attention in the United States because of American cyclist Lance Armstrong's quest to set—and then break— the world record for Tour victories. Armstrong is arguably the reason an American sports network broadcasts the Tour de France at all, since the race received only limited attention from American audiences before his participation. This actually works to the benefit of Crédit Lyonnais, since if it were not for the American telecast, Crédit Lyonnais might not enjoy the increased level of awareness it has garnered in the United States.

While ensuring more widespread awareness of an international identity might be the goal of a great number of organizations, other groups might simply prefer to reinforce an existing identity among a select group. An example of this type of reinforcement of identity elements is reflected in the approach taken by Clemson University.

CASE VIGNETTE: Clemson University

Clemson University, located in Clemson, South Carolina, is home to the Clemson Tigers. The university's athletic teams wear orange and rally around the school's mascot, a tiger, and the university's athletics logo, a tiger paw. Yet, in a world where universities often have long and storied histories behind their mascots, Clemson University is a sort of anomaly. The university's tiger paw logo is relatively new, having come about only in 1970, when it was designed by the advertising agency of a university alumnus.

The university distinguishes its tiger paw logo from many other schools' tiger paw logos through its authenticity: the design was based on the paw print of an actual tiger. In the years since the logo was designed, the university has incorporated it widely into its licensing program, and the logo appears on both the basketball court and football fields. The university also has an affiliated public golf course, the Walker Golf Course, which opened in 1993. Like many university golf courses, it is nicely maintained as a way of reflecting both the quality of the course and the institution it represents. Unlike most courses, however, the Walker Golf Course contains a signature hole that also perfectly reflects Clemson's tiger paw logo. The seventeenth hole—The Tiger Paw, as it is known—is just that: the green is the shape of the large pad of the tiger's paw, and four sand traps, or bunkers, make up the remaining four pads of the paw.

Clemson University considers itself a place that remembers its history and tradition, no matter how recent. The Tiger Paw Hole is a tangible example of that

61

tradition. While the tiger paw logo is a constant and specific reinforcement of just a singular element of the university's identity, the Walt Disney Company has taken the concept of alternative expressions of identity to a new level.

CASE VIGNETTE: Celebration, Florida

The Walt Disney Company, a firm that works diligently to project a "picture-perfect" identity as a family theme park, made a decision to strategically extend this identity by developing a new town created in its mold. While not representative of a typical non-traditional expression of identity (since Disney does not take discrete elements of its identity and project them in a unique way), the town of Celebration, Florida, illustrates the Disney gestalt.

Located in Osceola County, Florida, adjacent to the Walt Disney World property, Celebration is a planned community developed by the Walt Disney Company. The town was founded in 1994 on the ideals of "New Urbanism," a movement based on the notion that towns should be built as fully integrated communities that include places to live, work, shop, go to school, and be entertained.

Celebration might never have received much attention from the press or public if it were not owned by the Walt Disney Company (it has since been sold to a private real estate investment firm). Like many other planned subdivisions in the United States, there are a number of rules associated with owning a home in Celebration. For example, residents wishing to paint their houses must obtain pre-approval of the color from the town's architectural board, and there are regulations against keeping lawn ornaments in front yards. Critics contended that Celebration differed from other American subdivisions, however, because there was no town government making the town's rules and regulations. Rather, the Walt Disney Company was making the rules and regulations based on business decisions rather than on what was best for the public good.

From an aesthetics viewpoint, critics contend that Disney was simply trying to "imagineer" the perfect town: scrubbed clean and concerned with style over substance—much like Disney World itself. The evidence of this might be reflected in an annual winter holiday tradition: on the town's main street, the town manufactures snow every evening for 10 minutes on the hour between 6 and 9 p.m. Perhaps more than anything else, this tradition reflects the Disney identity of storybook perfection. While the merits of a profit-driven firm developing a town might be debatable, the mechanics and consistency with which Walt Disney World reflects its identity in Celebration is commendable.

CASE VIGNETTE: Boise State University—The "smurf turf"

Every day, a handful of tourists travel to Boise State University (BSU) in Boise, Idaho—not to check it out as a prospective school for themselves or for their children—but to ask permission to step onto the football turf, and maybe even have their picture taken on it. Although BSU has a notable football team, the tourists' attraction to the field has nothing to do with sports, but with color: they want their pictures taken on the only blue college football field in the United States.

In 1986, Athletic Director Gene Bleymaier was faced with having to replace the school's Astroturf. Because the school was beginning to attract a larger student population and aspired to move up into a more prestigious athletic conference, Bleymaier was looking towards the future and a way to distinguish the athletic program. After having conducted some feasibility research, he broached his idea for new turf at a meeting with his staff. The bright blue turf was installed later that year.

Over the past 20 years, the blue turf has made the university unique among college athletic programs. There's no threat of competition, either, since after BSU installed its turf, the National Collegiate Athletic Association (NCAA) instituted a rule that forbids colleges and universities from installing any turf that is not green. Boise State is "grandfathered" in under the old rules, where the NCAA did not dictate turf color. If Boise State ever decided to install a green turf again, however, it would not be allowed to return to blue. For that reason, BSU Sports Information Director Lori Hayes does not foresee a time when the school would return to traditional green turf.

When the turf was new, back in 1986, it received a lot of attention from the local media, but gradually the attention began to taper off. Then, when the team moved into a more prestigious athletic conference and eventually earned a Top 25 ranking, the blue turf became a national story.

In the realm of athletics, the turf becomes a conversation piece for BSU's competitors and the press covering the games. The success of the BSU team also helps to fuel the media coverage, but it also tends to "color" the coverage when the team is not playing well. During this period, the press is more likely to refer to the football field rather cynically as "the smurf turf."

Outside the realm of athletics, the blue turf has become a strategic part of the school's marketing of itself. In fact, according to Hays, the blue turf has "become the university's identity." The school's most recent promotional campaign is titled "Beyond the Blue," and it alerts potential students, donors, etc., to the fact that, while the football field is a sight to behold, it does not represent the entirety of the university.

CONCLUSION

While Celebration is not a typical example of a non-traditional expression of identity as defined in this chapter, it does help to illustrate the nuances and benefits involved in employing such non-traditional expressions. Like other promotional activities related to the brand, however, marketers must ensure that all non-traditional expressions help to link positive associations to the brand in the minds of consumers, since association formation goes directly to the heart of building a positive reputation and brand equity.

Aaker (1991) defines brand equity as "a set of brand assets and liabilities linked to a brand, that add to or subtract from the value provided by a product or service to a firm and/or to that firm's customers" (p. 15), and Keller (1993) develops the notion of customer-based brand equity (CBBE), defining CBBE as the differential effect of brand knowledge—including awareness and image—on the consumer's reaction to marketing of the brand. Customer-based brand equity occurs when consumers form and hold in memory some unique, strong, and favorable brand associations.

Keller's contention that associations must be favorable, strong, and unique in order to help achieve brand equity is particularly appropriate in the context of non-traditional expressions of identity. Rather than simply inundating consumers with traditional advertising, such unique expressions can help to foster a sense of goodwill between consumers and the brand by linking positive associations to the brand. And that is really the point: reaching consumers effectively and uniquely with a non-traditional message in an increasingly cluttered marketplace of ideas.

ISSUES FOR FURTHER DISCUSSION

1   Discuss the benefits and drawbacks of employing non-traditional expressions of identity.
2   Is the idea of a non-traditional expression of identity valid? How might these expressions fit into Melewar's International Corporate Visual Identity (ICVI) scale?
3   Through web research, identify an organization (corporate, non-profit, etc.) that successfully employs a non-traditional expression of its identity. Keep in mind that the organization and not one of its publics must project the expression. How does the organization express itself? Why is the expression successful? How might it be improved?

REFERENCES

Aaker, D. A. (1991) *Managing Brand Equity: Capitalizing on the Value of a Brand Name*. New York: Free Press.
Aaker, D. A., and Joachimsthaler, E. (2000) *Brand Leadership*. New York: Free Press.
Abratt, R. (1989) "A new approach to the corporate image management process." *Journal of Marketing Management,* 5(1): 63–76.

Alessandri, S. W. (2001) "Modeling corporate identity: a concept explication and theoretical explanation." *Corporate Communications: An International Journal*, 6(4): 173–82.

Alessandri, S. W. and Alessandri, T. (2004) "Promoting and protecting corporate identity: the importance of oganizational and industry context." *Corporate Reputation Review*, 7(3): 252–68.

Bergen, J. D. (1996) "Beyond integrated marketing." *Management Review*, 85(5): 62.

Cornelissen, J. P. and Lock, A. R. (2000) "Theoretical concept or management fashion? Examining the significance of IMC." *Journal of Advertising Research*, 40(5): 7–15.

Gray, E. R. and Balmer, J. M. T. (1997) "Managing corporate image and corporate reputation." *Long Range Planning*, 31(5): 695–702.

Gray, E. R. and Smeltzer, L. R. (1985) "SMR Forum: Corporate image: an integral part of strategy." *Sloan Management Review*, 26(4): 73–8.

Gregory, J. R. and Wiechmann, J. W. (1999) *Marketing Corporate Image: The Company as Your Number One Product*. Chicago: NTC Business Books.

Keller, K. L. (1993) "Conceptualizing, measuring, and managing customer-based brand equity." *Journal of Marketing*, 57, January: 1–22.

Keller, K. L. (1996) "Brand equity and integrated communication," in E. Thorson and J. Moore (eds), *Integrated Communication: Synergy of Persuasive Voices*. Mahwah, NJ: Lawrence Erlbaum Associates: 103–32.

Leitch, S. and Motion, J. (1999) "Multiplicity in corporate identity strategy." *Corporate Communications: An International Journal*, 4(4): 193–9.

Leuthesser, L. and Kohli, C. (1997) "Corporate identity: The role of mission statements." *Business Horizons*, 40(3): 59–66.

Markwick, N. and Fill, C. (1997) "Towards a framework for managing corporate identity." *European Journal of Marketing*, 31(5/6): 396–409.

Melewar, T. C. (2001) "Measuring visual identity: a multi-construct study." *Corporate Communications: An International Journal*, 5(1): 36–41.

Ross, A. (1999) *The Celebration chronicles: life, liberty, and the pursuit of property value in Disney's new town*. New York: Ballantine Books.

Schultz, D. E. and Kitchen, P. J. (2000) "A response to 'theoretical concept or management fashion?'." *Journal of Advertising Research*, 40(5): 17–21.

Schultz, D. E., Tannenbaum, S. I., and Lauterborn, R. F. (1993) *Integrated Marketing Communications: Pulling It Together and Making it Work*. Chicago: NTC Business Books.

Topalian, A. (1984) "Corporate identity: Beyond the visual overstatements." *International Journal of Advertising*, 3: 55–62.

Chapter 4

Illustrations of the internal management of corporate identity

Cláudia Simões and Sally Dibb

AT THE END OF THIS CHAPTER READERS SHOULD BE ABLE TO:

1   Understand corporate identity and related concepts
2   Appreciate the features of corporate identity management
3   Specify internal corporate identity management dimensions

KEY POINTS

■   Identity embraces what the company conveys in order to differentiate and create a unique position in the environment in which it operates

■   Approaches to corporate identity stem from several research backgrounds: visual/graphic design, organizational studies, marketing, and interdisciplinary perspectives. Increasingly, researchers advocate an interdisciplinary view of corporate identity reflecting the diverse perspectives which managers hold about the construct

■   The internal management of corporate identity entails features such as the *dissemination of mission and values, consistent image implementation,* and *visual identity implementation*

■   The dissemination of mission and values establishes a strategic focus highlighting the need for consistency and for the organization to have a sense of continuity and purpose in its actions

■   The consistent image implementation concerns primarily the consistency with which all aspects of image are presented

■   Visual identity implementation emphasizes the coordination of physical/ visual aspects of the corporation that constitute symbols (e.g., logos and company name) and create tangible recognition for the organization

- The image of an organization is intertwined with its leaders as top managers are both organizational members and identity builders, key actors in organizational identity development
- Overall identity derives from the inner capability that the company has of matching internal and external beings, establishing a singular and coherent stance in its environment
- This chapter rekindles and underlines the internal management of corporate identity specifying aspects of its domain which are controllable

INTRODUCTION

Organizations act in increasingly complex settings and dynamic environments. Growing internationalization/globalization, mergers and acquisitions, fierce competition, and volatile markets are forcing companies to find new ways to compete. Within this context, organizations are increasingly developing competitive strategies that are underpinned at the corporate level. The stakeholders that influence organizations' activities are more interested than ever in knowing "who" is behind the products and services they encounter. Managers and researchers are therefore increasingly concerned with the dimensions of corporate management, such as corporate associations (Ellen et al. 2006) and identification (Bhattacharya and Sen 2003), corporate brand (Ind, 1997), corporate reputation (Weiss et al. 1999), corporate image (Zinkhan et al. 2001), and corporate identity (Balmer and Soenen, 1999).

This chapter examines the management of corporate identity. Identity can be defined as a mix of elements which distinguish one person or entity from another. Organizations have an identity in the sense that each has particular traits or features that make up its uniqueness. Corporate identity and the process by which it is managed are emerging as tools in the battle to create sustainable advantage. Given that organizations are more enduring than products, it can be much more difficult for competitors to imitate a strong identity than to develop new products or brands.

Identity has a number of controllable dimensions. These must be coherently managed so that when they are filtered by audiences a positive image emerges. Indeed, the wide-range of stakeholders and the similarities among offers in the marketplace is driving this desire for unique and distinctive traits. The creation of a strong identity is one possible route for managing the perceptions of a corporation among stakeholders (Dowling 1993; van Riel and Balmer 1997; van Riel 1995). By effectively managing corporate identity, organizations are able to create a clear individuality that distinguishes them from other players in the marketplace.

A strong theme of this chapter is to explore how different aspects of corporate identity can be internally managed by the company. In the following section, the concept of corporate identity is introduced and the main dimensions of internally managing that identity are explored. Short case examples are used to illustrate these aspects. The discussion concludes by exploring the role of managers in corporate identity management and then highlighting key issues which warrant further consideration.

UNDERSTANDING CORPORATE IDENTITY AND INTERNAL CORPORATE IDENTITY MANAGEMENT

Corporate identity and related concepts

The domain of corporate identity is not clearly specified in the literature. In fact, the notion of corporate identity has been confused with and linked to a range of related concepts, namely *image* and *reputation*. For the purposes of this chapter, the stance adopted is that *identity* "comprises the ways that a company aims to identify itself or position its product" (Kotler 1997: 292). As such, *identity* embraces what the company conveys in order to differentiate and create a unique position in the environment in which it operates. Identity is therefore mirrored by the company's *image,* where image concerns the perception publics hold of an organization or of the items it sells. The notion of *reputation* relates to the regard associated with the company. As Weiss et al. (1999: 75) explain: "an image reflects a set of associations linked to a brand or company name that summarises a brand or firm's identity . . . Reputation . . . reflects an overall judgement regarding the extent to which a firm is held in high esteem or regard, not the specific identity it has."

Approaches to corporate identity stem from several areas of the literature. These include research and publications from the field of visual/graphic design, organizational studies, marketing, and interdisciplinary perspectives. The *visual/ graphic design* approach is concerned with the visual presentation of the company and embraces the management of corporate symbols (e.g., logos) (van Riel and Balmer 1997; Olins 1991). *Marketing* insights are drawn mainly from brand management and integrated communications research (e.g., Chernatony 1999; van Riel 1995; Duncan and Everett 1993). The *organizational studies* perspective primarily concerns the way employees relate to the organization (Dutton et al. 1994). Finally, *interdisciplinary* studies support a wide-ranging view of corporate identity drawing on several branches of knowledge (van Riel and Balmer 1997). (For further discussion of these approaches to corporate identity see Simões, Dibb, and Fisk 2005.)

Support among researchers for the interdisciplinary view of corporate identity has recently increased (Simões et al. 2005; Brown et al. 2006). To some extent this reflects the diverse perspectives which managers hold about the construct. In

Schmidt's (1995) study conducted across several European countries, managers viewed corporate identity as being about *public image/external projection* (50 percent); *visual presentation* (27 percent); an *expression of culture/values philosophy* (20 percent); *internal projection/staff behavior* (18 percent); *product brand support* (4 percent); and *advertising/communication support* (4 percent).

Given the diversity of views about corporate identity, a strategic examination of its management that is grounded in different domains is appropriate. This means that any approach to corporate identity must be eclectic, encompassing visual dimensions, communication/image and the underlying philosophy of the business. As Schmidt (1995: VII) observes,

> From a company's understanding of its own purpose and values, through its culture and behaviour, to its outward expression, corporate identity deals with matters of core strategic concern. These matters affect everyone inside a company and everyone in its range of external contacts. Special management skills must be adopted.

Corporate identity management is inherently broad and cannot be fully covered in a single chapter. In order to manage its breadth, the focus of this chapter is on considering the internal management of corporate identity. The text is based on previous work examining the features of corporate identity that should to be managed from inside the organization (Simões et al. 2005). The next section will establish the domain of corporate identity management and explore its application in companies.

THE MANAGEMENT OF CORPORATE IDENTITY

The management of corporate identity embraces "(1) the endorsement of consistent behaviour through the diffusion of a company's mission, values, and goals; (2) the expression and pursuit of brand and image consistency in the organization's symbols and forms of communication; and (3) the implementation, support, and maintenance of visual systems" (Simões et al. 2005: 153). Using this definition as a basis, three main features of corporate identity management can be derived: the *dissemination of mission and values*, *consistent image implementation*, and *visual identity implementation*. These elements, each of which must be consistently specified and managed, connect to form the triangle of *corporate identity management* (see Figure 4.1).

The domain of the corporate identity management construct is concerned with the controllable aspects of corporate identity. There are dimensions within the company's control that affect its image. This discussion is therefore only concerned with dimensions that are featured and molded by the company. In this

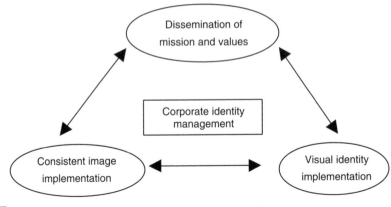

Figure 4.1 *Corporate identity management triangle*

respect, the stance adopted is comparable to the notion of the presented brand as denoted by Berry (2000: 129):

> The presented brand is the company's controlled communication of its identity and purpose through its advertising, service facilities, and the appearance of service providers. The company name and logo and their visual presentation, coupled with advertising theme lines and symbolic associations, are core elements of the presented brand. The presented brand is the brand message a company conceptualizes and disseminates.

A central assumption in the material presented here is that companies are able to develop an identity that is deliberately managed. In this respect, corporate identity management involves those activities that the company or business unit deliberately undertakes in order to enhance its image among its audiences (Simões, Dibb, and Fisk 2005). It is further argued that a well-specified and appropriately conveyed identity plays a vital role in establishing the desired corporate image.

MISSION AND VALUES DISSEMINATION

As corporate identity is developed, the link between identity and philosophy must be established via the corporate mission. Corporate philosophy concerns the business values and beliefs embraced by top executives and commonly expressed in a company's mission statement. This is a critical feature to convey internally, as the corporate culture—common values and beliefs held by organizational members—should ideally reflect the organizational philosophy (Gray and Balmer

1997). As Balmer (1996: 254) notes, "the acquisition of a favorable corporate image is dependent upon appropriately nurturing a distinct corporate culture by management which reflects the corporate mission and philosophy and as such becomes one of the dominant cultures within the organization (i.e., the desired corporate personality) which results in the desired corporate identity (i.e., where the innate character of the organization mirrors the corporate strategy and philosophy)".

The need for the shared mission and values to be properly communicated to and interpreted by employees is clear. This means that identity both encapsulates and forms a means of expressing corporate philosophy (Bernstein, 1984). Transposing the idea that mission is an aspect of the tangible image of vision and a "vocalization" of corporate philosophy to audiences, the communication and diffusion of the company's mission and values can be seen to be part of corporate identity management.

The mission and values dissemination dimension emphasizes the need for consistency and for the organization to have a sense of continuity and purpose in its actions. A strategic focus to the corporate identity construct is therefore established (Balmer, 1994). This suggests that managing corporate identity requires the definition of relevant corporate values and their sharing with organizational members. As Simões et al. (2005: 162) explain: "The rationale is that corporate identity is strategically driven by each organization's unique corporate philosophy, which is reflected in its mission, values, and goals. This dimension, which is a key element of corporate identity, internally diffuses the sense of purpose and singularity of the company motivating commitment to organizational goals . . . This creates a basis for developing consistent behaviours among employees emphasizing their role in conveying the right business messages." The illustrative case below shows how the mission, philosophy, and values of global fitness business Nike shape the company's identity.

CASE VIGNETTE: Nike

With more than 26,000 employees and net revenues of $13.7 billion in 2005, Nike is the world's biggest sports and fitness company. The company's identity is driven by a corporate philosophy centered on innovation and encapsulated in its mission statement: "To bring inspiration and innovation to every athlete in the world" (www.nikebiz.com). Nike's website expands on this sense of purpose, explaining that: "Our mission has always been to provide a competitive edge, to help athletes perform better. We climb inside the athletic mind. We feel every beat of the athletic heart. We flex, bend, twist, and torque every inch of athletic sinew and muscle. It's not easy, but it's natural for us. We're athletes" (www.nikebiz.com).

The stated mission and the philosophy and values on which it is based, is much broader than may at first be apparent. Despite the focus on innovation and athletic success, Nike's products are not just aimed at professional athletes. In the words of Bill Bowerman, co-founder of Nike, "If you have a body, you are an athlete." This articulates that the driving force to innovate and inspire, which has become central to all of Nike's activities, is for the benefit of all athletes everywhere.

The origins of Nike's philosophy can be traced back to 1971 and to the design of the Waffle outsole. This radical cushioned sole was to transform sporting footwear and provide the springboard for the Nike brand. At the same time, graphic designer Carolyn Davidson was busy creating the wing-like Nike Swoosh. Her brief was to design a logo that reflected movement and which could be featured on the company's footwear. The result, inspired by the winged Greek Goddess Nike, enjoys widespread recognition among consumers, being described as "a universal beacon for athletes from all walks of life who wish to enhance their physical performance."

It is possible to feel this "action" throughout the company. In fact, Nike's driving values ("do the right thing" and the recognition that "consumer decides") are wide spread and experienced by Nike's employees (Porter et al. 2002). Indeed, Nike's employees genuinely like sports and support athletes' achievements (La Salle 2006).

Today, the desire for innovation is reflected in all of Nike's activities: in the advancement of footwear cushioning such as in Nike Shox, and in high-performance fabrics designed to help athletes manage extreme temperature and other conditions. Nike's chairman refers to this as "evolution," explaining that "new and better is the way" and arguing that this is achieved by consultation with both professional athletes and regular consumers (Nike 2005 Annual Report: www.nike.com).

Sources: www.nike.com; www.nikebiz.com; Nike Annual Report, 2005 (www.nike.com); www.trizera.com/jsp/nikehist.html; Danenberg, J., Evanski, J., Ruszkowski, G., Coscarelli, P., and A. Lezon, Dimensions of Nike, http://homepages.wmich.edu/~j1evansk/bus270.htm; La Salle, Guy, 2006, (http://ec.europa.eu/comm/consumers/cons_safe/presentations/20−02/nike.pdf); Porter, Jeff, Harris, Mark, and Yeung, Gavin, 2002 (http: //www.cs.ucla.edu/~gavin/pub/IntlBusMgmtNike.pdf).

CONSISTENT IMAGE IMPLEMENTATION

The consistent image implementation dimension is concerned with the consistency with which all aspects of image are presented. Companies need to have a broad understanding of every form or representation of image if they are to successfully manage their corporate identity. Each member of staff has a role to play in this process and so needs to understand all of the elements used to create the image. As Kennedy (1977: 123) notes: "realising that every employee is a potential salesman for the company, and that the company is selling much more than its conventional product range, brings employees into the centre of the image formation process."

At the business unit level it is crucial to take account of the breadth and consistency of all aspects of the image. In order to achieve this, ongoing scrutiny is needed of facets such as marketing and promotional activities, staff, and the visual presentation of branding through the logos and symbols that are used. As Simões et al. (2005: 163) explain, consistent image implementation "captures communications and brand dimensions through various degrees of tangibility." They go on to emphasize the particular role of employees in relation to the more intangible items, explaining that this factor "focuses on the creation and diffusion of a consistent brand image, shapes the impressions of external stakeholders and affects how employees construe corporate identity" (p. 163). These issues and the difficulties sometimes associated with them are explored further in the Fair Trade case study below.

CASE VIGNETTE: Fair Trade

The International Fair Trade Association (IFAT) has well-established principles which shape the activities and behaviour of the organization and its members. These involve creating opportunities for economically disadvantaged producers, ensuring transparency and accountability in all dealings with trading partners, building capacity to encourage the independence of producers, ensuring the payment of fair prices, supporting equity between genders, ensuring safe and healthy working conditions, and supporting environmentally responsible production practices (www.ifat.org/ftrinciples.shtml).

Those working in Fair Trade recognize the importance of responsible consumption and the need to promote Fair Trade principles and transparent working practices. Although these principles are becoming better established, a unified identity for Fair Trade is only just beginning to emerge. Managers and other staff increasingly recognize the role which a strong identity could play in helping achieve the organization's aims. For these reasons IFAT is working to build the identity of Fair Trade by promoting the Fair Trade Organization (FTO) mark. This identifier guarantees that organizations displaying the mark have achieved particular standards in relation to their Fair Trade activities. IFAT believes that businesses with the mark will 'stand out from the crowd' and be able to set themselves apart from other organizations (www.ifat.org/theftomark.shtml). IFAT also supports the Fair Trade Label, a logo attached to products produced and traded under Fair Trade conditions. The logo is co-ordinated by the Fair Trade Labelling International (FLO-I), which is seeking greater international consistency in the use of such labelling.

73

Building the Fair Trade identity is an ongoing process. Effective communication of the Fair Trade identity requires coordination and consistency across a diverse range of internal and external activities and stakeholder groups. These stakeholders include Fair Trade consumers, producers, public institutions (such as local government agencies), and community bodies (such as schools). As an ethical organization, IFAT is committed to transparency and openness in all of these communications. The organization's extensive website provides a detailed explanation of Fair Trade principles and lists all organizations with IFAT membership. This is just one part of the external communications, which include the labels and logos used by those engaged in Fair Trade, as well as all education programs and community projects, both at the international and local level.

There is also an internal dimension to how the Fair Trade identity is communicated. Staff and volunteers who work for Fair Trade are a key audience for communicating the organization's identity. The way in which Fair Trade inducts new staff and volunteers helps to ensure consistency in approach. As a Fair Trade representative from Portugal explains: "every time we have new volunteers we organise a one-day initial training session . . . We show documentaries, videos, etc. that illustrate the movement, showing the producers, products. . . . [This] entails training in the political and commercial aspects of FT [and] attendees gain an initial grasp on how this movement works." A good deal of the communication is word-of-mouth, with internal information flowing between the organization's associates, using the Internet and training events which encourage interaction between members. This continuous training and diffusion of information is a way to reinforce members' interest and commitment to the organization/movement. Overall, these internal activities supplement and strengthen communications with external stakeholder groups.

Sources: http://www.ifat.org/; http://www.fairtrade.org.uk; interview with Miguel Pinto, Fair Trade representative in Portugal.

VISUAL IDENTITY IMPLEMENTATION

Visual identity is widely regarded as a key dimension of corporate identity. Physical aspects of the corporation such as logos and company name are essential features of an organization's identity. These elements form physical symbols and create tangible recognition for the organization (Olins 1991; Melewar and Saunders 1998). Not surprisingly, visual and graphic aspects of identity play an important role in corporate identification, acting as a kind of identity card for the organization. As such, visual identity implementation ought to be considered in corporate identity management.

When managed in a coordinated way, a company's aesthetics may enhance the appeal of the organization and its offers (Schmitt et al. 1995). Given the business implications of visual identity, it is important to carefully define and operationalize the construct. If a company's visual identity is to be effectively implemented, clear support for managing the visual elements is required. For example, it is important to conduct visual audits, to actively seek consistency across visual/tangible aspects and to establish specific guidelines for how the company is visually presented. Simões et al. (2005: 163) explain that "[t]his can be regarded as the 'hard' aspect of identity (Morison, 1997) and the most practical or action-oriented CIM [corporate identity management] dimension." As the McDonald's case illustrates, the extent of the visual aspects to be managed can be extremely broad, adding to the challenge of ensuring a consistent company-wide approach.

CASE VIGNETTE: McDonald's

Global fast-food giant McDonald's is recognized by consumers everywhere. The famous "Golden Arches" have achieved iconic status, marking out more than 30,000 outlets in five different continents. This highly visible signage is just one of many aspects that make up the visual part of McDonald's corporate identity. Others include the McDonald's logo on its menu, the distinctive design of its packaging, drinking straws and napkins, and the red and yellow corporate colours. Even the well-known character Ronald McDonald and the distinctive litter bins positioned around the chain's restaurants are part of the company's identity make-up.

The company has invested heavily and worked tirelessly to build the visual aspects of its identity, which are consistent across the company's facilities, equipment, products, personnel, and marketing. Such consistency is essential if consumers are to take away the image which McDonald's has worked so hard to develop. This fits with McDonald's desire to connect with customers in an integrated way, ensuring a consistent and customer-focused message across all aspects of the marketing mix. Such consistency is backed up and encapsulated in the "I'm lovin' it" theme. A theme which also connects with a stated desire to respond to consumer concerns about living healthy and active lives. As the company explains "Through 'I'm lovin' it' customers express their individuality and celebrate their commonalities. They describe what they love about life and how McDonald's fits into it" (www.mcdonalds.com).

The integrity of this visual dimension of corporate identity must be carefully controlled. For McDonald's, the fact that many outlets are franchises adds a layer of complexity. The company would find itself in an unsustainable position if franchise holders failed to uphold the visual parts of its image. Not surprisingly, under the terms of their agreements, franchise holders are required to maintain the consistent identity with which McDonald's has become associated. The use of a variety of tools assists this process. These include the provision of written guide-lines and visual auditing, which can be achieved using head-office staff or mystery shoppers. All visual elements of the internal and external presentation of the restaurant must be covered, including staff, products, marketing materials, and consumables. Adopting a rigorous approach to these activities helps McDonald's to ensure that the consistent identity it is seeking is maintained and protected.

Sources: www.mcdonalds.com; www.mcdonalds.co.uk; www.agilisys.co.uk

THE ROLE OF MANAGERS IN CORPORATE IDENTITY MANAGEMENT

In this final section, the role which corporate identity players undertake in building and managing identity and image is explored (Balmer 1995; Bernstein 1984). The importance of top management in the process is closely scrutinized. This reflects the fact that managers have long been considered an important symbolic instrument of corporate identity. It is widely recognized that the way in which managers connect with the organization affects how groups, such as employees and other publics, see and feel about an organization (Hatch and Shultz 1997).

For example, at a business unit level, the unit manager's role is to communicate company rules and values throughout the business unit. The business unit manager is the "guardian of the brand" (Gilbert and Guerrier 1997: 124). This involve-ment of senior managers in the integration of actual and desired corporate identity is paramount, making the process more strategic. As van Riel and Balmer (1997: 341) note, "senior managers can narrow the gap between the actual and desired corporate identity through marshalling the corporate identity mix (communications, symbolism and behaviour)."

The pivotal role of top management and its relevance to image development is therefore increasingly featured. The image of an organization is intertwined with its leaders (Sutton and Callahan 1987). Top managers are both organizational members and identity builders, key actors in organizational identity development. Although stakeholders themselves, they also represent the organization in its interaction with other stakeholders. In this sense, they have a particular role in the construction of organizational identity. It is top managers' responsibility to manage organizational identity, aiming for the promotion of favorable organiza-tional images to attain organizational goals (Scott and Lane 2000).

Moreover, managers play a critical role in influencing stakeholders' identifi-cation with the organization by presenting images that are attractive to those audiences. Their stipulation of goals, mission, organizational practices, values, and action contribute to shaping organizational identity. These features differentiate organizations in the eyes of managers and stakeholders. Organizational identity can therefore be seen as the common set of beliefs that top managers and stakeholders hold about what is central, enduring and distinctive in an organization (*op. cit.*).

As such, a managerially centred approach helps to support the construction of organizational images. Although all organizational members, including employees, are involved in the building and conveying of desired organizational images, it is managers who are most visible and who have the responsibility and resources to pursue this aim. As Scott and Lane (2000: 47) note, "managers act together to form a consensus on core values and organizational purpose and to furnish a consistent view of what the organization is all about to the world. In doing so, they collectively reinforce each other's beliefs regarding the organization, and they collectively present their view of reality to stakeholders".

The identities of managers and organizations are more likely to coincide than those held by employees. This is because the public visibility which managers enjoy means that these individuals are more likely to identify with their respective organization (*op. cit.*). Most managers are well aware of, for example, the need to be perceived as credible by organizational audiences. A damaged managerial image erodes target audiences' faith in the organization and may lead to their withdrawal of support (Sutton and Callahan 1987). Of course, as the following illustrative case demonstrates, some top managers are more credible than others in this regard.

CASE VIGNETTE: Richard Branson and Virgin

The Virgin brand, a banner name for businesses ranging from entertainment and travel, to publishing and soft drinks, is well known by people everywhere. Richard Branson is the man behind the brand, the individual whose entrepreneurial values and strong leadership have been pivotal in establishing the Virgin identity. Virgin's success story began with a student magazine and a record mail-order business. The record label Virgin Records which Branson established in 1972 and later sold to EMI soon followed. In the 1980s, Branson moved Virgin into transport, forming Virgin Atlantic Airways and, in 1997, set up Virgin trains. Today, as the company's portfolio continues to grow, the strong Virgin identity is a consistent feature at the heart of all that they do.

So how did the Virgin identity become so strong? Branson is happy to talk about the secrets of the company's success. Among the insights he offers, Branson stresses the need to "Do the right things for the brand." His desire to build and protect the Virgin brand is reflected in both his activities and his business style. In Branson's own words "If you get your face and your name out there enough, people will start to recognize you. Many people know the Virgin brand better than the names of the individual companies within the group" (www.virgin.com/uk/entertainment/richard-branson.asp).

Branson has ensured that those within the corporation understand the role that identity plays in its success and about how this connects with the values around which the Virgin brand is based. In the words of the Virgin website: "We believe in making a difference. In our customers' eyes, Virgin stands for value for money, quality, innovation, fun and a sense of competitive challenge" (www.virgin.com/aboutvirgin/allaboutvirgin/whatweresbout/default.asp). The importance of talented managers and skilled employees is also readily acknowledged, and there is a pride in what Virgin calls "the trademark management style, skills, and experience. These people resources are vital to the effective management of the company's image, playing an important part in the diffusion of that image within and outside the business."

The role that Branson himself has played in establishing this image cannot be overstated. The company's website cites Branson's personal reputation as a key success factor. This reputation extends far beyond pure business acumen, to include his passion for breaking records and high-profile, daredevil adventures. Through his association with adventurer Per Lindstrand, Branson was involved in the first hot air balloon crossing of the Atlantic in 1987 and, in 1991, broke records for crossing the Pacific from Japan to Arctic Canada. What is important for Virgin's identity is that these activities influence things that the company does and helps shape its image with stakeholders. Virgin Galactic, a space tourism business which Branson set up in 2004, is a typical expression of the spirit which lies at the heart of this identity.

Sources: www.virgin.com; www.virginbrand.com; http: //en.wikipedia.org/
wiki/Richard_Branson; www.cptelecom.net/~ennyman/branson.html;
Branson, Richard. *Sir Richard Branson: The Autobiography*, 2002,
Longman, ISBN 0582512247

CONCLUSION

Overall identity derives from the inner capability that the company has of matching internal and external beings, establishing a singular and coherent stance in its environment. As such, corporate identity can be used by organizations to generate the organization's behavioural consistency and to highlight its uniqueness among constituents. Every company has an identity whether it is specified, emerging, or informal. If the potential of that identity is to be maximized, the pillars on which it is based must be accurately defined and molded. This constitutes the controllable realm of corporate identity management.

Throughout this chapter the aims have been to rekindle and underline the management of corporate identity and specify aspects of its domain which are controllable. The features of corporate identity which can be managed at the internal level have been specified. The construct of corporate identity management has been depicted as a spiral of three, intertwined elements: mission and values dissemination, consistent image implementation, and visual identity implementation. The role of managers in managing and implementing corporate identity within the company has also been identified.

An important feature of the organizational environment is the extent to which it continually evolves and changes. As such the expression of an identity may alter or be transformed throughout the organization's lifetime. Organizations must be vigilant in detecting the depth of such changes so that a measured response can be made. Indeed the management of identity is an ongoing and continuous process. As organizations seek to respond to their changing organizational environment, the corporate identity needs to become the organization's reality.

ISSUES FOR FURTHER DISCUSSION

1 How do identities evolve over time?
2 What other internal controllable and uncontrollable facets of identity can be specified and how can these be managed?

REFERENCES

Balmer, J. (1994) "The BBC's corporate identity: myth, paradox and reality." *Journal of General Management,* 19(3): 33–49.

Balmer, J. (1995) "Corporate Branding and Connoisseurship." *Journal of General Management,* 21(1): 22–46.

Balmer, J. (1996) "The nature of corporate identity: an explanatory study undertaken within BBC Scotland." Doctoral dissertation, University of Strathclyde.

Balmer, J. and Soenen, G. (1999) "The acid test of corporate identity management." *Journal of Marketing Management,* 15(1–3): 69–92.

Bernstein, D. (1984) *Company Image and Reality.* London: Cassel Educational.

Berry, L. (2000) "Cultivating service brand equity." *Journal of the Academy of Marketing Science,* 28(1): 128–37.

Bhattacharya, C. B. and Sen, S. (2003) "Consumer–company identification: a framework for understanding consumers' relationships with companies." *Journal of Marketing,* 67(April): 76–88.

Brown, T., Dacin, P., Pratt, M., and Whetten, D. (2006) "Identity, intended image, construed image, and reputation: an interdisciplinary framework and suggested terminology." *Journal of the Academy of Marketing Science,* 34(2): 99–106.

Chernatony, L. (1999) "Brand management through narrowing the gap between brand identity and brand reputation." *Journal of Marketing Management,* 15(1–3): 157–79.

Dowling, G. R. (1993) "Developing your company image into a corporate asset." *Long Range Planning* 26(2): 101–19.

Duncan, T. R. and Everett, S. (1993) "Client perceptions of integrated marketing communications." *Journal of Advertising Research* (May–June): 30–9.

Dutton, J. E., Dukerich, J. M., and Harquail, C. V. (1994) "Organizational images and member identification." *Administrative Science Quarterly*, 39: 239–63.

Ellen, P., Webb, D. J., and Mohr, L. A. (2006) "Building corporate association: consumer attributions for corporate social responsible programs." *Journal of the Academy of Marketing Science*, 34(2): 147–57.

Fombrun, C. and Shanley, M. (1990) "What's in a name? Reputation building and corporate strategy." *Academy of Management Journal*, 33(2): 233–58.

Gilbert, D. and Guerrier, Y. (1997) "UK hospitality managers past and present." *Service Industries Journal*, 17(1): 115–32.

Gray, E. R. and Balmer, J. M. T. (1997) "Corporate identity: a vital component of strategy." Working paper, University of Strathclyde.

Hatch, M. and Schultz, M. (1997) "Relations between organizational culture, identity and image." *European Journal of Marketing*, 31(5/6): 356–65.

Ind, N. (1997) *The Corporate Brand*. London: Macmillan.

Kennedy, S. H. (1977) "Nurturing corporate images: total communication or ego trip?" *European Journal of Marketing*, 11(1): 120–64.

Kotler, P. (1997) *Marketing Management: Analysis, Planning, Implementation and Control*, 9th edn. London: Prentice Hall International.

Melewar, T. C. and Saunders, J. (1998) "Global corporate visual identity systems: standardisation, control and benefit." *International Marketing Review*, 15(4): 583–98.

Melewar, T. C. and Saunders, J. (1999) "International corporate visual identity: standardization or localization?" *Journal of International Business Studies*, 30(3): 583–98.

Olins, W. (1991) *Corporate Identity*. Toledo: Thames and Hudson.

Schmidt, K. (1995) *The Quest for Identity: Corporate Identity, Strategies, Methods and Examples*. London: Cassel.

Schmitt, B., Simonson, A., and Marcus, J. (1995) "Managing corporate image and identity." *Long Range Planning*, 28(5): 82–92.

Scott, S. G. and Lane, V. R. (2000) "A stakeholder approach to organizational identity." *Academy of Management Review*, 25(1): 43–62.

Simões, C., Dibb, S., and Fisk, R. P. (2005) "Managing corporate identity: an internal perspective." *Journal of the Academy of Marketing Science*, 33(2): 153–68.

Sutton, R. I. and Callahan, A. L. (1987) "The stigma of bankruptcy: spoiled organizational image and its management." *Academy of Management Journal*, 30(3): 405–36.

Van Riel, C. B. M. (1995) *Principles of Corporate Communications*. London: Prentice Hall.

Van Riel, C. B. M. and Balmer, J. (1997) "Corporate identity: the concept, its measurement and management." *European Journal of Marketing*, 31(5/6): 340–55.

Weiss, A. M., Anderson, E. and MacInnis, D. J. (1999) "Reputation management as a motivation for sales structure decisions." *Journal of Marketing*, 63(October): 74–89.

Zinkhan, G. M., Ganesh, J., Jaju, A., and Hayes, L. (2001) "Corporate image: a conceptual framework for strategic planning," in G. Marshall and S. Grove (eds), *Enhancing Knowledge Development in Marketing*. Chicago: American Marketing Association, vol. 12, 152–60.

Part II

Corporate communications

Chapter 5

Corporate communications and corporate reputation

Understanding how (best) practices make a difference

Tibor van Bekkum, Joep P. Cornelissen, and Betteke van Ruler

AT THE END OF THIS CHAPTER READERS SHOULD BE ABLE TO:

1 Distinguish between "best practices" and "signature practices"
2 Understand "why" signature practices make a difference
3 Understand the issues and challenges communication professionals face

---

KEY POINTS

■ A *practice* perspective on corporate communications and reputation management focuses upon how branding and communications professionals carry out their work and are (more or less) effective in making a contribution to their organizations

■ A *practice* perspective suggest that "best" or high-performing practices emerge from a complex interplay between the roles and backgrounds of practitioners, their activities, the political and cultural situation surrounding their work, and the way in which they are organized

■ Our research demonstrates that the practices of branding and communications professionals are to a large extent idiosyncratic and reflect their company's unique culture and belief systems, rather than being universal and generally applicable across different companies and industries

INTRODUCTION: A PRACTICE PERSPECTIVE ON
CORPORATE COMMUNICATIONS

The field of corporate communications (CC) and corporate brand management (CBM) is gradually developing into a fully fledged and strategic managerial function. This development is partly a reflection of the widespread belief that the future of any company depends critically on how the company is viewed by key stakeholders such as consumers, investors, employees, and the local community in which the company resides (Cornelissen 2004). The reputation of the corporation is indeed now widely regarded as an important strategic asset that creates differentiation from competitors and preference among internal and external stakeholders of the company. Not surprisingly, therefore, corporate brand management (CBM) and corporate communications (CC) are recognized as important functions to build and maintain reputations with important stakeholder groups upon which the organization is dependent (e.g. Schultz et al. 2005).

In line with these developments, academics have been suggesting frameworks and models that prescribe steps towards the "strategic" use of the corporate brand and communications towards stakeholders, including ideas such as "integrated marketing communications" (e.g., Kitchen and Schultz 1999), "corporate identity management" (e.g., Van Riel and Balmer 1997), "reputation management" (e.g., Fombrun 1996), "stakeholder communications" (e.g., Christensen and Cheney 1994), and "excellent public relations" (e.g., Grunig and Grunig 1998). Much of this work has been prescriptive in suggesting frameworks for managing communications and for managing firm–stakeholder interactions, as opposed to a more grounded and detailed understanding of the practices of branding and communications professionals and how these may make a difference in the management of firm–stakeholder relationships. The latter, we argue, is particularly important given the rift between the importance placed by CEOs and senior executives upon *strategic* CC and the perceived huge under-performance by brand and communication professionals in the US, the UK, and continental Europe (e.g. Van der Jagt 2005; Murray and White 2004).

Prior research on CBM and CC has largely focused on macro outcomes (i.e. strong and favorable reputations with stakeholders) of activities carried out by branding and communication professionals instead of the activities themselves. As such, research has been deducing the effectiveness of activities from reputation and brand value measurements across firms, rather than tracking the development of a strong corporate brand or reconstructing the development of a strong corporate brand from the inside-out. Inductive accounts that describe, instead of prescribe, the steps taken and decisions made by companies with excellent reputations have been largely lacking from the literature.

These observations point to shortcomings in the "traditional" perspective on CBM and CC. They also lead us to suggest an alternative and complementary perspective on the subject. We argue that a "practice perspective" on CBM and CC provides a lens to describe and understand how organizations actually build and maintain strong corporate reputations with stakeholders. This alternative and so far unexploited perspective accounts, we argue, for a deeper and more intimate understanding of the micro activities (practices) that take place within a certain organizational context and that explain (at least partly) the macro outcomes of the strength and favorability of reputations with stakeholders. Table 5.1 outlines the differences between the traditional perspective on corporate communications and our practice perspective.

A practice perspective regards managerial functions such as CBM or CC within firms as areas of practice; as activities and work being carried out by practitioners in an organizational context with the latter referring to the political, cultural, and structural aspects related to the practice of CBM and CC within the firm. Although there are various ways to investigate CBM and CC as a practice, scholars who have followed the "practice turn" in related managerial fields as strategy (e.g. Whittington 2003) and accounting (Hopwood and Miller 1994), have been guided by a shared list of questions in their research. These include questions of where and by whom work is actually done and the tools and techniques that are being used (i.e. *practitioners and activities*), the roles and skills required of practitioners and how these are acquired (i.e. *practitioners and their professional development*), the ways in which practitioners and the work involved are organized (i.e. the *organization of communication work*), political and cultural issues that contextualize and mediate these practices and activities (i.e. *political and cultural issues*), and the way in which the process and products of practices and activities are communicated and consumed (i.e. the *contribution and use of practices and activities*) (cf. Whittington 2003). Taken together, these questions equally provide a template for our present purposes to consider CBM and CC as a practice, and to map and conceptualize these functions in a more comprehensive manner than previous work has done.

Table 5.1 *A practice perspective versus traditional perspectives on corporate communications*

	Traditional perspectives on CC	A practice perspective on CC
Explanations of performance	*Deductive*: infer best practices from reputation scores across firms	*Inductive*: grounded in the actual activities of professionals and how these add value and make a contribution to a firm
Primary focus	*Macro*: strategic outcomes (reputations and reputation measurement)	*Micro*: practitioners, processes and structures within the organization
Key strategic processes	"Alignment" between the reputation and the identity or positioning communicated	Strategic positioning and cultural accommodation within the firm

Clearly, a practice perspective makes some important contributions to our theorizing about CBM and CC. First of all, it gives us an understanding of what is actually going on in the organization. It brings the internal organizational dynamics into the fore rather than considering CC or CBM as a strategy problem that is detached from the organization itself. Second, it takes the everyday perspective of the communication professional into account and populates the field with acting human beings. It "humanizes" the field. At the end of the day, human action constitutes all activities within organizations and equally within the management of the corporate brand and reputations. Third, and this is supported by the results of our study, it sheds light on the cultural and political surroundings of the communication function that mediate the input of communication professionals into the corporate strategy and subsequently into the interactions of a firm with its environment. Fourth, the practice perspective demonstrates that different practice dimensions (activities, political and cultural surroundings, the practitioners, and their professional development, etc.) have clear interrelations. For example, if professionals aspire to a developmental shift from a "tactical' or "craft" orientation to communications, characterized by technician role enactment and communications service departments or units carrying out low-level communication mechanics, to a strategic management function, they need to enact managerial roles through management activities like environmental scanning, counseling, and strategic planning that demonstrably add value to the corporation, and they need to vie for an organizational arrangement that gives them a central, recognizable place in the firm from where to counsel and support senior management as well as managers in other functional areas. In this sense, then, a practice perspective extends prior research that has focused on just one dimension in isolation. This accounts for a comprehensive and realistic insight into CC and CBM. Fifth, and lastly, a practice perspective makes a clear "practical" contribution as it informs professionals how corporate communications and the corporate brand can indeed be better managed.

IN SEARCH OF "BEST" PRACTICES

Against this background we conducted empirical research on the corporate branding and communication practices of three multinational corporations with European origins that by and large have highly reputed corporate brands: Philips, Siemens, and Nokia. We selected these corporate brands for our research based on the appearance of these brands in (1) the reputation quotient list of companies with very high top of mind awareness scores (2001/2) and in (2) the interbrand top 100 ranking of most valuable brands (2003/4). We argue that since these brands appeared on both lists, these organizations appear to be able to capitalize on the power of their corporate brand.

Within each organization we interviewed 3 to 4 communications and branding professionals who had a formal responsibility in managing the corporate brand and communications. The interviews took place in 2004 and were guided by a topic list with questions about the areas that are central to a practice perspective as mentioned above. We also asked respondents to indicate what they felt were "best" practices that had made an important contribution to the strength of their corporate brand and reputation.

So what are in fact "best practices" in CBM and CC? This question puzzled us even after we had collected and analyzed the data. Each of these three corporations is very different in their practices, and also the opinions of professionals on what practices they regarded as "best" practices were quite diverse.

Within Philips, for example, optimization of work processes via standardization and output measurement is central to many of the practices of communications and branding professionals and indeed is seen as making an important contribution to the company's brand building success. As the head of communications management explains: "A signal of good reputation management is that you have standardized your reputation measurement system, to make sure that that won't be a subject of discussion." Other examples of the drive for standardization, optimization, and output measurement within Philips are the use of process survey tools, philosophies like Six Sigma, handbooks and guidelines to improve and demonstrate the overall contribution of the communication function to the organization.

Within Siemens the practices that are seen to have successfully contributed to building a strong corporate brand include mechanisms that have facilitated dialogue between professionals. These mechanisms include Brandville (an online platform for communications and branding professionals to consult and add information to), the *Value Proposition Guide* (an inspirational document explaining the brand strategy and the ways in which different business units can relate to it), and annual meetings with representatives of all communications departments in Siemens worldwide. Instead of standardization, control, or optimization, these mechanisms aim to inspire professionals across the corporation to share knowledge and best practices. Siemens also organizes a global competition which invited all communication professionals in the different business units of the corporation to showcase their best practices in corporate communications and design. All of these mechanisms, which are regarded by Siemens as important for maintaining the strength of their corporate brand, differ fundamentally from the practices put in place by Philips.

"Best" practices within Nokia revolve around the informal coordination between professionals and the absence of rigorous protocols or brand charters. Instead, a "can do" and "informal" culture is regarded as one of *the* practices that has a significant impact on the success of the Nokia brand and the company's reputation. Practices within Nokia are completely distinct from those in Siemens and Philips. The director of corporate brand management explains:

> Although we have a brand charter in place, we very much want to retain the [can-do] culture that we currently have. We are emphasizing the importance of our culture, emphasizing the importance of people making the decisions where they work, on the spot, not sort of, you know going into brand books and in different kinds of manuals and look for the right answer and the wrong answer, because you simply cannot manage a global brand with guidelines and policies. So, our view is that it is much more important that the people have the culture and the values, and have the essence of the brand in the back of their heads, so that they actually can put that into practice in their everyday work rather than having to refer to very strict guidelines and policies and processes and with people coming to you looking for the right answer to every single question [about branding and communications]

Accordingly, there are few formalized working patterns. Communication and branding professionals within Nokia frequently liaise with one another to co-ordinate their brand building efforts.

Our research questions whether there are any "best practices" in CBM and CC in terms of general models or principles that are and indeed can be adopted across firms and industries. Instead, the practices in each of these corporations appeared to reflect something about the organizational context in which they seem to work.

BEST PRACTICES VERSUS SIGNATURE PRACTICES

When we delved once more into our research data, we found that the practices within Philips, Nokia, and Siemens are linked to the core of their business, history, or culture. This may point to what Gratton and Ghoshal (2005) call signature practices; practices and processes that embody a company's character and are therefore somewhat unique and idiosyncratic, rather than general and universal for the entire industry. Signature practices are linked with the core values of the organization and evolve from a specific company history. Thus, "signature practices" fundamentally differ from "best practices." The latter are regarded as universal standards that are applicable across firms. Signature practices, on the other hand, are unique to a particular organization. Whereas best practices focus on bringing successful practices from elsewhere into the corporation, signature practices focus on developing practices internally (see Table 5.2).

Branding and communication practices within Philips, for example, are rooted in a technocratic and engineering-led culture. Standardization and output measurement do not only guide the practices within the communication function, they also guide many of the practices throughout the entire corporation. The focus on output measurement is, for example, integrated into the company's reward system. For example, the process of business alignment under the banner

Table 5.2 *The differences between best practice and signature practices*

	Best practice	Signature practice
Origin	"Bringing the outside in": starts with external and internal search for general best practices	"Bringing the inside out": evolves from a company-specific history and culture
Development	Needs careful adaptation and alignment to the company and industry context	Needs championing and further refinement by professionals
Core	Shared knowledge from across the sector	Cultural values
Applicability	Across different companies	Company-specific
Impact	As a "tool" (direct and instrumental impact)	As a "process" (diffuse and indirect impact)

"Towards One Philips" requires employees to commit themselves to contribute to this process of alignment and to show at the end of each year how they have helped to realize this company goal. These are criteria on which decisions for rewards are made. The technocratic and engineering-led culture, then, provides the organizational context in which CC and CBM practices take place.

Siemens is one of the largest companies in the world (operating in 192 countries and employing over 400,000 people) with business units operating on a more or less autonomous basis. Its sheer size and complexity call for mechanisms that aim to inspire rather than control. The Director of Communications, Corporate Brand and Design explains: "We can't send out 'sheriffs' with guns killing everyone who doesn't comply." As such, the corporate branding department decided to use coordination mechanisms that facilitate dialogue instead of, as mentioned, giving directives. This practice is embedded in the culture of the organization and is a result of the company's size and complexity.

Nokia fosters an "innovative," "can do," and "improvising culture" as a result of the rapid growth that the company experienced in the beginning of the twenty-first century. As the vice president, corporate brand management, explains: "In 1997, when I joined Nokia, mobile telecommunications was not the global consumer business that it is today, it is only towards the end of 2002 that it took off and we managed [at that time] to present a credible story of Nokia as a company transforming itself into a high-tech producer of handsets. In those days, the communications taskforce was literally 24 hours a day, and the global media were interested in our story; first of all because they were interested in the wireless Finland story, like what is happening in this obscure country up in the north, close to the North Pole, where school children are using mobile phones, and, secondly, they were interested in the Nokia success story: like how come a company coming from this small country that no one knows is all of a sudden transformed into a global leader of mobile telecommunications." Such a turbulent environment called for structures and mechanisms that allowed professionals to cope with rapid change. Nokia found these mechanisms in its corporate culture (see Table 5.3).

Thus, central to the practices in use within these companies is the adaptation of practices to the circumstances of the organization; its culture, history, size, and structure. In effect, this adaptation appears to be central to an effective use of corporate communications and corporate branding in these corporations and also demonstrates the "added value" of communications internally with managers from other functions. The latter is important to convince senior management and others in the corporation of the added value and contribution of CBM and CC.

Table 5.3 Signature practices in three European corporations

	Philips	Siemens	Nokia
Signature practice	Process survey tools	Democratic decision making	Informal coordination
What is it?	A tool that documents and standardizes work processes, so that these can be constantly monitored, updated, and optimized	A process in which decisions are made collectively and multiple views are shared on a certain subject	An informal arrangement of working together
Core (cultural value)	"Process optimization'	"Equality"	"Flexibility"
Origin	Engineering tradition	■ Size of the company ■ Relative autonomous basis on which business units operate	■ Finnish values of openness ■ Common bond between professionals
Development	Supported by company (ISO certification) and driven by senior VP corporate communications	Actively supported and managed by the senior brand manager(s) at the company's headquarters	Nurtured and endorsed by senior corporate branding and communication professionals
Impact	■ Improved coordination, efficiency and effectiveness of activities ■ Increased standing with CEO and senior executives	■ Alignment between business units that operate on an autonomous basis ■ Sharing best practices ■ Mutual inspiration	■ Enabled coordination between professionals ■ Knowledge sharing ■ Strong cultural bond between professionals

Our research indicates that the practices employed by communications and branding professionals are unique and tied to the history, culture, size, and structure of their company, rather than applicable and universal across industries and organizations. Practices are to a large extent idiosyncratic and reflect the company's unique "signature."

LESSONS FOR STRATEGIC CORPORATE COMMUNICATIONS: DIFFERENT PRACTICES, SAME ISSUES

Despite these differences, we found that communication professionals are at the same time concerned with largely the same issues. These issues include building a coherent and clear image (consistency in messaging), strategic internal positioning (showing the added value of the communication function to the company) and coordination of work and activities. However, the ways in which companies deal with these issues depends on the organizational context. What is however important is that companies *do* address these common issues in communications, although they may find very different ways of dealing with them.

Issue 1: building a coherent image

Clarity about what the company stands for and what stakeholders can expect when interacting with the company is generally seen as a crucial topic for brand and communications managers (e.g. Schultz et al. 2005; Fombrun and Van Riel 2004). As such, consistency in the messages sent out by a company is considered as important to create clarity about what the company stands for and what stakeholders can expect (Fombrun and Van Riel 2004). This issue is recognized by communications professionals in each of the three companies studied. Within Siemens, this issue is addressed with mechanisms such as Brandville (an online platform for communications and branding professionals to consult and add information to) and the *Value Proposition Guide* (an inspirational document explaining the brand strategy and the ways in which different business units can relate to it). Rather than aiming to control, these mechanisms, as mentioned, aim to inspire. In contrast, within Philips the focus is much more on regulation via formal coordination mechanisms such as rigorous process descriptions and payment and reward systems. As already mentioned, this is a direct result of the company's history and related technocratic and engineering culture. Within Nokia, there are no formal mechanisms to address the issue of consistency nor are instruments such as Brandville installed. Instead, it is the specific corporate culture that facilitates the alignment of communications to ensure consistency. A corporate culture that has its roots in the national culture of Finland as well as the specific company history; the company having grown so fast in a very turbulent industry has made improvisation key to its communication success.

Issue 2: strategic internal positioning and the added value to the company

Generally across Europe, many communication professionals still lack the requisite knowledge and skills to fully enact a broad strategic managerial role, particularly in areas such as financial management, the strategy-making process, and the use of communications in organizational development and change. As a result, these practitioners and the communication departments that they represent may be sidelined by companies and treated as a peripheral management discipline—one viewed as unimportant to the overall functioning of the corporation. Indeed, at times corporate communications has been seen as adding little to corporate performance and as a "fluffy" discipline that is insufficiently focused on the practicalities and demands of the business. Professionals, particularly ones in senior positions, bear a responsibility to show and communicate the value of communications in terms of what it contributes to a company. A general theme emerging from this is the importance of showing the *added value* of communications to the firm, through process survey tools such as in Philips or indeed other key practices such as environmental scanning and formalizing a brand charter. In Siemens, environmental scanning of stakeholder views of the company and brand equity research is channeled into management decision-making as a set of value-added activities that help senior managers make decisions about the acquisition of businesses. In general, each and every function within a company is evaluated and scrutinized by senior management for its contribution to the company and to the achievement of corporate objectives. When the contribution or "added value" of a particular function to the organization is seen as high and is also visible, it is more likely that the function will be granted input into strategic decision-making. The same goes for corporate communications, which like every other function (human resources, finance, etc.) is measured with the same stick. Capturing and quantifying the contribution of communications to the company and to the commercial bottom-line is thus key, although, unfortunately, not always commonplace. The added value of communications within Nokia, for example, is evident to senior managers. Communications has been central to the telling of "the Nokia story" and has helped the company to develop its business.

Issue 3: organizing work and activities

The visibility and status of corporate communications may vary across firms and industries, and reflects certain generic issues around the developing state of communications as a managerial profession and its acumen. At the same time, it appears that corporate communications as a practice area is often usefully and effectively given shape, in line with the wider cultural and professional context of the firm of which it is part. Within Philips, as mentioned, corporate communications is seen as a part of an organization-wide technocratic engineering culture where every function and the work processes involved are documented and stand-ardized, so that these can be constantly monitored, updated, and optimized. Within Nokia, in contrast, the corporate vision of "connecting people" together with the fact that members of the company have a strong bond between them ("having embarked on the technological journey together") has led to an "informal," "innovative," and "can-do" culture of knowledge-sharing and of coordinating work processes. There are no formalized work patterns or lines of communication between communication professionals within Nokia; they, rather, liaise frequently and informally with one another. Siemens uses a mixture of these two different approaches. Coordination mechanisms exist but largely function to enable professionals to discuss their work and make decisions between them, and are not used as formal protocols for control and performance management.

CASE VIGNETTE: Practices in Nokia

Until the early 1990s, Nokia was a conglomerate with businesses as diverse as rubber products, paper, and computers. The company transformed itself during the 1990s into a focused telecommunications firm supplying telecommunications network equipment and mobile phones. At the heart of this radical transformation lies the modular, flexible structure of the Nokia organization and the Finnish "informal," "innovative," and "can-do" culture of knowledge-sharing and of coordinating work processes. There are in fact little formalized work patterns or lines of communication between communication professionals within Nokia; these professionals instead liaise frequently and informally with one another. The director of corporate branding explained that this situation had evolved in this way because of the strong understanding of everyone in the company about the corporate story of Nokia.

> In 1997, when I joined Nokia, mobile telecommunications was not the global consumer business that it is today, it is only towards the end of 2002 that it took off and we managed [at that time] to present a credible story of Nokia as a company transforming itself into a high-tech producer of handsets. In those days, the communications taskforce was literally 24 hours a day, and the global media were interested in our story; first of all because they were interested in the wireless Finland story, like what is happening in this obscure country up in the north, close to the North Pole, where school children are using mobile phones, and secondly, they were interested in the Nokia success story: like how come a company coming from this small country that no one knows is all of a sudden transformed into a global leader of mobile telecommunications.

Because of this strong sense of Nokia's corporate story which is based upon its recent history and its country of origin, communications professionals have a clear sense of what messages need to be communicated; in other words, their shared history and understanding of Finnish values is such that no strict formal coordination is necessary. As the director of corporate branding explains: "Although we have a brand charter in place, we very much want to retain the [can-do] culture that we currently have. We are emphasizing the importance of our culture, emphasizing the importance of people making the decisions where they work, on the spot, not sort of, you know going into brand books and in different kinds of manuals and look for the right answer and the wrong answer, because you simply cannot manage a global brand with guidelines and policies. So, our view is that it is much more important that the people have the culture and the values, and have the essence of the brand in the back of their heads, so that they actually can put that into practice in their everyday work rather than having to refer to very strict guidelines and policies and processes and with people coming to you looking for the right answer to every single question [about branding and communications]."

CONCLUSION

A practice perspective extends a focus on corporate brand management (CBM) and corporate communications (CC) as strategic outcomes of what goes on in organizations to the activities that constitute them. This perspective is concerned with the same strategic issues of importance to branding and communications professionals (i.e. *how to build and maintain strong corporate reputations with stakeholders of the firm?*), but in terms of the organizational activities and practices which are their fabric. As such, it provides a more comprehensive and detailed picture of how communications is, and indeed, can be managed. Understanding the relationships between the practice dimensions (i.e. between the roles and skills of practitioners, their activities, the political and cultural situation surrounding their work, and the way in which they are organized) and knowing what practices work best in what circumstances provide professionals with concrete factors or attributes that can be understood and, if needed, challenged or manipulated. To branding and communications professionals, the profound implication is not only a greater understanding of their work but also suggestions and prescriptions for how their work can be changed or improved. In particular, the practice perspective recommends that professionals develop practices that "fit" with their organizational contexts; that is, in line with their company's culture, history, size, and structure. Such "signature" practices may be crucial to manage and coordinate branding and communications activities in an effective way and to demonstrate the added value of these activities to the company as a whole.

ISSUES FOR FURTHER DISCUSSION

1 What in your opinion are the practices that appear to work within Nokia?
2 Would it be possible to transfer these practices to other corporations in the same industry or other industries?

REFERENCES

Argenti, P. A., Howell, R. A., and Beck, K. A. (2005) "The strategic communication imperative." *MIT Sloan Management Review*, 83–9.

Christensen, L.T., and Cheney, G. (1994) "Articulating identity in an organizational age," in S. A. Deetz (ed.), *Communication Yearbook*. Thousand Oaks, CA: Sage, no. 17, 222–35.

Cornelissen, J. (2004) *Corporate Communications: Theory and Practice*. London: Sage.

Fombrun, C. (1996) *Reputation: Realizing Value from the Corporate Image*. Cambridge: Harvard Business School Press.

Fombrun, C. J. and Van Riel, C. B. M. (2004) *Fame and Fortune: How Successful Companies Build Winning Reputations*. Upper Saddle River, NJ: Financial Times/ Prentice Hall.

Gratton, L., and Ghoshal, S. (2005) "Beyond best practice." *MIT Sloan Management Review*, 6(3): 49–57.

Grunig, J. E., and Grunig, L. A. (1998) "The relationship between public relations and marketing in excellent organizations: evidence from the IABC study." *Journal of Marketing Communications*, 4: 141–62.

Hopwood, A. and Miller, P. (1994) *Accounting as Social and Institutional Practice*. Cambridge: Cambridge University Press.

Kitchen, P. J. and Schultz, D. E. (1999) "A multi-country comparison of the drive for IMC." *Journal of Advertising Research*, 39: 21–38.

Murray, Kevin and White, John (2004) *CEO Views on Reputation Management: A Report on the Value of Public Relations, as Perceived by Organizational Leaders* (UK survey of CEO views of reputation management).

Schultz, M., Antorini, Y. M., and Csaba, F. F. (2005) *Corporate branding: Purpose/ People/Process*. Copenhagen: Copenhagen Business School Press.

Van der Jagt, Ron (2005) *Executives on Reputation* (Dutch survey of CEO views of reputation management).

Van Riel, C. B. M., and Balmer, J. (1997) "Corporate identity: The concept, its measurement and management." *European Journal of Marketing*, 31: 340–56.

Whittington, R. (2003) "The work of strategizing and organizing: for a practice perspective." *Strategic Organization*, 1: 119–27.

Chapter 6

How specific should corporate communication be?

The role of advertising language in establishing a corporate reputation for CSR

Guido Berens and Johan van Rekom

AT THE END OF THIS CHAPTER READERS SHOULD BE ABLE TO:

1 Understand the importance of providing factual information in advertising on corporate social responsibility

2 Appreciate the trade-off between persuading external stakeholders through factual information and fostering the identification of internal stakeholders through impressionistic information

---

KEY POINTS

- One striking aspect of many corporate advertisements focusing on corporate social responsibility (CSR) is the degree of factualness with which CSR information is displayed. Some ads use only general wordings, while others describe very specific examples

- Ads about CSR using specific wording are perceived as more credible than ads using only general wording

- Ads about CSR using specific wording are perceived as more diagnostic for judging the company's CSR than ads using only general wording

- This increased credibility and diagnosticity of specific ads translates into more favorable perceptions of the company, i.e., a more favorable corporate reputation

INTRODUCTION

Corporate advertising is a widely used and highly visible form of corporate communication. Each year, organizations spend billions of dollars on corporate advertising campaigns (Blankenhorn 1998). These advertisements focus on a *company as a whole* instead of specific products. They are generally aimed at improving the company's image among the general public, often with respect to corporate social responsibility (CSR). Several studies have confirmed that corporate advertising focusing on CSR can have a positive influence on corporate reputation (Davis 1994a; Winters 1988). For example, Chevron's "People Do" campaign, which focused on the company's environmental efforts has run for many years. It has substantially improved Chevron's image, even among sceptical audiences (Winters 1988). However, not all such campaigns have been so successful. Therefore, an important question is what factors determine the success of a CSR ad campaign in terms of the establishment of a favorable corporate reputation.

Table 6.1 provides an overview of corporate CSR ad messages that have appeared in leading international business and opinion magazines, such as *Fortune, Time, the Economist, Business Week*, and the *Far Eastern Economic Review*. One thing that is striking from this overview is that while a number of ads make specific, verifiable claims, others do not. For example, software company Computer Associates communicates in one ad that it has been recognized as one of the top ten companies for working mothers. Similarly, Toyota provides us with details about the environmental performance of its "Hybrid Synergy Drive technology." On the other hand, chemical company BASF provides a general description of their principles regarding sustainable development, without providing specific examples or results. Table 6.1 shows how many ads do not make any verifiable claims.

Table 6.1 *Examples of advertisements in corporate communication*

Company	Sample text
Altana	We are laying the foundation for innovation by establishing a genomics research center near Boston, USA, and by increasing our research investments annually by a double-digit percentage.
BASF	BASF is at home all over the world. So we think and act globally, based on values and principles applied worldwide. They cover sustainable development and include safety, health, labor standards, and environmental protection.
Bayer	All around the world, harvests are under threat from pests and disease. In many regions, these dangers are also compounded by enduringly poor conditions such as drought, excessive heat and soil salinization, resulting in huge losses. Bayer CropScience is working to minimize these problems and find lasting solutions—productive plants and varieties that are better suited to their environment and more resilient to the stresses of climate extremes. *Continued overleaf*

Continued overleaf

97

Table 6.1—continued

Company	Sample text
BP	As part of our goal to double our global manufacturing capacity, we've invested over $25 million in BP Solar's Maryland plant, making it the largest integrated solar panel manufacturing facility in North America.
CA Computer Associates	. . . we've been recognized as one of the top ten [for working mothers]. Maybe it's because of our subsidized child development program. Or our adoption assistance program, which helps employees through the process of adopting a child.
Cigna	At Cigna we realize obesity can affect the home as well as the workplace. With the Healthy Kids Challenge we're working with families and physicians alike on the importance of eating healthy and exercising at a young age.
Daimler Chrysler	If nature had one wish, what do you think it would be? A car that doesn't produce exhaust? We thought so too. That's why our hydrogen powered Fuel Cell vehicles only emit water.
Esso	That's why, for decades, Esso has consistently led the industry in research and technology. And why we're now making the largest ever investment in independent climate and energy research that is specifically designed to look for new breakthrough technologies.
GE	. . . the GE Innova 2000 can help surgeons pinpoint coronary blockages with such precision that they may find alternatives to bypass surgery.
Haworth	Haworth's commitment to sustainability and dedication to adaptability helps create great spaces that work for both our clients and the environment. Great spaces designed around LEED certification adapt to change, reduce energy costs, and improve air quality.
Honda	In 1974, Honda introduced the ingeniously simple Civic CVCC. World-changing for its fuel efficiency and low emissions, the CVCC demonstrated our spirited commitment to environmentally responsible technology.
Norilsk Nickel	Our goal is to strengthen Stillwater and our own company for the benefit of our shareholders, customers, employees and communities
Permata Bank	Trust, integrity, professionalism, service and excellence are our values to build long lasting relationships
Shell	. . . it has actually led to cleaner, greener fuels capable of greatly reducing CO_2 emissions. Which has proven potential to significantly lessen these emissions in cities around the world. In effect, it represents the creation of a forest more than 100 times the size of Manhattan.
Sonatrach	For sustainable development and better future for the next generations.
Siemens	Helping people get ahead means opening the door to young talent. It's what we do every day. Creating opportunities for students and employees.
Toyota	Take Toyota's Hybrid Synergy Drive technology: it cuts fuel consumption by almost 45 percent, compared to a conventional petrol engine, and its emissions are 80 percent below the European standards for 2005.
United Technology	UTC Power's customers benefit from reliable, energy-saving alternatives that power buses, cars, and buildings around the world, keeping the air that we breathe cleaner.

Even more strikingly Banerjee, Gulas, and Iyer (1995) showed that the majority of "green ads" published between 1987 and 1991 only made general, vague statements about a company's commitment to the environment, without discussing specific environmental actions of the company. Vague claims may give managers ample leeway to choose their own course of action, taking advantage of the flexibility such general claims offer. However, the question arises whether such a strategy is effective. Can organizations create a favorable reputation by publishing such vague general claims? Might it be better to communicate about concrete, verifiable facts? In this chapter, we will tackle this question of whether the factualness of information provided in advertising about corporate social responsibility (CSR) influences the reputation of a company.

FINDINGS IN PREVIOUS STUDIES

Several studies have addressed the effectiveness of corporate advertising about CSR as a way to create a favorable corporate reputation (see Rossiter and Percy 1997; Roznowski 2002; Schumann, Hathcote, and West 1991). Most studies found that advertising favorably influences corporate reputation. Grass, Bartges, and Piech (1972) addressed the effectiveness of a corporate campaign by Du Pont that focused on the company's "interest in the welfare of society" and public safety. They found that this campaign positively affected people's opinion of the company's commitment to society. Similarly, Winters (1977; 1982; 1986; 1988) investigated the effectiveness of several corporate ad campaigns by Chevron. One interesting finding was that ads mentioning specific actions regarding the environment (e.g., constructing wooden platforms above electricity wires to protect eagles) were perceived more favorably than ads that merely stated the company's commitment to the environment (Winters 1988). More recently, Sheinin and Biehal (1999) found that corporate advertising focusing both on a company's manufacturing expertise and its CSR influenced people's attitudes toward the company's brands.

While previous studies have compared the effectiveness of advertising campaigns, most have not systematically investigated what—perceived—aspects of the content of the corporate advertising message may influence its effectiveness. Specifically, Davis (1994a) compared the effectiveness of three different environmental advertising messages. He found that for companies with a positive environmental reputation, communicating about environmentally friendly production methods was most effective, whereas for companies with a negative environmental reputation, communicating about monetary donations to environmental organizations was most effective. Reeves and Ferguson-DeThorne (1980) looked at the effects of communicating different corporate motivations. They found that describing the company as mainly motivated by serving stakeholder interests was perceived most favorably, and that describing the company as mainly motivated by profit-making was perceived least favorably. Describing the company as striving to serve the interests of society as a whole took an intermediate position.

In product advertising, more research has been devoted to the issue of message content (Darley and Smith 1993; Debevec, Meyers, and Chan 1985; Holbrook 1978). Objective, factual product claims lead to more favorable brand attitudes than subjective, impressionistic claims. A factual claim can be defined as a claim that "includes specific data that can be measured by a standard scale *not* subject to individual interpretation." The opposite of a factual claim is an impressionistic claim, which can be defined as a claim that uses "descriptions that *are* subject to individual interpretations" (Darley and Smith 1993: 101). For example, "we reduced our CO_2 emissions by 20 percent" is a factual claim, because it is expressed on a scale that is not subject to individual interpretations. By contrast, "we behave responsibly toward the environment" is an impressionistic claim, because both "responsibly" and "toward the environment" are subject to individual interpretations. Factualness can make a claim appear *objective* (Darley and Smith 1993: 101). Researchers have examined the effects of message factualness in the context of product quality (Darley and Smith 1993; Holbrook 1978), product innovativeness (Debevec et al. 1985), product health effects (Kozup, Creyer, and Burton 2003), and product environmental effects (Chan and Lau 2004; Davis 1994b; Maronick and Andrews 1999). Recently, Feldman, Bearden and Hardesty (2006) found positive effects of factualness in recruitment advertisements. However, the impact of message factualness has not yet been examined in the area of corporate CSR ads. More strikingly, recipients of factualness have not often been the focus of research. Factualness in corporate ads may have a completely different effect, because they have a goal that is much broader in scope than is the case with product ads. Product ads aim to persuade people to buy the product, whereas corporate CSR ads aim to create a favorable impression of a whole company. Recipients may appreciate more generalized, "impressionistic" information because of the general scope of subjects at the corporate level. Product ads have a far more specific goal than corporate ads. This may lead to differences in the way people react to the two types of ads.

HINTS IN THE LITERATURE ABOUT FACTUALNESS IN CORPORATE ADVERTISING

What effect may we expect from factual claims, as opposed to impressionistic claims in corporate advertisements? Given the scarcity of studies on corporate communication, we draw upon literature about product and personnel communication. Studies in product advertising that looked at the effect of message factualness have generally found that providing factual information about product attributes produces more favorable attitudes towards products (Darley and Smith 1993; Debevec et al. 1985; Holbrook 1978). Davis (1994b), investigating environmental claims, found that factual claims are perceived more favorably. Similarly, Feldman et al. (2006), in their recent study in job advertising also found that specific information increases attitudes toward the company, but only for the most relevant attributes, i.e., for attributes of the job itself rather than those of the company and the work context. Factual information is generally perceived as more *credible* than impressionistic information, because it is objectively verifiable (Darley and Smith 1993; Holbrook 1978). However, these findings might not hold for every context. Maronick and Andrews (1999), who investigated environmental product claims, found no significant effect of factualness on product attitudes. Furthermore, Chan and Lau (2004) found that for Chinese consumers, the effect of the factualness of environmental claims depended on the country of origin. When the product was from a country that people regarded as a credible source of environmentally friendly products, factual claims were perceived more favorably than abstract claims. However, when the country of origin of the product was not perceived as a credible source, abstract information was perceived more favorably. Apparently respondents did not even trust specific, factual claims from an untrustworthy country.

THE EFFECT OF FACTUALNESS ON CSR REPUTATION

We may expect that these findings in the field of product and job advertising can be generalized to corporate advertising about CSR. Providing factual information about CSR, e.g. about the company's environmental programs or philanthropic donations, is likely to be perceived as more credible by stakeholders than providing impressionistic statements like "we act responsibly toward the environment." This increased credibility could lead stakeholders to be more easily persuaded by the message, and therefore to develop more favorable perceptions regarding the company's CSR. This latter expectation is consistent with findings in the advertising literature, i.e. that the credibility of an ad influences brand attitudes (MacKenzie and Lutz, 1989). We therefore formulate the following hypotheses.

Hypothesis 1: Factual CSR ad information will be perceived as more credible than impressionistic CSR ad information.

Hypothesis 2: To the degree that factual CSR ad information is perceived as more credible than impressionistic CSR information, it will lead to a more favorable CSR reputation.

However, factualness may also have other effects besides increasing the credibility of a message. Semin and his colleagues (Semin and de Poot 1997; Semin and Fiedler 1988; Wigboldus, Semin, and Spears 2000) have investigated the effects of the abstractness of language on people's inferences regarding other people. Abstractness can be defined as the degree to which words "maintain an immediate reference to concrete behavioural events" (Semin and Fiedler 1988: 560), and is therefore almost synonymous to factualness. Similar to the research on advertising objectivity, this research has shown that people perceive abstract language as providing less credible information than concrete language. However, it also shows that people perceive abstract words as providing *more* information about a person than concrete words. Abstract words suggest a generalization beyond the immediate situation under discussion, or in other words, they give more information about the attributes of an actor than about the attributes of the situation. By contrast, specific words give more information about the situation than about the actor. For example, when a company provides facts about its waste reduction program, people may not automatically perceive this to imply that the company will display pro-environmental behavior in other situations as well. They may attribute the behavior to situational circumstances, like pressure from stakeholders. Therefore, the facts that are provided do not imply that the company is an "environmentally responsible" company. By contrast, the statement that a company is "acting to preserve the environment" may automatically imply a generalization across a whole range of situations (even though it may be perceived as less credible than the statement about the waste reduction program). The claim implies that the company is truly "environmentally responsible," i.e., acting from a commitment to preserve the environment, rather than from situational pressures. Although it may be relatively easy for people to make the step of generalizing factual information about a company's CSR activities to situations other than those discussed, this step may be even easier for impressionistic CSR information.

In terms of inference-making theories (Lynch, Marmorstein and Weigold 1988; Schum 1977), it may be that impressionistic information is more *diagnostic* (i.e., useful) than specific information for making inferences about companies. The diagnostic value of an information input can be defined as "the degree [to which] consumers believe that the decision implied by that input alone would accomplish their decision goals" (Lynch et al. 1988: 171). As suggested above, the information *implied* in impressionistic information (independently of its credibility) would be more useful than specific information to evaluate the company's CSR. Based on this reasoning, we formulate the following hypotheses.

Hypothesis 3: Factual CSR ad information will be perceived as less diagnostic for evaluating the company's CSR than impressionistic CSR ad information.

Hypothesis 4: To the degree that factual CSR ad information is perceived as less diagnostic for making inferences about CSR than impressionistic CSR information, it will lead to a less favorable CSR reputation.

What overall effect of factualness on the favorability of CSR associations could we expect? Schum (1977) has argued that the diagnostic value and credibility of information jointly determine the degree to which people use the information to make inferences. However, it is hard to predict which factor will have a larger weight in determining the favorability of CSR associations. Previous studies in product advertising have found a positive effect of factualness on product attitudes (Darley and Smith 1993; Holbrook 1978). Because it may be relatively easy for people to generalize facts about a company's actions to similar situations, we hypothesize that the overall effect of factualness will be positive.

Hypothesis 5: Overall, factual CSR ad information will lead to a more favorable CSR reputation than impressionistic information.

THE INFLUENCE OF FACTUALNESS ON REPUTATION REGARDING CORPORATE ABILITIES

When people see a corporate CSR ad, they may also use it to make inferences regarding other attributes of the company than its CSR. Specifically, they infer something about the company's expertise in its core business, i.e. their "corporate abilities" (Brown and Dacin 1997). When Goldberg's (1998) respondents saw favorable information about the company's CSR, they also evaluated the company's CA more favorably. When people infer something about a company's CA from a CSR ad, it seems likely that these inferences will be more favorable when the ad is perceived as more credible. Therefore, we expect that:

Hypothesis 6: The more factual CSR information in the ad is perceived as credible, the more it will lead to a favorable CA reputation.

On the other hand, the smaller diagnostic value of a factual message may be more pronounced when people make inferences about a company's CA than when they infer CSR associations. Although a factual CSR message presumably provides less information about the company than an impressionistic CSR message (Semin and Fiedler, 1988), it still would be straightforward to infer at least something about the company's CSR from such a message. A factual CSR message provides no information at all about CA, whereas an impressionistic message, being subject to multiple interpretations, may make it easier for people to make a step from the information about CSR to other attributes (Maronick and Andrews 1999).

Research in social judgment (Srull and Wyer 1989) has shown that when people are provided with abstract words describing a person's character, they more easily form an overall favorable or unfavorable impression of that person, than when they are provided only with descriptions of concrete behavior. Once people have formed an overall impression, this impression serves as the basis for making inferences about traits about which no information is provided. Therefore, it seems likely that impressionistic claims in a corporate CSR ad make it easier for people to establish an overall (favorable) impression of the company, and therefore to make inferences about the company's CA. Based on these considerations, we formulate the following hypotheses.

Hypothesis 7: Factual CSR ad information will be perceived as less diagnostic for evaluating the company's CA than impressionistic CSR ad information.

Hypothesis 8: To the degree that factual CSR ad information is perceived as less diagnostic for making inferences about CA than impressionistic CSR information, it will lead to a less favorable CA reputation.

We might expect that in the case of CA associations, the "balance" of the effect of factualness may be shifted more in the direction of the negative effect on the diagnostic value of the message. The reason is that we assumed that this negative effect of factualness is stronger for CA associations than for CSR associations. We therefore formulate the following hypothesis.

Hypothesis 9: Overall, factual information will lead to less favorable evaluations of a company's CA than impressionistic information.

Figure 6.1 summarizes our reasoning into an overall research model. Also, our nine hypotheses are listed together in Table 6.2.

METHOD

To test the hypotheses formulated above, we conducted a classroom experiment in which two groups of students were asked to evaluate an ad about a company's CSR. One group saw an ad containing only factual information, and the other group saw an ad containing only impressionistic information. After viewing the ad, subjects were asked questions regarding their evaluations of the company's CSR and CA, the diagnostic value of the information in the ad (for evaluating CSR and CA), the credibility of the ad, and the degree to which they perceived the ad to be factual versus impressionistic (a manipulation check). Finally, some

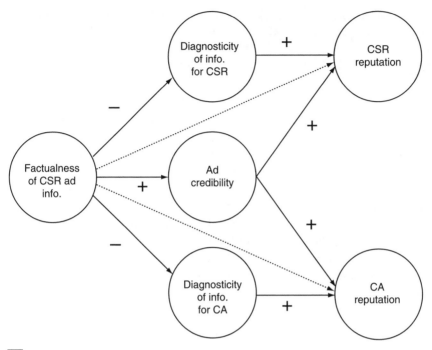

Figure 6.1 *The influence of perceived CSR ad factualness on diagnostic value, ad credibility, and corporate associations*

Table 6.2 *Overview of hypotheses*

1	Factual CSR ad information will be perceived as more credible than impressionistic CSR ad information.
2	Hypothesis 2: To the degree that factual CSR ad information is perceived as more credible than impressionistic CSR information, it will lead to a more favorable CSR reputation.
3	Factual CSR ad information will be perceived as less diagnostic for evaluating the company's CSR than impressionistic CSR ad information.
4	To the degree that factual CSR ad information is perceived as less diagnostic for making inferences about CSR than impressionistic CSR information, it will lead to a less favorable CSR reputation.
5	Overall, factual CSR ad information will lead to a more favorable CSR reputation than impressionistic information.
6	The more factual CSR information in the ad is perceived as credible, the more it will lead to a favorable CA reputation.
7	Factual CSR ad information will be perceived as less diagnostic for evaluating the company's CA than impressionistic CSR ad information.
8	To the degree that factual CSR ad information is perceived as less diagnostic for making inferences about CA than impressionistic CSR information, it will lead to a less favorable CA reputation.
9	Overall, factual information will lead to less favorable evaluations of a company's CA than impressionistic information.

demographic questions were asked (gender, age, and nationality). The materials, measures and procedures used are described in more detail below.

Materials

Two corporate CSR ads were prepared, one of which included only factual content, while the other included only impressionistic content. The ad was presented as a test ad for a large chemical company, which was dubbed "Laurec." We chose to focus on a chemical company because CSR issues are particularly salient in this industry. To ensure sufficient realism, the "impressionistic" ad was adapted from a real ad by the chemical company BASF. The two ads are shown in Figure 6.2. Through pretesting, we assessed whether these two versions were perceived to be sufficiently different in terms of the degree of factualness, and also whether they were not significantly different in terms of other variables (i.e., potentially confounding). Specifically, we assessed potential differences in realism (since only the impressionistic ad was directly adapted from a real ad) and in the favorability of the information given (i.e., how "objectively" positive the information is). In the final versions, there appeared to be no significant differences on these variables.

Respondents

One hundred and twenty-seven undergraduate students in the International Business Administration program at the Erasmus University Rotterdam participated in this study. They were recruited at the entrance of two lecture halls and received a sandwich and a drink in return for a filled-out questionnaire. Of these people, 61.4 percent were male, and 72.7 percent had Dutch nationality. Altogether, there were 20 different nationalities represented in the sample, with the largest groups (after Dutch) being Chinese (6 people or 4.5 percent) and German (also 6 people). Most other nationalities were represented by only 1 person. The age of the respondents ranged between 18 and 38, with a median of 21.

Procedure

Students were assigned randomly to one of the experimental groups. To avoid effects of the order in which questions about CSR and CA were asked (CSR first, or CA first), this order was counterbalanced between subjects. The respondents were instructed to carefully look at the ad, and then fill in the questionnaire without looking back at the ad.

This year, the World Health Organization established that our CO_2 emissions have decreased by 10% since 1992, as a result of our global greenhouse gas management program. In addition, due to our work–life balance programs, the number of stress-related illnesses among our employees was reduced by 15%.

Chemicals, Plastics & Fibers, Performance Products, Agricultural Products & Nutrition **LAUREC**

Laurec is at home all over the world. So we think and act globally, based on values and principles applied worldwide. These cover sustainable development and include safety, health, labor standards and environmental protection. That's how Laurec lives up to its responsibilities and builds confidence.

Chemicals, Plastics & Fibers, Performance Products, Agricultural Products & Nutrition **LAUREC**

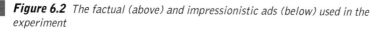 *Figure 6.2* The factual (above) and impressionistic ads (below) used in the experiment

Measures

All relevant constructs in this study were measured using 7-point semantic differential or Likert scales. All items and the reliability coefficients of the composite scales are provided in the Appendix 6.1. The means, standard deviations, and correlations of the items for each of the two experimental groups are shown in Tables 6.3 and 6.4.

Dependent measures

The dependent variables are CSR and CA reputation. CA reputation was measured by items from two subscales of the "Reputation Quotient" questionnaire (Fombrun, Gardberg and Sever 2000), namely, "Products and Services" and "Workplace Environment." To measure CSR reputation, we used two items from the "Social and Environmental Responsibility" subscale.

Mediator measures

The diagnostic value of the ad content for making inferences about the company's CSR and CA was assessed with questions about the information's usefulness, relevance, and importance for judging the company's CSR and CA, respectively (cf. Aaker and Sengupta 2000). The credibility of the ad was measured by three items used by MacKenzie and Lutz (1989). We also included another item asking about the ad's "reliability."

Manipulation check measure

We measured the perceived factualness of the information given in the ad with a single semantic differential scale adapted from Darley and Smith (1993), which asked how "factual" versus "impressionistic" the message was. Following these authors, we also provided definitions of these terms below the labels.

RESULTS

To test the hypotheses, we ran a structural equation model using the partial least squares (PLS) estimation method (Bagozzi, Yi, and Singh 1991). We first examined whether the presence of multiple nationalities could bias the results. The covariances of the variables in the model turned out to be equal for Dutch and non-Dutch respondents. We also tested whether the results of the path model were substantially different when only the data from the Dutch students were analyzed. This was not the case. The size and significance of the coefficients was comparable across the two analyses. We therefore used the pooled data for testing our hypotheses.

Next, we tested whether our manipulation of factualness actually influenced perceived factualness. This was the case: respondents who saw the factual ad rated its factualness 3.60 on average, whereas the respondents who saw the impressionistic ad gave an average rating of 2.92 ($t = 2.75$, $p = 0.01$). Thus, our manipulation had the intended effect on perceived factualness. Because this study is interested in the degree to which perceptual effects play a role, and wants to focus on how respondents' perceptions of factualness influenced the other effects, we used the manipulation check as the independent variable in the subsequent analyses.

Figure 6.3 shows the estimated path coefficients of the model. All coefficients in Figure 6.3 are unstandardized regression coefficients, significant at the 5 per-cent level. The first hypothesis stated that the factual message would be perceived as more credible than the impressionistic message. The manipulated factualness of the message (mediated through perceived factualness) indeed has a significant positive effect on ad credibility ($b = 0.25$, $t = 2.89$, $p = 0.01$). We also predicted that factualness would have a *negative* effect on the degree to which the message was perceived as diagnostic for evaluating the company's CSR and CA (hypotheses 3 and 7). The effect of factualness on the diagnostic value for inferring CSR is significant. The coefficient, however, is positive, i.e. the more factual the message is perceived to be, the more respondents think it informative regarding the organization's CSR policy ($b = 0.19$, $t = 2.18$, $p = 0.03$). The effect of factualness on the diagnostic value for inferring CA is not significant at the 5 percent level ($b = 0.17$, $t = 1.93$, $p = 0.06$).

■ 108

Table 6.3 *Means, standard deviations, and correlations for the impressionistic ad*

| | Descriptives | | Correlations | | | | | | | | | | | | | | |
	Mean	Std. dev.	Perc. factual-ness	Ad cred. (1)	Ad cred. (2)	Ad cred. (3)	Diagn. for CSR (1)	Diagn. for CSR (2)	Diagn. for CSR (3)	Diagn. for CA (1)	Diagn. for CA (2)	Diagn. for CA (3)	CSR (1)	CSR (2)	CA (1)	CA (2)	CA (3)
Perceived factualness	2.92	1.44															
Ad credibility (1)	3.91	1.34	0.19														
Ad credibility (2)	3.97	1.45	0.22	0.69													
Ad credibility (3)	4.31	1.25	0.08	0.49	0.64												
Diagnostic value for CSR (1)	3.69	1.75	0.29	0.25	0.50	0.23											
Diagnostic value for CSR (2)	4.09	1.69	0.15	0.32	0.42	0.17	0.60										
Diagnostic value for CSR (3)	4.34	1.72	0.17	0.41	0.47	0.25	0.56	0.75									
Diagnostic value for CA (1)	3.45	1.47	0.35	0.43	0.58	0.44	0.52	0.51	0.62								
Diagnostic value for CA (2)	3.72	1.46	0.24	0.37	0.53	0.33	0.26	0.28	0.39	0.56							
Diagnostic value for CA (3)	3.81	1.57	0.14	0.32	0.42	0.23	0.39	0.45	0.61	0.70	0.60						
CSR reputation (1)	4.63	1.70	0.19	0.26	0.29	0.28	0.52	0.50	0.34	0.36	0.07	0.19					
CSR reputation (2)	4.88	1.09	0.26	0.23	0.37	0.25	0.58	0.42	0.38	0.34	0.06	0.11	0.70				
CA reputation (1)	4.70	1.14	0.08	0.36	0.48	0.27	0.42	0.23	0.36	0.41	0.33	0.26	0.27	0.28			
CA reputation (2)	4.61	0.92	−0.14	0.14	0.41	0.30	0.24	0.30	0.19	0.29	0.26	0.14	0.30	0.27	0.36		
CA reputation (3)	4.83	0.99	0.07	0.17	0.33	0.24	0.47	0.55	0.32	0.30	0.11	0.17	0.49	0.38	0.48	0.40	
CA reputation (4)	4.75	1.09	0.05	−0.07	0.12	0.02	0.39	0.43	0.22	0.13	−0.20	−0.02	0.43	0.30	0.14	0.26	0.72

Table 6.4 Means, standard deviations, and correlations for the factual ad

	Descriptives		Correlations														
	Mean	Std. dev.	Perc. factual-ness	Ad cred. (1)	Ad cred. (2)	Ad cred. (3)	Diagn. for CSR (1)	Diagn. for CSR (2)	Diagn. for CSR (3)	Diagn. for CA (1)	Diagn. for CA (2)	Diagn. for CA (3)	CSR (1)	CSR (2)	CA (1)	CA (2)	CA (3)
Perceived factualness	3.60	1.31															
Ad credibility (1)	4.00	1.31	0.30														
Ad credibility (2)	4.18	1.37	0.21	0.64													
Ad credibility (3)	4.53	1.16	0.26	0.50	0.64												
Diagnostic value for CSR (1)	4.40	1.49	0.07	0.39	0.29	0.25											
Diagnostic value for CSR (2)	4.32	1.53	0.05	0.36	0.45	0.36	0.71										
Diagnostic value for CSR (3)	4.26	1.62	0.10	0.50	0.53	0.46	0.63	0.57									
Diagnostic value for CA (1)	3.26	1.40	0.03	0.24	0.42	0.25	0.29	0.40	0.38								
Diagnostic value for CA (2)	3.40	1.48	0.08	0.42	0.55	0.47	0.34	0.40	0.42	0.63							
Diagnostic value for CA (3)	4.06	1.52	0.08	0.37	0.51	0.41	0.35	0.43	0.58	0.63	0.64						
CSR reputation (1)	5.18	1.29	0.07	0.36	0.38	0.18	0.36	0.36	0.35	0.19	0.28	0.25					
CSR reputation (2)	5.15	1.07	0.07	0.32	0.21	0.00	0.29	0.32	0.22	0.04	0.09	0.17	0.58				
CA reputation (1)	5.11	1.12	0.00	0.10	0.33	0.16	0.13	0.34	0.13	0.24	0.22	0.26	0.48	0.65			
CA reputation (2)	4.79	1.06	0.06	0.26	0.50	0.28	0.41	0.47	0.43	0.41	0.41	0.32	0.34	0.26	0.38		
CA reputation (3)	4.73	1.12	−0.02	0.20	0.31	0.28	0.14	0.33	0.19	0.21	0.16	0.24	0.21	0.35	0.42	0.42	
CA reputation (4)	4.95	1.22	−0.08	0.13	0.28	0.24	0.14	0.26	0.07	0.23	0.17	0.20	0.21	0.22	0.43	0.37	0.56

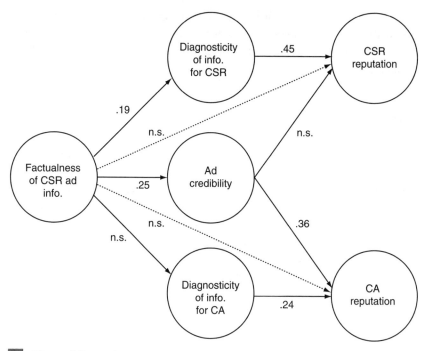

Figure 6.3 *Results*

To what degree does the effect of factualness on ad credibility "pass through" to the favorability of people's corporate associations? The perceived diagnostic value of the message for evaluating CSR has a strong significant effect on CSR reputation ($b = 0.45, t = 5.06, p = 0.00$). However, surprisingly, the credibility of the ad does not have a significant effect on CSR reputation ($b = 0.11, t = 1.28, p = 0.20$). On the other hand, CA reputation is significantly influenced both by the diagnostic value for inferring CA ($b = 0.24, t = 2.39, p = 0.02$), and by ad credibility ($b = 0.36, t = 3.68, p = 0.00$).

Consistent with this pattern, the indirect effect of the factualness on CSR reputation, mediated through the diagnostic value for inferring CSR, is also significant ($b = 0.09, t = 2.21, p = 0.03$). Because the effect of ad credibility on CSR reputation is not significant, the indirect effect of specificity on CSR reputation, as mediated by credibility, is also not significant ($b = 0.03, t = 1.14, p = 0.26$). On the other hand, the effect on CA reputation, as mediated through ad credibility, is significant ($b = 0.09, t = 2.52, p = 0.01$). Because factualness does not significantly influence the diagnostic value for inferring CA, the effect of factualness on CA reputation, as mediated through diagnostic value, is not significant ($b = 0.04, t = 1.74, p = 0.08$). There are no significant direct effects of factualness on CSR and CA reputation, implying that the effect of factualness on reputation is mediated completely by the diagnostic value and credibility of the ad. The effect of factualness on CSR reputation is mediated by diagnostic value for the organization's CSR activities, while the effect of factualness on CA reputation is mediated by ad credibility.

DISCUSSION

We have investigated whether the factualness of corporate communication about corporate social responsibility (CSR) influences a company's reputation. Our results show that factualness positively influences the diagnostic value of a corporate advertising message for inferring the organization's CSR, and, via this path, leads to a significantly more positive reputation regarding CSR. In addition, the results show that message factualness has a positive influence on the credibility of the message, which, in turn, significantly enhances the organization's reputation for corporate ability. Interestingly, providing factual information in a CSR ad thus led respondents to believe that the company was able to do a better job in its core business.

THEORETICAL IMPLICATIONS

The findings of our study have generated important insights into the way people respond to corporate advertising about CSR. The finding that factual ads are perceived as more credible than impressionistic ads is consistent with studies in product advertising that have looked at message factualness (Darley and Smith 1993; Holbrook 1978). Factual ads provide information that is not subject to multiple interpretations, and that therefore is more verifiable than impressionistic information. Hence, people are more likely to perceive this information as reliable. Providing facts may give consumers and other stakeholders the assurance that a company applies a "no-nonsense" approach, acting in a straightforward manner without trying to mislead them.

The finding that factual messages were perceived as more diagnostic for making inferences about the company's CSR was contrary to our original expectation. We had expected that factual ads would be perceived as *less* diagnostic than impressionistic ads, because their information should be perceived as less generalizable across situations and across a company's different attributes. A recent study by Semin, Higgins, Gil de Montes, Estourget and Valencia (2005) suggests one explanation for this unexpected finding. They found that concrete messages are more effective when people focus on preventing harm, while abstract messages are more effective when people focus on promoting benefits. The reason is that focusing on details is particularly important when trying to prevent harm, while focusing on the (abstract) desired end state is more important when trying to promote benefits. Many forms of CSR, and in particular a chemical company trying to take care of the environment like in our experiment, focus on preventing harm to society. This prevention focus might be a reason why people regard factual CSR information as more diagnostic than impressionistic CSR information.

Analogous to findings in research on factualness in product advertising, the results of the present study suggest that in corporate advertising on CSR, "being factual" also leads to a more favorable reputation for CSR. The reason for this effect is the increased diagnostic value of the information. Also, the increased credibility of a factual ad in turn can result in other positive perceptions of the company, like the perception that it is also doing a good job in its core activities. While factualness does not increase the diagnostic value of the message for inferring such other attributes, people might reason that if a company is trustworthy in its communication about CSR, it is likely to be trustworthy in other respects as well.

LIMITATIONS AND SUGGESTIONS FOR FUTURE RESEARCH

There are some limitations to this research. The first limitation is constituted by our focus on corporate advertising. Corporate advertising cannot be seen in isolation from other communication tools. In practice, companies do not profile themselves *only* through corporate advertising. The brevity of the corporate ad copy that was provided to respondents in this study may have created an artificial situation. In fact, some respondents remarked that it was very hard for them to infer anything from such a brief text. While the length of the text was quite representative for real corporate ads, in reality people can generally supplement this information with what they know about the company through other sources. Future studies could examine corporate ads in the context of other corporate communication efforts that provide additional information about the company, like a corporate website.

Second, we used a convenience sample of international undergraduate students. The respondents were relatively homogeneous with respect to age and educational background, even though they came from widely different cultural backgrounds. There is an important positive side to this sample, however: many of the students might, a few years later in their career, exactly fall into the group at which many corporate advertisements are aimed. Replication among corporate decision makers and other stakeholder groups of real organizations with real advertisements would be desirable, though.

Third, the manipulation of factualness that we used may to some extent have confounded factualness with other variables such as third-party endorsement (as the World Health Organization was mentioned only in the "factual" ad) or the broadness of the issue discussed in the ad (environmental protection in general versus greenhouse gasses in particular). Our reliance of the perceived factualness as the independent variable avoids in large part this possible confusion, but nevertheless this kind of confounding may have influenced our results.

Finally, the ad focused on a chemical company trying to prevent harm to the environment and to its employees. The reason we chose a chemical company is that CSR issues (especially the environment) are particularly salient in this industry. However, people may believe that the chemical industry is somewhat "suspect" because of the very nature of its activities, and may therefore react with more scepticism when a chemical company announces positive environmental principles or behaviors. In addition, because the advertisement mainly focused on preventing harm, it may be easier to generalize the results to other CSR messages with a prevention focus, like saving the environment or sparing personnel, than to CSR messages with a promotion focus, e.g., about a community outreach project like Pillsbury's (Bartel 2001). Further research is needed in order to establish whether being factual is as important to corporate communication in the latter case as it is in the former.

PRACTICAL IMPLICATIONS

The results of this study suggest that corporate communication about CSR should include factual information in order to be effective in creating a favorable reputation. Being factual may be particularly essential for audiences who are strongly involved with the issue discussed in an ad, such as "socially conscious" consumers and NGOs. While such audiences will have other sources of information about the company besides its advertising (e.g. its annual report and website), they may perceive impressionistic corporate advertising as a form of deceit, which may negatively influence their opinion of the company. This is consistent with recent work by Heugens (2001) on advertising campaigns aimed at defending the company's position on controversial issues like genetically modified foods. He suggested that the reason why many such campaigns are ineffective is that they are too general. The highly involving nature of the topic may make people less likely to accept non-factual messages.

Our recommendation to be factual in corporate communication may run counter some other advice in this field. For instance, Roznowski (2002) argues that the message sometimes *needs* to be vague and impressionistic, because corporate advertising may serve goals other than persuading stakeholders outside the organization. In particular, companies may use corporate advertising to convey to internal stakeholders (i.e., their employees) an image of the company with which they can all identify. When trying to achieve this goal, the advantage of an impressionistic message is that everyone can interpret it in his or her own way. This is what Eisenberg (1984) calls "strategic ambiguity." Based on our results, however, we would caution managers to keep the leeway they strategically need, but otherwise be as factual as the situation allows. In most cases, it may not be too complicated to provide examples that are factual without consuming this strategic freedom. In the long run, the gain in credibility and reputation may outweigh advantages of a short-term leeway in strategic maneuvering.

CASE VIGNETTE: Shell's "experts" campaign

In a recent advertising campaign, Royal Dutch Shell wanted to highlight its efforts to invest in sustainable sources of energy. As the company declares on its website, the goal of this campaign was to "tell Shell's business story and position ourselves at the heart of the energy debate. . . . It's not just a matter of behaving responsibly but also communicating about how we do business, inviting people to comment, share views and feel included in the debate" (http://www.shell.com/home/Framework?siteId=tellshell-en&FC2= &FC3=/tellshell-en/html/iwgen/advertising/advertising.html). This declaration is a logical outgrowth of Shell's concerted efforts since the mid-1990s to maintain a structural dialogue with its stakeholders (Fombrun and Rindova, 2000).

One part of this campaign features local experts, who are working with Shell to minimize the impact of the company's activities on the local community and environment. The ads explain exactly how Shell collaborates with these individuals in order to accomplish this task. One ad shows how the company, before felling trees in the Philippines for a deep water gas project, contacted local botanists to inquire about the likely impact of this project on the local ecosystem, and recruited experts to replant trees afterwards. Another example is an ad about the Blyth offshore wind project in the UK, in which Shell was a partner. In the ad, the company explains that the opinion of several experts with a stake in the project, including the Royal Society for the Protection of Birds and local fishermen, was consulted before making a decision on the location of the wind turbines. These ads highlight not only Shell's investments in projects involving alternative energy sources (deep water gas and wind energy), but also show how the company engages in a dialogue with all stakeholders involved, in order to limit any damage to the local environment as a result of the projects.

What is striking about this campaign is the concreteness of the examples that the ads display. Taken individually, they seem relatively minor contributions to specific problems, but as a whole they create an impression of a company that exerts efforts on all kinds of useful initiatives. In addition, and as suggested by the results of the study reported in this chapter, the concreteness of the examples might enhance their credibility and diagnostic value for judging the behavior of the company. The concreteness of what Shell does signals their genuineness in meeting stakeholders' interests and in the values shared—which favorably reflects upon the company's reputation (Fombrun and Rindova, 2000). Rather than a broad story about the company's values or mission, people see concrete, lively examples of what the company actually does.

ISSUES FOR FURTHER DISCUSSION

1   In what kinds of situations could factual information be less important for the company's reputation among consumers, or even detrimental to this reputation?
2   What other factors, besides factualness, could influence the credibility of corporate communication among consumers?

REFERENCES

Aaker, J. L. and Sengupta, J. (2000) "Additivity versus attenuation: the role of culture in the resolution of information incongruity." *Journal of Consumer Psychology,* 9: 67–82.

Bagozzi, R. P., Yi, Y., and Singh, S. (1991) "On the use of structural equation models in experimental designs: two extensions." *International Journal of Research in Marketing,* 8: 125–40.

Banerjee, S., Gulas, C. S., and Iyer, E. (1995) "Shades of green: a multidimensional analysis of environmental advertising." *Journal of Advertising,* 24(2): 21–31.

Baron, R. M. and Kenny, D. A. (1986) "The moderator–mediator variable distinction in social psychological research: conceptual, strategic, and statistical considerations." *Journal of Personality and Social Psychology,* 51: 1173–82.

Bartel, C. A. (2001) "Social comparisons in boundary-spanning work: effects of community outreach on members' organizational identity and identification." *Administrative Science Quarterly,* 46: 379–413.

Blankenhorn, D. (1998) "Corporate ad budgets up 18 percent in '97." *Advertising Age's Business Marketing,* 83: 2.

Brown, T. J. and Dacin, P. A. (1997) "The company and the product: corporate associations and consumer product responses." *Journal of Marketing,* 61: 68–84.

Chan, R. Y. K. and Lau, L. B. Y. (2004) "The effectiveness of environmental claims among Chinese consumers: influences of claim type, country disposition and ecocentric orientation." *Journal of Marketing Management,* 20, 273–319.

Churchill, G. A. (1979) "A paradigm for developing better measures of marketing constructs." *Journal of Marketing Research,* 16(February): 64–73.

Darley, W. K. and Smith, R. E. (1993) "Advertising claim objectivity: antecedents and effects." *Journal of Marketing*, 57: 100–13.

Davis, J. J. (1994a) "Consumer response to corporate environmental advertising." *Journal of Consumer Marketing*, 11: 25–37.

Davis, J. J. (1994b) "Good ethics is good for business: ethical attributions and response to environmental advertising." *Journal of Business Ethics*, 13: 873–85.

Debevec, K., Meyers, P. W., and Chan, K. K. (1985) "The effects of knowledge and imagery on advertising responses to an innovation," in M. Holbrook (ed.), *Advances in Consumer Research*. Provo, UT: Association for Consumer Research, vol. 12, 273–8.

Eisenberg, E. M. (1984) "Ambiguity as strategy in organizational communication." *Communication Monographs*, 51: 227–42.

Feldman, D. C., Bearden, W. O., and Hardesty, D. M. (2006) "Varying the content of job advertisements: the effects of message specificity." *Journal of Advertising*, 35(1): 123–41.

Fombrun, C. J. and Rindova, V. P. (2000) "The road to transparency: reputation management at Royal Dutch Shell," in M. Schultz, M. J. Hatch, and M. H. Larsen (eds), *The Expressive Organization, Linking Identity, Reputation and the Corporate Brand*. Oxford: Oxford University Press, 77–96.

Fombrun, C. J., Gardberg, N. A., and Sever, J. M. (2000) "The reputation quotient: a multi-stakeholder measure of corporate reputation." *Journal of Brand Management*, 7: 241–55.

Garbett, T. F. (1988) *How to Build a Corporation's Identity and Project Its Image*. Lexington, MA: Lexington Books.

Goldberg, R. (1998) "Corporate image: Business competency versus social conscience," Unpublished doctoral dissertation, Harvard University, Cambridge, MA.

Grass, R. C., Bartges, D. W., and Piech, J. L. (1972) "Measuring corporate image ad effects." *Journal of Advertising Research*, 12(6): 15–22.

Green, S. B. (1991) "How many subjects does it take to do a regression analysis?" *Multivariate Behavioral Research*, 26: 499–510.

Heugens, P. P. M. A. R. (2001) "Strategic issues management: implications for corporate performance." Doctoral dissertation, Erasmus University, Rotterdam.

Holbrook, M. B. (1978) "Beyond attitude structure: toward the informational determinants of attitude." *Journal of Marketing Research*, 15: 545–56.

Kozup, J. C., Creyer, E. H., and Burton, S. (2003) "Making healthful food choices: the influence of health claims and nutrition information on consumers' evaluations of packaged food products and restaurant menu items." *Journal of Marketing*, 67: 19–34.

Li, Y. (2005) *PLS-GUI: A Graphic User Interface for Lvpls (PLS 1.8 PC) (Version 2.0.1)*. Columbia, SC: University of South Carolina (available at: http: //dmsweb.moore.sc.edu/yuanli/PLS-GUI).

Lynch, J. G., Marmorstein, H., and Weigold, M. F. (1988) "Choices from sets including remembered brands: use of recalled attributes and prior overall evaluations." *Journal of Consumer Research*, 15: 169–84.

MacKenzie, S. B. and Lutz, R. J. (1989) "An empirical examination of the structural antecedents of attitude toward the ad in an advertising pretesting context." *Journal of Marketing*, 53: 48–65.

Maronick, T. J. and Andrews, J. C. (1999) "The role of qualifying language on consumer perceptions of environmental claims." *Journal of Consumer Affairs*, 33(2): 297–320.

Reeves, B. and Ferguson-DeThorne, M. A. (1980) "Measuring the effect of messages about social responsibility." *Public Relations Review*, 6: 40–55.

117

Rindskopf, D. and Rose, T. (1988) "Some theory and applications of confirmatory second-order factor analysis." *Multivariate Behavioral Research*, 23: 51–67.

Rossiter, J. R. and Percy, L. (1997) *Advertising Communications and Promotion Management*. Boston: Irwin/McGraw-Hill.

Roznowski, J. L. (2002) "A review of corporate advertising and an agenda for future research with a theoretical twist." Paper presented at the AMA Summer Marketing Educators' Conference, San Diego, CA.

Schum, D. A. (1977) "Contrast effects in inference: on the conditioning of current evidence by prior evidence." *Organizational Behavior and Human Performance*, 18: 217–53.

Schumann, D. W., Hathcote, J. M., and West, S. (1991) "Corporate advertising in America: a review of published studies on use, measurement, and effectiveness." *Journal of Advertising*, 20(3): 35–56.

Semin, G. and Fiedler, K. (1988) "The cognitive functions of linguistic categories in describing persons: Social cognition and language." *Journal of Personality and Social Psychology*, 54: 558–68.

Semin, G. and de Poot, C. (1997) "The question–answer paradigm: you might regret not noticing how a question is worded." *Journal of Personality and Social Psychology*, 73: 472–80.

Semin, G. R., Higgins, E. T., Gil de Montes, L., Estourget, Y., and Valencia, J.F. (2005) "Linguistic signatures of regulatory focus: how abstraction fits promotion more than prevention." *Journal of Personality and Social Psychology*, 89: 36–45.

Sheinin, D. A. and Biehal, G. J. (1999) "Corporate advertising pass-through onto the brand: some experimental evidence.", *Marketing Letters* 10: 63–74.

Srull, T. K. and Wyer, R. S. (1989) "Person memory and judgment." *Psychological Review*, 96: 58–83.

Tenenhaus, M., Vinzi, V. E., Chatelin, Y.-M., and Lauro, C. (2005) "PLS path modeling." *Computational Statistics and Data Analysis*, 48: 159–205.

Voss, G. B. and Parasuraman, A. (2003) "Conducting measurement validation with experimental data: cautions and recommendations." *Marketing Letters*, 14: 59–73.

Wigboldus, D., Semin, G., and Spears, R. (2000) "How do we communicate stereotypes? Linguistic bases and inferential consequences." *Journal of Personality and Social Psychology*, 78: 5–18.

Winters, L. C. (1977) "Should you advertise to hostile audiences?" *Journal of Advertising Research*, 17(6): 7–14.

Winters, L. C. (1982) "Comparing pretesting and posttesting of corporate advertising." *Journal of Advertising Research*, 23: 25–32.

Winters, L. C. (1986) "The effect of brand advertising on company image: implications for corporate advertising." *Journal of Advertising Research*, 26(2): 54–59.

Winters, L. C. (1988) "Does it pay to advertise to hostile audiences with corporate advertising?" *Journal of Advertising Research*, 28(June–July): 11–18.

APPENDIX 6.1: MEASURES

Scale	Items	Coefficient alpha
Perceived factualness	How would you describe the information given in the ad? 1 Factual—impressionistic 2 Factual: everyone can agree on the meaning of the information in the ad 3 Impressionistic: the meaning of the information in the ad is subject to interpretation	—
Ad credibility	How would you describe the information given in the ad? 1 Unreliable—reliable 2 Unconvincing—convincing 3 Unbelievable—believable	0.82
Diagnostic value for CSR	1 How useful do you find the information given in the ad for judging Laurec's social responsibility? 2 How relevant do you find the information given in the ad for judging Laurec's social responsibility? 3 How important do you find the information given in the ad for judging Laurec's social responsibility?	0.83
Diagnostic value for CA	1 How useful do you find the information given in the ad for judging Laurec's overall expertise / social responsibility? 2 How relevant do you find the information given in the ad for judging Laurec's overall expertise? 3 How important do you find the information given in the ad for judging Laurec's overall expertise?	0.84
CSR reputation	1 Do you think that [company] supports good causes? 2 Do you think that [company] maintains high standards in the way it treats people?	0.76
CA reputation	1 Do you think that [company] develops innovative products and services? 2 Do you think that [company] offers high-quality products? 3 Do you think [company] is well-managed? 4 Do you think that [company] employs talented people in comparison with competitors?	0.73

Note: the numbers correspond to those in Tables 6.2 and 6.3.

Chapter 7

Corporate communication
Reputation in action

Tom Watson and Philip J. Kitchen

AT THE END OF THIS CHAPTER READERS SHOULD BE ABLE TO:

1 Understand notions and definitions of reputation and the debate about them
2 Discuss reputation management and its relationship with communication strategy
3 Appreciate the factors that comprise best practice in reputation management

---

KEY POINTS

- Reputation is of immense importance to all organizations as it paves the way to acceptance and approval by stakeholders. It underpins competitive advantage by demonstrating differences from other similar organizations
- Reputation does not occur by chance. It relates to leadership, management, and organizational operations, the quality of products and services, and—crucially—relationships with stakeholders. Reputational performance is also connected to communication activities and feedback mechanisms
- Reputation is a collective representation of images and perceptions that involves relationships with stakeholders. It is gained, maintained, enhanced, or detracted from over time. All members of an organization make a contribution to building and sustaining a reputation
- Brand, identity, and reputation are sometimes used interchangeably but inaccurately. Image is an organization's self-presentation; brand is its offer in terms of products, services, and customer relationship; whereas reputation is bestowed by the perceptions and interactions of others
- Reputation management is a term whose validity is contested. There are those

who consider that reputation cannot be managed and that it is an outcome of interactions between the organization and its stakeholders; others make the case that it can be developed in a planned manner by organizations that are fully aware of their operating environment and respond constructively to it

- Closely allied to reputation is relationship management, which is being strongly advocated as the new paradigm for public relations. This moves public relations away from message creation and dissemination to the development of mutually beneficial relationships between organizations and stakeholders (publics). Strong, positive relationships are the bedrock of good reputations

- Case studies show how positive and negative aspects of corporate decision-making, communication and operation performance affect reputation. In some instances, a good reputation has a defensive halo effect in protecting an organization in a crisis; whereas a poor or declining reputation limits an organization's operational freedom and can lead to its failure

- Best practice in reputation management has found that CEOs (or equivalent leaders) are very important in reputational matters in some countries (Italy, Canada, and the USA) but much less so in others (Belgium, France, and the UK)

A good reputation is an excellent calling card: It opens doors, attracts followers, brings in customers and investors—it commands our respect.

(Fombrun and Van Riel 2004: 4)

INTRODUCTION

Reputation is of immense importance to all organizations, whether they be commercial, governmental, or not-for-profit. To achieve goals, remain competitive, and prosper, good reputation paves the organizational path to acceptance and approval by stakeholders. It also underpins competitive advantage by demonstrating distinctive differences from other [similar] organizations. Even those operating in difficult ethical environments—perhaps self-created—need to sustain a positive reputation.

Dowling (1994) reports that a good corporate reputation can help underpin better profitability than those of competitors by:

- inhibiting the mobility of rival firms;
- acting as a market entry/penetration barrier;
- signaling quality of the firm's products to customers and consumers and possibly enabling the firm to exercise price leadership;

- attracting better job applicants;
- enhancing access to capital markets;
- attracting investors (Brown and Reingen 1987, quoted in Dowling 1994: 16).

Argenti and Druckenmiller argue that, "organizations increasingly recognize the importance of corporate reputation to achieve business goals and stay competitive" (Argenti and Druckenmiller 2004: 368). While there are many recent examples of organizations where poor leadership and unethical business practice behavior have destroyed their reputation, such as Enron, Arthur Andersen, Tyco, and WorldCom, the positive case for reputation is that it does foster the continued expansion of companies such as Johnson and Johnson and Philips and innovators such as Cisco Systems, who appear regularly in the top percentile of rankings of the most respected organizations in the US and Europe.

Thus, corporate reputation is not just a matter of academic or arcane management discussion. However, US public relations industry leader David Drobis noted from the Wall Street Journal in the first 10 months of 2000 that 38 CEOs from the US's 200 largest companies had left their jobs to "pursue other interests." That is a 1 in 5 turnover rate (Jolly 2001: 4). Meanwhile, another PR industry leader, London-based Adrian Wheeler, commented that market research by MORI has persistently found that barely a quarter of people "trust business leaders to tell the truth . . . there is a gulf between the principles which companies espouse and how they operate" (Jolly 2001: 9). Thus, while reputation is important, the need for leaders and organizations to be "appear to be (and actually be) ethical and truthful" is more urgent now in the twenty-first century, than at any other point since the 1950s.

What is evident is that reputation *does not occur by chance*. It relates to leadership, management, and organizational operations, the quality of products and services, and—crucially—relationships with stakeholders. It is also connected to communication activities and feedback mechanisms.

This chapter will look at reputation in action and as a key driver of corporate communication. It will explore notions of reputation and of reputation management. It will consider case studies of reputation and examine best practice in reputation-led corporate communication.

MANAGEMENT OF REPUTATION

What is reputation?

The dictionary definitions of reputation, while normally focused on individuals, give strong indications of the elements that are relevant to organizations. An example is:

1. What is generally said or believed about a person or thing. 2. The state of being well thought of.

(*Oxford Current English Dictionary* 1990)

In the corporate world, reputation is seen as a major element of an organization's provenance alongside and included in financial performance and innovation.

Dowling (1994) defines corporate reputation as:

the evaluation (respect, esteem, estimation) in which an organization's image is held by people.

(p. 8)

Argenti and Druckenmiller (2004) define it as:

The collective representation of multiple constituencies' images of a company built up over time and based on a company's identity programs, its performance and how constituencies have perceived its behavior.

(p. 369)

Dowling's definition is simpler and links to his definition of corporate image as the "total impression an entity makes on the minds of people" (p. 8). The elements to note in his definition and the Argenti and Druckenmiller equivalent are that reputation is a "collective representation" of images and perceptions, not merely a self-promotional message. It involves relationships with all stakeholders ("constituencies") and . . . is gained, maintained, and enhanced, or detracted from over time.

Murray and White's research among UK CEOs found similar characteristics:

It is the role of public relations to make sure that the organization is getting credit for the good it does. Great reputations are built on doing this consistently over a period of time in which a track record of delivering on promises and engendering trust is evident to everyone. All members of an organization have a contribution to make to building and sustaining reputation.

(Murray and White 2004: 10)

The elements of promoted yet sustainable image and performance are again identified, but a holistic factor—"all members of an organization"—is added. Later in this chapter, the role of CEOs in defining and driving reputation is discussed. However, it is broadly accepted that good reputation is unsustainable without internal organizational support. Neglect of reputation by means of apathy, indifference, or ineffective communication, is leaving a key communication to the vagaries of other market forces. Even worse is the promotion of an apparent ethical, truthful, and open reputation, until the forces of publicity unmask the exact opposite. The result of such poor communication is evident as cited in many examples (see earlier citations).

Murray and White also point to relationship management as being "at the heart of creating, enhancing and retaining a good reputation" (p. 10). They see strong communication performance by organizational leaders and effective feedback mechanisms from stakeholders as essential for articulating relevant messages and making better informed decisions that retain the support of stakeholders.

BRAND, IDENTITY, AND REPUTATION

These three terms are sometimes used interchangeably—brand and image; image and reputation. Van Riel and Berens (2001) say, "corporate identity can be defined as a company's *self-presentation*, that is, the managed cues or signals that an organization offers about itself to stakeholders" (p. 45). It also defined by Argenti and Druckenmiller (2004) as consisting of "a company's defining attributes, such as its people, products, and services" (p. 369). Van Riel and Berens also point to corporate symbolism as part of the identity, which includes logos, house style, staff uniforms, etc. (p. 45). The transmitted corporate identity is received by stakeholders as image, "a reflection of the organization's identity and its corporate brand" (Argenti and Druckenmiller 2004: 45). This image or set of images thus contributes to the reputation of the organization.

The corporate brand is also an expression of the organization's presentation to others. Argenti and Druckenmiller define it as: "a brand that spans an entire company which can have disparate underlying product brands; and. . . . Conveys expectations of what the company will deliver in terms of products, services, and customer experience" (p. 369).

As can be seen, the primary (and important difference) between image and reputation is that reputation is a two-way relationship with stakeholders and thus open to managerial intervention and planning.

CORPORATE COMMUNICATION

Can reputation be managed?

The question of the validity of the term "reputation management" is also at the core of debate on corporate communication. There is a body of knowledge and academic research in this field, an academic journal, *Corporate Reputation Review*, as well as the rebranding of public relations by some consultancies with this term

(Hutton et al. 2001: 247–8). There is also the assumption that all organizations have a reputation be it good, neutral, or bad. But, how well can this be managed, controlled or directed? Hutton et al. (2001) describe the dilemma tersely:

> [US public relations academics] David Finn, Doug Newsom, and others have pointed out that concepts such as "reputation" and "image" are not generally something that can be managed directly, but are omnipresent and the global result of a firm's or individual's behavior. Attempting to manage one's reputation might be likened to trying to manage one's own popularity (a rather awkward, superficial and potentially self-defeating endeavour). On the other hand, some advocates see reputation management as a new guiding force or paradigm for the entire field, in keeping with Warren Buffet's admonition that losing reputation is a far greater sin for an organization than losing money.
>
> (p. 249)

Charles Fombrun argues a different case that reputation can be developed in a planned manner by organizations taking necessary notice of the environment in which they operate.

> Better-regarded companies build their reputations by developing practices which integrate social and economic considerations into their competitive strategies. They not only do things right—they do the right things. In doing so, they act like good citizens. They initiate policies that reflect their core values; that consider the joint welfare of investors, customers, and employees, that invoke concern for the development of local communities; and that ensure the quality and environmental soundness of their technologies, products, and services (Fombrun 1995: 8).

This paradigm of reputation management is that the organization's reputation is dependent on its behavior as a corporate citizen, part of the societies in which it operates, and not above or apart from these. Reputational considerations are embedded in policy and actions, not just bolted on when convenient.

GOOD AND BAD REPUTATION

The definitions of reputation tend to favor the positive with emphasis placed on "being well thought of," "in public esteem," and "delivering on promises." But, as all readers know, reputation has two sides. In early 2000, Gardberg and Fombrun investigated the reputation of companies at both ends of the reputational spectrum. They sought the views of a sample of Americans and Europeans in 11 countries on companies with the best and worst corporate reputations (Gardberg and Fombrun 2002: 385). Using a combination of telephone and online polling, they garnered over 10,000 nominations. Their conclusions were:

> Positive nominations are given to companies with strong corporate brands that have identifiable subsidiary brands often of the same name. The gaining of favorable "top-of-mind" visibility speaks to the historical associations created in the minds of the public through strategic communications.

Negative associations with some equally strong mega-brands whose names have become synonymous with crisis speak to the inability these companies have in adjusting public perception (p. 391).

Later, Fombrun and van Riel (2004) noted that strong financial and trading performance does not necessarily result in a good reputation. They also conclude that branding is a subset of reputation management.

It's often true, therefore, that a good reputation sits on the bedrock of a strong product or corporate brand. However, brand and reputation are not synonymous—and they differ in importance. On one hand, the brand describes the set of associations that customers have with the company's products. A weak brand has low awareness and functional appeal to customers, whereas a strong brand has high awareness and functional appeal. Reputation on the other hand involves assessments that multiple shareholders make about a company's ability to fulfill their expectations. A company may have strong product brands or even a strong corporate brand—its brands can have high awareness and appeal—but can still have a weak or poor reputation . . . (The example of Nike sports products was given) . . . Succinctly put, branding affects the likelihood of a favorable purchase decision by consumers. Reputation, however, affects the likelihood of supportive behavior from all the brand's stakeholders. Branding therefore is a subset of reputation management (p. 4).

Nike is an example of an organization that has been severely damaged by criticism of its work and employment practices in low-cost supplier countries. However, this is an aspect of its reputation which it has persistently sought to remedy. Failure to remedy this negative image, however, will continue to bedevil its competitive advantage and its ability to improve sales and profit potential.

LINKS TO RELATIONSHIP MANAGEMENT

A theme in public relations and corporate communications theory is whether the paradigm should be changed from message delivery-type process activities to management of relationships. There have been parallel tracks of development that emphasize the use of negotiation techniques (Watson et al. 2002), the embedding of corporate social responsibility in corporate policies, and symmetrical (equal two-way) communications (Grunig and Hunt 1984). These were previously brought together by Ledingham and Bruning who proposed that relationship management is at the core of a general theory of public relations. This moved theory and practice away from message creation and dissemination to a problem-solving management function. It fits into a framework of mutual understanding and can be closely associated with negotiation techniques where the outcome sought is mutual gain. Relationship management fits closely with community relations, corporate social responsibility, and consultative processes used in corporate issues management.

As noted earlier, the development and maintenance of reputation is based on numerous relationships with internal and external stakeholders, so relationship management as a new paradigm of public relations can be aligned with reputation management. Ledingham and Bruning (2000)'s argument is based on very similar grounds to those expressed for best practice in reputation management.

Organizations that develop a relationship management program that focuses on mutual benefit will maximize the influence that relationships can have on consumers while concurrently acting as a good citizen because the organization will be engaging in activities, actions, and communications that are in the best interests of both the consumer and the organization (p. 169).

Although some public relations academics, notably Hutton et al. (2001), strongly question reputation management as a separate discipline, there appear to be strong enough operational and applied theoretical links between reputation management and relationship management to indicate the need for closer dialogue.

These case studies show reputation and corporate communication under the closest examination.

CASE VIGNETTE: Johnson and Johnson

Reputation speeds recovery after a deadly crisis

The case study of the Johnson and Johnson Company and the pain relief drug, Tylenol, is one most frequently referred to. Although it happened two decades ago, it illustrates the value of a strong brand image, a strong company reputation, and an ethical core to the business which was immediately operationalised once a problem arose. Note that the managerial response to this case is a response which few firms seem to carry out nowadays. A few capsules of Tylenol were contaminated with cyanide by an unknown person and the top-selling analgesic was immediately withdrawn from the market. Market research showed that a high level of confidence in both the Johnson and Johnson name and the Tylenol brand,

and this trust was used as the basis to relaunch the drug after the packing had been redesigned to make it tamper-proof. The company's speed of response and highly effective communications throughout the crisis process—closely allied to its decision to take its best-selling product off the market—has become the management template for product withdrawal and ethically prompt corporate communication. Jim Burke, then chairman of Johnson and Johnson, said "the reputation of the corporation, which has been carefully built over 90 years, provided a reservoir of goodwill among the public, the people in the regulatory agencies, and the media, which was of incalculable value in helping to restore the brand" (ten Berge 1988, quoted in Dowling 1994: 215). Even now, Johnson and Johnson continually heads the list of most respected corporations in the USA. Yet, some two decades, on, we still find many companies offering excuses rather than solutions to managerial issues, ethical problems, and sheer "bad management." Perhaps Johnson and Johnson is the exception rather than the norm?

CASE VIGNETTE: Rover

Reputation affected by management behavior
Public support for the British car maker Rover, which had been bought back from BMW for £1 by management, fell like a stone when it was revealed in the media that the chief executive was one of the best paid motor executives in Europe at a time when the company's sales were in steep decline. A pension fund for senior executives was boosted by £13 million at the same time that the employee pension fund was an estimated £60 million in deficit. "The rewards to this [managerial] group were judged by the media and many opinion leaders to be out of proportion to the rewards to others—and certainly counter to the disappointing sales and financial performance of the company. The media and opinion leaders may just be one group but market performance seemed to suggest that customers were no more impressed" (Haywood 2005: 3). Yet, how often do senior managerial groups accrue rewards to themselves without actually delivering anything by way of improved sales, profits, return on investment, or corporate performance?

CASE VIGNETTE: Australian Airline

Reputation loss leads to corporate failure
The long-established Australian airline Ansett collapsed in 2001 after a series of aircraft maintenance crises that eroded public confidence. McDonald applied attribution theory to Ansett's problems and using a qualitative research approach found the dominant attitude to the airline had been passengers' anger directed at it and distrust in the senior executive staff to manage and tell the truth. Because of a period of maintenance problems which had seen the airline grounded by the government civil aviation watchdog, passengers and potential passengers had largely perceived the airline as responsible for its own fate. Her research also

found that a \$A20 million advertising campaign after one crisis had a boomerang effect with one interviewee commenting that "it drives me nuts those ads, so I think they're going to crash the plane and they're trying to convince that they're not" (McDonald 2006: 7). Another said that the \$20 million would have been better spent on aircraft maintenance. This period became known as "Chance it on Ansett."

> Additionally, when crisis messages, such as that delivered by the Ansett CEO, were perceived as lies, anger resulted and negative character attributions were made about company management. Such dispositional attributions revealed strong negative attitudes to those companies caught lying and contribute to the public's lack of trust in the integrity of organizations.
>
> (McDonald 2006: 10)

CASE VIGNETTE: General Motors and Toyota

Reputation leads to differential purchase decisions
General Motors and Toyota produced identical cars through a joint venture in the US. "The Toyota Corolla and Chevrolet Prizm, though built side by side from identical components and with only minor trim differences, had quite different fates: Only one-quarter as many Prizms were sold, their trade-in value depreciated more quickly, and the Prizm required up to \$750 more in buyer incentives to support its sales. Having Toyota's name on the Corolla attracted customers; while the Prizm was lost among the Chevy dealer's other offerings."
> Source: McQuire, J. B., Schneeweis, T., and Branch, B. 1990,
> quoted in Fombrun and van Riel 2004: 9.

CASE VIGNETTE: BBC

Reputation aids employment
A poll of 6,000 final year UK university students was asked to name the five organizations they would most like to work for. The BBC topped the list, followed by Foreign and Commonwealth Office, British Airways, Andersen (now defunct) and Accenture. Four of these organizations are major graduate recruiters, but the BBC doesn't have a formal graduate recruitment process and recruits 300 people annually. It had run on-campus communication programs to dispel the notion that it is elitist and undertook talent recruitment aimed at young presenters, producers, and technicians which emphasized its innovation and interest in "edgy" programming.

> Clearly, a good reputation attracts interest from potential employees, even if you don't hire much. It also reinforces the commitment of in-

house employees to the company's values, beliefs, mission, and objectives. By building identification with the company, reputation as a good employer fuels employee loyalty, motivation, engagement, and commitment.

(Fombrun and van Riel 2004: 10)

REPUTATION'S VALUE IN A CRISIS

Fombrun and van Riel (2004) argue that crisis costs are one way to estimate reputation capital. The value of a corporate reputation is magnified at such times because of the tragic loss of physical assets and human lives that occur and the expected clean-up and legal costs associated with the crisis. "Over time, some companies recover dissipated value quickly and the crisis fizzles. Others experience more extended damage. Research suggests that the enduring difference may well lie in how the crisis is handled and what the reputation of the company was beforehand" (Fombrun and van Riel 2004: 34–5).

Oxford University research (Knights and Pretty 1999, quoted in Fombrun and van Riel 2004: 34–5) studied the impact of major manmade crises on 15 large companies, ranging from the Tylenol tampering to Heineken's recall of bottled beer because of rumours of glass shards in its bottles. On average, the stocks took an 8 percent hit in value. However, their preparedness and speed of response categorized the companies into "recoverers" and "non-recoverers." The recoverers' stock sagged only 5 percent in the first few weeks, while non-recoverers dropped an average 11 percent. After 10 weeks, the recoverers rose an average of 5 percent and stayed in "positive territory" for the balance of the year. The non-recoverers, by contrast, stayed down and finished the year down by 15 percent. "Overall, the reputational losses associated with crises are substantial and, on average, amount to 8–15 percent of the market values of affected companies" (Fombrun and van Riel 2004: 38).

COSTS OF CRISES

The financial and reputational cost of catastrophe can be extremely high and may not be fully apparent for months and years after the event, according to examples given by Regester (in Jolly 2001: 93)

Exxon (*Valdez* spill)	$13 bn
PanAm (Lockerbie crash)	$652m
P&O Ferries (Zeebrugge sinking)	$70m
Union Carbide (Bhopal)	$527m

Perrier (benzene accident)	$263m
Occidental Oil (Piper Alpha explosion)	$1.4m
Barings Bank (collapse)	$900m

The consequence of crises were

- product/service boycott or abandonment (numerous pharmaceutical products);
- share price collapse (e.g. Perrier, which was taken over by Nestlé);
- loss of competitive advantage (Monsanto and GM crops in Europe);
- damaging legacy issues (Railtrack and the rail crash at Southall, near London);
- imposition of new, restrictive legislation (numerous sectors).

BEST PRACTICE IN REPUTATION MANAGEMENT

In an eight-country study, Kitchen and Laurence (2003) explored corporate reputation management practice, with an emphasis on the role of the CEO and the management of reputation across cultures and national borders. Corporate reputation was found to be of the greatest importance in achieving corporate objectives, with the highest ranking in the US, Canada, and the UK.

CORPORATE REPUTATION MEASUREMENT

As for measurement of this "very important" element, Kitchen and Laurence comment, "despite, the apparent importance devoted to corporate reputation, sustained increase in systematized formal measurement procedure was not in marked evidence in the countries concerned" (p. 108). More than half the respondents in Netherlands and Canada undertook formal measurement, but there was little or no progress in other countries. It should be noted that this situation of low investment measurement is similar for measurement of public relations and corporate communications programs in general.

Where evaluation took place, the majority of companies in the eight countries nominated "custom research" as both their main method of monitoring and measuring reputation and the one metric that is "Most Meaningful." Kitchen and Laurence comment that "custom research" is a category that covers a wide range of quantitative and qualitative research techniques that can be undertaken by in-house facilities and external suppliers (p. 110). However, the very interesting factor identified was that "media coverage" is much less important than "custom research" and "informal feedback" in most countries, and was lowly ranked as a Most Meaningful metric in only three out of eight countries (Netherlands

7 percent, USA and UK 5 percent each). As media relations is the main activity in most corporate communications programs, it is revealing that it appears to have so little importance in the measurement of (and thus contribution to) corporate reputation.

THE CEO'S ROLE IN REPUTATION MANAGEMENT

A theme of this study is the weight given to the CEO's reputation in determining corporate reputation. Citing van Riel (1999) that there is a close interrelationship between corporate reputation and the reputation of the CEO, Kitchen and Laurence's data found (p. 113) that it is "most important in Italy, closely followed by Canada, then the USA." On the reverse, it "is . . . least likely to impact on corporate reputation in Belgium, the UK and France" (p. 113). See Table 7.1 below.

"The CEO's reputation becomes more important when choosing a successor to move the company on to new and better heights" (pp. 113–14), with the USA (64 percent), Germany (55 percent) and Italy (52 percent) placing greatest weight, with Canada (38 percent) and France (34 percent) placing least emphasis on this factor.

Summarizing the eight country study, Kitchen and Laurence offer six conclusions:

1   Corporate reputation has increased and is increasing in importance
2   The need for a recognized measurement is growing in importance
3   The key influencers on reputation are—despite some caveats—customers, employees, and then the CEO
4   A good corporate reputation precedes and helps business grow internationally and in preparing the ground in new markets among key constituencies

Table 7.1 What % of your company's corporate reputation is based on the CEO's reputation?

Country	50 to 100
Italy	83
Canada	66
USA	54
Netherlands	44
Germany	42
France	36
UK	33
Belgium	26

5   CEO reputation and corporate reputation are increasingly intertwined. The CEO is inevitably cast in the role of chief communicator

6   The responsibility for managing reputation is a key management responsibility and—led by the CEO—it must be managed in an integrated manner (pp. 115–16).

Kitchen and Lawrence concluded that it was clear that if the organization or its CEO could not communicate its mission, brands, or values, some other organization, stakeholder, or irate public with communication capabilities could and would. Thus, corporate communication must be mastered by the corporation and those duly appointed to speak on its behalf; or it will master the corporation (p. 116).

The role of the CEO as corporate spokesman has also been anecdotally buttressed by two of Britain's best-known business leaders of the late twentieth century. The late Lord Hanson's best practice advice was:

> Do not delegate the key elements. You may get (a consultant) to give you advice or set up the procedures—but never let them become the spokesman for your organization. That is the job that senior executives must undertake themselves. Creative people may be able to develop great advertising for you, but this principle should not be applied to public relations. This is essentially a personal skill and a senior responsibility.
>
> (Haywood 2005: 23)

Former ICI chief, Sir Denys Henderson added:

> The most skilful use of "smoke and mirrors" can disguise fundamental problems for no more than a limited period. In the end, there must be substance behind the promise—truth will undoubtedly out, regardless of any camouflage efforts by the most expert "spin" doctor. Management has to accept to responsibility not only for the success or otherwise of the message but also for the facts behind it.
>
> (Haywood 2005: 24)

Fombrun and van Riel (2004: 87–94), using the results of their reputation studies in North America, Europe, and Australia, propose five principles that create a strong, sustainable and positive reputation. They are, in summary:

■   *Be visible*: High reputation companies spend more on communication, as found in the US by the Council of PR Firms in 2000.

■   *Be distinctive*: BP's "beyond petroleum" stance and visual image has given it a different image to competitors in the oil-led energy sector.

- *Be authentic*: The then independent ice-cream maker, Ben and Jerry's, was ranked as a top-five reputation in the US in 1999 because consumers and business leaders saw it as an authentically-voiced organization.
- *Be transparent*: In 2002, Enron and other scandals had an indirect cost of $35 billion, according to the Brookings Institute.
- *Be consistent*: GM is seen as a bad example of brand silos that conflict with each other.

MULTI-NATIONAL REPUTATION MANAGEMENT

Trans-national enterprises (TNE) have to defend their reputations with speed and understanding of local situations if they are to retain their high standing. Kitchen and Laurence (2003) reinforce the point that corporate reputations of TNEs are open to scrutiny around the clock.

> Corporations in the global economy need to exercise social responsibility and exercise due accountability for their actions and if not at their peril. And all forms of communication offer global potentiality. As the multiple medias undergo further development, so the imperative will be to monitor what is communicated, how it is communicated, through which media and with what potential outcomes. That means measuring outcomes by all media contacts including the WorldWideWeb.
>
> (p. 116)

This argument brings reputation management back to corporate communication structures that operate 24/7 and which have a direct line of responsibility to the highest levels of management or preferably are managed by those at board level.

MEASURING EFFECTIVENESS IN CORPORATE COMMUNICATION

Although Kitchen and Laurence's (2003) eight-country study found that the majority of organizations do not measure reputation well, there is a wide range of literature from academics and practitioners that indicates existing evaluation practices are apparently sufficient for measurement of communication programs and reputation without the need for new and specialized tools. Indeed, as Murray and White (2004) found, CEOs are not demanding exact metrics but seek better planning of relations with stakeholders and monitoring of information.

CEO'S ATTITUDES TO EVALUATION

Murray and White's (2004) research amongst chief executives into their attitudes towards public relations brought a different and potentially confounding result. They interviewed 14 CEOs and chairpersons from major UK and international organizations and discovered that they "intuitively" valued corporate communication. Indeed, CEOs saw it as an essential cost of business, and essential to business and organizational performance. The business leaders also felt that it was "not amenable to precise measurement, being long-term and iterative in effect, or being an aid to avoiding surprises or mistakes. They do not feel a great need to demonstrate a return on investment in their PR" (Murray and White 2004: 4).

While thinking that practitioners needed to use available measures more confidently and to be able to make the case for the value of their contribution more effectively, CEOs are used to handling information that is not exhaustive. They need enough information to make sensible decisions, but the quest for definitive information on the performance of public relations appears to be a practitioner's obsession.

"MOST ADMIRED" COMPANIES

Research by Gregory and Edwards (2004) into the practice of public relations by companies in the UK *Management Today* magazine's "Most Admired" company list and by Gregory, Morgan and Kelly (2005) on "Most Admired" companies and public sector organizations, found that a range of evaluation metrics were used, (usually between four and eight) and the most frequently used metrics were informal and/or qualitative such as journalist feedback and discussions with stakeholders. It is as if the respondents were "just checking" that everything was on track. This supports the proposition in the Murray and White (2004) research which indicated an intuitive sense of what is or was working. As such it reflects life in business generally where, besides solid research, intuition and a general sense of purpose and direction are regarded as vital to success. The one consistent hard quantitative measure for private sector companies was the share price.

It was discovered that status of the senior public relations practitioner was high in these admired organizations with 43 percent on the Board or Executive Committee and many others reporting directly to the CEO. Asked why public relations was regarded so highly, it appeared that the handling of crises had been key to the recognition of public relations as a vital and valued activity. Either these organizations had recognized that good public relations had been essential to preserving their reputation in a crisis (reflected also by Murray and White 2004) or that a lack of such a function had left them dangerously exposed. Once having passed such a credibility test, the value of public relations was recognized and the need for the function constantly to prove its contribution diminished.

CASE VIGNETTE: James Hardie Industries

Loss of reputation damages competitive freedom

From the early twentieth century onward, asbestos was mined in Australia and processed into building materials, principally for internal and external wall-boards. Indeed, houses built with the external materials were given the generic nickname of "fibro houses" after the fibrous asbestos source minerals and there are hundreds of thousands of these humble abodes across the country. In the latter part of the twentieth century, it became apparent that many thousands of miners and building workers were suffering from the lung disease mesothelioma, which is caused in many instances by exposure to asbestos fibers. One of the major producers of these asbestos products (from 1917 to 1987) is James Hardie Industries (JHX) which was faced with increasingly large compensation demands.

In a defensive move, the company shifted its ownership offshore in 2001 to Holland and at the same time created a body called the Medical Research and Compensation Foundation which took over the rump of its Australian interests and was to handle compensation claims. At the time of the corporate split, JHX issued a news release which stated that the $A293 million made available to the Foundation "was sufficient to meet all legitimate compensation claims anticipated from people injured by asbestos products manufactured in the past" (NSW Government 2004: 354–5). It also indicated that the move to Holland was to facilitate its international expansion.

Actuarial assessments, however, estimated the liability over the next 40 years at $A1.5 billion (*Sydney Morning Herald*, August 17, 2004: 10). In 2004, the state government in New South Wales convened a special committee of inquiry into the medical research and compensation foundation whose aim was to investigate the company's conduct. It found the foundation did not have sufficient funds to meet all anticipated legitimate compensation claims and was massively under-funded; and that JHX's statement that returns from the foundation's investments would cover future liabilities was "fanciful" (NSW Government 2004: 358).

Commissioner Jackson, who led the inquiry, found that senior management were deliberately dishonest and "prepared to be deceitful" about the extent of asbestos claims. He also found that two senior executives were not credible witnesses (*Sydney Morning Herald*, October 1, 2004: 16). One of his determinations was that the corporate communications activity in 2001 had been deliberately misleading (Howell et al. 2005: 5) and had been planned as such. These activities were undertaken to support JHX's reputation in the international building materials market and Jackson said that "public relations played a larger than healthy part in the activities of the James Hardie Group" (NSW Government 2004: 358–9).

The outcomes of this period of organizational behavior and its investigations were that a new chairperson was appointed and after a considerable delay the main executives criticized by Commissioner Jackson left the company. In the meantime, several other Australian states proposed legislation specifically targeted at JHX including its removal from all tender lists, while the national trade union movement ran an angry campaign against it. JHX has since agreed to extend its compensation package and to reduce legal restrictions applied to claimants.

JHX has not failed, nor has it lost its place in the worldwide market for building products but it has lost the trust of many as an ethical and responsible business. Although the union campaign has ended, many contractors are reluctant to order Hardie products, a doubt that will take many years to eradicate. The company's share price has remained solid, although it consistently trails below the benchmark ASX200. Its attempt to manage reputation in 2001 failed because of the behavior of senior executives and the inability of the organization to correct them quickly. Subsequently, JHX's ability to operate freely has been severely limited by vastly increased government oversight, union antipathy, and increased costs for compensation and legal services.

CONCLUSION

This chapter demonstrates that reputation is at the heart of all organizations, irrespective of stakeholders' perspectives as to whether these organizations are good or bad. Reputation is organic and ever changing which means that it must be monitored, understood, and nurtured. The companies with the strongest and most resilient reputations are those that have close, interactive relationships with their stakeholders. They also have policies and practices that offer continuing, ongoing, and mutual benefit to these stakeholders who include employees, customers, shareholders, regulators, and suppliers.

Companies with good reputations have strong communication cultures, both internally and externally. They are prepared to listen and be flexible in their operations. Their CEOs are the lead communicators and their communication staff are involved in high-level decision-making. These companies understand that their reputation has great value, not just in leveraging financial performance; and their executives take a "long view" in decision-making. Managing reputation is an integral part of the organization's operations and not confined to a special group.

Poor reputations are a necessary consequence to organizations which are poorly led with low levels of engagement with stakeholders and weak ethical performance. In the short term, many of these companies may still enjoy good financial performance, but the cost of their operations will become greater as they ignore reputational issues, or engage in reputation management initiatives which are at odds with actual marketplace behaviors. The loss of competitive advantage comes from increased regulation and litigation, the loss of belief in the company by its employees and suppliers and the wariness of customers. Moreover, continued poor communication may mask managerial inefficiency for a while, but market performance will undoubtedly unmask pretensions in this area.

ISSUES FOR FURTHER DISCUSSION

1. Track media coverage of a major organization in print, broadcast and World Wide Web for a month. Identify the reputational issues that impact upon it. Using the data from the tracking study, draft a short report offering corporate communications advice to the organization's CEO.
2. If you are working in a classroom or online situation, poll fellow students for their list of organizations with positive and negative reputation and prepare a report on the outcomes.
3. Discuss why some organizations—even with poor or negative reputation—may still have good sales and profit. Does that mean that reputation can be treated with disdain? (Justify your response with examples.)
4. Why do so many companies and/or executives seem to get away with unethical or unprofessional business behavior for so long? In what way(s) can linkages be made between unethical business behaviors and societies that permit these behaviors to continue?

REFERENCES

Argenti, P. A. and Druckenmiller, B. (2004) "Reputation and the corporate brand." *Corporate Reputation Review*, 6(4): 368–74.

Brown, J. J. and Reingen, P. H. (1987) "Social ties and word-of-mouth referral behaviour." *Journal of Consumer Research*, 14: 611–25.

Dowling, G. (1994) *Corporate Reputations*. Melbourne: Longman Professional.

Fombrun, C. J. (1995) *Reputation: Realising Value from Corporate Image*. Cambridge, MA: Harvard Business School Press.

Fombrun, C. J. and van Riel, C. B. M. (2004) *Fame and Fortune: How Successful Companies Build Winning Reputations*. New Jersey: Financial Times/Prentice Hall.

Gardberg, N. A. and Fombrun, C. J. (2002) "For better or worse: the most visible American corporate reputations." *Corporate Reputation Review*, 4(4): 385–91.

Gregory, A. and Edwards, L. (2004) *Patterns of PR in Britain's "Most Admired" Companies*. Leeds: Leeds Business School for Eloqui Public Relations.

Gregory, A., Morgan, L., and Kelly, D. (2005) *Patterns of PR in Britain's "Most Admired" Companies and Public Sector Organizations*. Leeds: Leeds Business School for Eloqui Public Relations.

Grunig, J. E. and Hunt, T. (1984) *Managing Public Relations*. New York: Holt, Rinehart & Winston.

Haywood, R. (2005) *Corporate Reputation, the Brand and the Bottom Line*. London: Kogan Page.

Howell, G., Miller, R., and Bridges, N. (2005) "Cardinal rule of the media release: get your facts right." Paper presented to the PRIA05 Academic Forum, Brisbane, October.

Hutton, J. G., Goodman, M. B., Alexander, J. B., and Genest, C. M. (2001) "Reputation management: the new face of corporate public relations." *Public Relations Review*, 27: 247–61.

Jolly, A. (2001) *Managing Corporate Reputations*. London: Kogan Page.

Kitchen, P. J. and Laurence, A. (2003) "Corporate reputation: an eight-country analysis." *Corporate Reputation Review*, 6(2): 103–17.

Knights, R. F. and Pretty, D. J. (1999) "Corporate catastrophes, stock returns, and trading volume." *Corporate Reputation Review*, 2(4): 363–81.

Ledingham, J. A. and Bruning, S. D. (2000) "Background and current trends in the study of relationship management," in: J. A. Ledingham and S. D. Bruning (eds), *Public Relations as Relationship Management: A Relational Approach to Public Relations*. Mahwah, NJ: Lawrence Erlbaum Associates.

McDonald, L. (2006) "Perceiving is believing: How consumers' attributions about the cause of Ansett Airlines' safety crisis impacted outcomes." *Asia Pacific Public Relations Journal*, 6(2), available at http://www.deakin.edu.au/arts/apprj/currenti.php#7

McQuire, J. B., Schneeweis, T., and Branch, B. (1990) "Perceptions of firm quality: a cause or result of firm performance." *Journal of Management*, 16(1): 167–81.

Murray, K. and White, J. (2004) *CEO Views on Reputation Management*. London: Chime Communications. Available at http://www.insightmkt.com/ceo_pr_briefing/

Regester, M. (2001) "Managing corporate reputation through crisis," in A. Jolly (ed.), *Managing Corporate Reputations*. London: Kogan Page.

ten Berge, D. (1988) *The First 24 Hours*. Oxford: Basil Blackwell.

Van Riel, C. B. M. (1999) *Corporate Communications*. New Jersey: Prentice Hall.

Van Riel, C. B. M and Berens, G. (2001) "Balancing corporate branding policies in multi-business companies," in P. J. Kitchen and D. E. Schultz (eds), *Raising the Corporate Umbrella: Corporate Communications in the 21st Century*. Basingstoke: Palgrave.

Watson, T., Osborne-Brown, S., and Longhurst, M. (2002) "Issues negotiation: creating competitive advantage through stakeholder investment." *Corporate Communications: An International Journal*, 7(1): 54–61.

Chapter 8

Employing effective leadership in a crisis

A case study of Malden Mills, corporate reputation, and the limits of socially responsible public relations

Richard Alan Nelson and Ali M. Kanso

AT THE END OF THIS CHAPTER READERS SHOULD BE ABLE TO:

1 Determine how corporate reputation is understood and evaluated
2 Recognize the importance (and limitations) of public relations in managing a business crisis
3 Apply the case study method to other corporate identity challenges

KEY POINTS

- Corporate reputation is based not just on what companies say, but also what they do
- Corporate reputation is a long-term viewpoint held by various publics about the perceived behavior of a firm
- A single individual can make a major difference in terms of personal and institutional reputation
- Reputation can be enhanced by effective public communication
- Positive employee, media, and government relations are dependent on fiscal realities

INTRODUCTION

Importance of corporate reputation

A business, whether it be local or global, has a personality or image that gels into its reputation. Many researchers have pointed out that reputation is a major factor in achieving organizational goals and competitively differentiating one corporation from another (see, for example, Stuart 1999; Melewar and Saunders 2000; Schultz and Kitchen 2004). There is general agreement that a "corporate brand" as well as specific product brand names have value ("brand equity"). But individual perceptions of an organization may differ depending on the conditions, and these many images can complicate our understanding of what a corporation's reputation is.

An emerging body of literature has introduced many different approaches to the study of corporate reputation as well as more precise definitions (among recent scholars, see Marwick and Fill 1997; van Riel and Balmer 1997; Greyser 1999; Christensen and Askegaard 2001; Cornelissen and Elving 2003; Gotsi and Wilson 2001; Siegbahn and Öman 2004; and Schwaiger 2004). Helm (2005: 95), for instance, points out that the concept of reputation "has attracted much attention among researchers and practitioners alike." But she also notes, "The growing body of literature in this area has led to a wide variety of measurement approaches. . . . It is not clear (1) if reputation is a formative or reflective construct and (2) how it should be conceptualized using a formative approach."

Westcott Allessandri (2001) suggests that image and reputation, while overlapping, are not the same. She says those elements over which the business has no direct control but which still influence public perception of the firm help create the establishment of *corporate image* through interaction or experience. On the other hand, *corporate reputation* emerges over time through repeated impressions of corporate image, whether they be positive or negative.

Reputation as defined by Fombrun (1996: 37), as "the overall estimation in which a company is held by its constituents . . . the net affective or emotional reaction . . . to the company's name" is widely cited in the literature. Podnar (2004) adds that to be a major factor, the overall "core" reputation of the firm must be consistent with how people interact with that business in a competitive environment (its "branch identity").

A recent definition suggests that while corporate branding involves how the business wants to be perceived, its actual business reputation is dependent on others. This means corporate reputation is "The collective representation of multiple constituencies' images of a company, built up over time and based on a company's identity programs, its performance and how constituencies have perceived its behavior" (Argenti and Druckenmiller 2004: 369). We believe this makes sense. After all, the factors that influence corporate reputation are based on multiple factors, mostly external. But internal actions taken by managers and employees based on the corporate mission moving outward through communication efforts are also important (see Figures 8.1 and 8.2).

Figure 8.1 demonstrates how a company's corporate reputation is influenced by external as well as internal factors. External forces include political, economic, social, technological, and competitive issues. Internal factors—all interrelated—involve the company's behaviour, communication, and symbolic efforts.

Figure 8.2 shows the development of a company's reputation. This is based on how the management sees the firm and how the company's actions are perceived. A corporate mission is established not just as a written statement but through the company's visuals and behaviour which help form its "corporate identity." While "corporate image" refers to how various publics perceive the company, corporate identity exemplifies how the firm presents itself. From the integration of image and identity over time, corporate reputation is established.

Gray and Balmer's (1998) research has demonstrated that effectively managing corporate identity (including all its component elements) is critical in the process of differentiating the corporation from competitors and insuring a distinctly branded corporate reputation. According to Siegbahn and Öman (2004: 8),

The corporate identity and communication are managed with two primary objectives in mind; to create the intended image in the minds of the

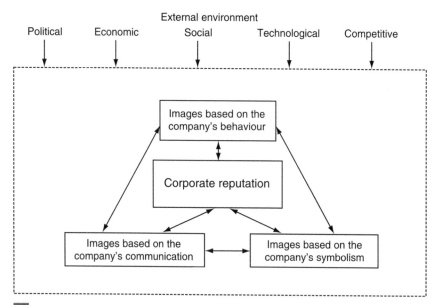

Figure 8.1 *Factors influencing corporate reputation*

Source: Adapted from Gotsi and Wilson (2001).

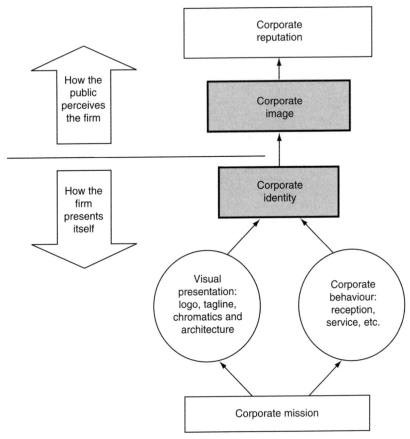

Figure 8.2 *A model of how corporate reputation develops*

Source: Adapted from Alessandri (2001: 178) and Siegbahn and Öman (2004: 2).

company's main constituents, and to create a favorable reputation in the minds of important stakeholders. The former means to create a widespread name recognition among the company's target stakeholder[s] as well as among the company's business field and principal products. Since the second objective, to create a favorable reputation, often takes years to accomplish, it requires more than just effective communication efforts. It is achieved via consistent performance and also sometimes via a well-coordinated communication program which in the end might reinforce and promote a positive reputation [see Figure 8.3].

A company's organizational culture is a key component to the company's reputation. Figure 8.3 presents a way of looking at the internal structure of a firm's organizational culture. Aspects such as personality, strategy, and identity

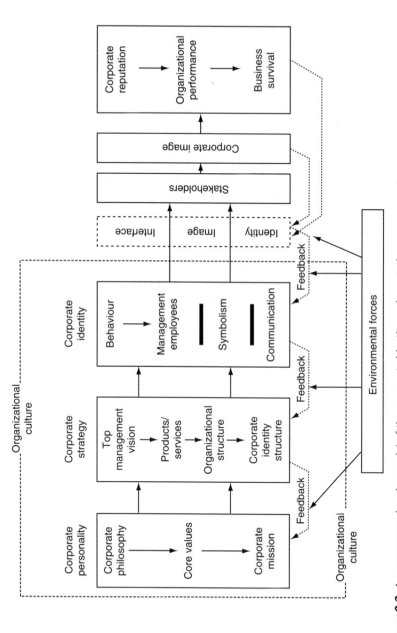

Figure 8.3 *A more comprehensive model of the corporate identity and reputation management process*

Source: Adapted from Stuart (1999: 206); and Siegbahn and Öman (2004: 9).

play an important role in the company's reputation. The organizational culture as a whole impacts the company's identity, image, and interface. Stakeholders (those with an interest in the business) consider these three elements. From such adaptation a corporate reputation is established, keeping the company's performance and survival in mind.

With this general overview of some major trends in corporate reputation research, let us turn to an example where a firm's reputation, combined with expert public relations work, made a difference.

 CASE VIGNETTE: About Malden Mills

On December 11, 1995, a fire struck Malden Mills' main textile plant, a sprawling complex that straddles the borders of Lawrence and Methuen, Massachusetts, in the northeastern United States. Known as the Immigrant City, Lawrence has long been a multi-ethnic and multi-cultural location with its current population of 70,000, largely Hispanic. The city still maintains a 35 percent manufacturing-based economy, of which Malden Mills is a key factor.

In a stretch of a few hours, the inferno overturned lives, created controversy, and changed a business tragedy into a public communication triumph. This triumph occurred with little appearance of "spin doctors" on the job. Malden Mills public relations strategists used all the tools necessary for ethical two-way communication success: immediate response, honesty, integrity, and concern for human relations.

The blaze began on a cold New England winter night. Aaron Feuerstein, the owner of Malden Mills and grandson of its founder, was celebrating his 70th birthday when the news reached him. He immediately went to the scene and was appalled at the devastation. The fire was consuming three of the mill's buildings. Officially ruled an "industrial accident," the fire injured 36 employees, 8 seriously. Feuerstein's initial reaction was, "We're going to continue to operate in Lawrence. . . . We had the opportunity to run to the south many years ago [by outsourcing in cheaper overseas factories]. We didn't do it then and we're not going to do it now" (*Boston Globe*, December 15, 1995, p. B1). Two days later, he announced plans to pay worker salaries and extend health benefits for 30 days. "We have to think creatively," Feuerstein announced. "There will be a Malden Mills tomorrow" (quote from subsequent article in *Boston Globe*, September 8, 1996).

Initially, the firestorm looked to be the end of an era for Feuerstein, his workers, and textile-making in New England. Besides the injured workers, about 1,400 others were left without jobs. However, once Feuerstein realized that some buildings were spared, he started a rebuilding campaign. This effort became a public relations case study of astounding measures.

The most inspiring part of the study was the intent of the leader. Nine months after the incident, the *Boston Globe* commented, "In the days and months ahead, a third-generation mill owner driven by pride, [his orthodox Jewish] religion, and a sense of family would battle insurance companies, government officials, and competitors ... to do something nobody in modern times had attempted: rebuild a giant textile plant in an old New England mill city" (*Boston Globe*, September 8, 1996).

Background

Malden Mills Industries, Inc., founded in 1906 by Henry Feuerstein, is a leader in the international textile industry. It produces fabrics for apparel, upholstery, home furniture, and military markets. In the early 1980s the company revolutionized the way the world dresses for cold weather with the invention of performance fabrics sold under the Polartec® brand. The company is widely known for employing some of the highest-paid textile workers in the world (Brokaw 1996). Malden Mills has not only shown a strong commitment to its employees but has also spread this commitment throughout New England with its support of local charities, including homeless shelters, sports clubs, and police and fire departments (Slaboda 1998).

One of Malden Mills' mission statements from that period reads as follows: "Devoted to creating high-quality fabrics with unique capabilities, and committed to its work force, environmental responsibility, and customer satisfaction, this is the Malden Mills. . . . A family tradition—a leader in American industry" (Fact Sheet 1998).

Research method

A case study is one major research method used to answer questions which require an explanatory approach. The case study technique has a distinct advantage over other methods when asking "how" or "why" questions about contemporary events and related organizational decision-making. For example, what happened?, why were certain decisions taken?, how were they implemented?, and what was the result? (Yin 2003).

Our analysis is based on data collected through in-depth interviews with two public relations strategists at Malden Mills, James Gillett and Jen Slaboda, and a thorough review of subsequent media coverage of the fire and the company's ownership struggles.

Discussion

Public communication efforts

The role of public relations at Malden Mills was narrowly defined prior to the fire. Although there were individuals responsible for the image of the organization and its products, the focus was mostly on the marketing aspect of the company. Malden Mills was more than prepared to deal with the promotion of its high-tech fabrics (Martins 1997). To handle the situation, the company established a crisis team. The team consisted of 1 spokesperson (Brand Manager Jeffery Bowman), 5 company employees, and 20 volunteers.

The campaign was crucial for three main reasons. First, Malden Mills sought to assure its commitment to all employees. From the very morning after the fire, Feuerstein stated that he would rebuild and showed his support for employees by paying their wages for the next 90 days. He also reassured his employees that their safety was of prime importance. Second, the company wanted to affirm its social responsibility toward the community and the region. If a firm like Malden Mills laid off several hundred employees in a depressed city like Lawrence, myriad problems would have occurred (Ryan 1996). Third, Malden Mills desperately needed to get the message across that it was dedicated to serving its customers. The company used the media to assure its buying public that: (1) production would be running soon, (2) several machines escaped damage, and (3) factories were being commissioned to dye fabric in order to meet its production orders.

Target publics

There was an eclectic mix of target publics for the campaign. Although every public was important, three key publics were considered the integral part of the campaign. These publics included: the employees, the Malden Mills customers (e.g., Victoria's Secret, Eddie Bauer, Lands' End, etc.), and the media (e.g., *Boston Globe, Boston Herald, Lawrence Eagle-Tribune*, National Public Radio, CBS News, ABC News, NBC News, etc.). Various local, state, and federal government agencies were also contacted for funds, tax assistance, and retraining. Many other publics were important to the campaign. Such publics involved: the employees' family members, especially the families of the burn victims; local hospitals that remained on code red awaiting emergency patients for hours after the blaze; local and regional fire departments that assisted in battling the blaze; local and state police departments that helped evacuate residential areas close to the fire; local businesses that provided food and monetary donations; banks that lent millions of dollars to expedite the rebuilding effort; area residents; politicians such as President Bill Clinton, former Secretary of Labor Robert Reich, Senator John Kerry, and Senator Ted Kennedy; religious organizations; and cultural and neighborhood leaders and groups (Gillett 1998).

Research

Malden Mills public relations strategists did not have much of a proactive approach. Their campaign to rebuild and rehire was a situational incident that could not be controlled or predicted. Therefore, the need for proactive research was quite unforeseeable. The reactive research was costly. A missed step in the campaign could have crumbled the fragile plans for reconstruction. Malden Mills hired LUCE, a news clipping service, to gather all fire related stories. These stories were circulated to the management and staff, then bound and filed.

Strengths

The Malden Mills campaign had a number of strengths. Several factors contributed to the campaign's success. First, Malden Mills products were popular. Second, employee morale remained high. The company made the employees the number one priority. This position was monumental in securing the relationship between the employees, the company, and the community. Third, the company encouraged a family atmosphere. Fourth, Feuerstein was perceived as an important community leader. Fifth, Malden Mills had a proven record of solid community relations. Sixth, the company received immediate public support for responding to the people's concerns. Seventh, the owner met with the employees to reinforce his commitment through continuation of compensation and benefits and assured his promise to rebuild. Feuerstein's socially responsible actions as a corporate citizen were evidenced through the continuing assistance he provided his employees. Furthermore, by rebuilding the mill with high-tech machinery, he was able to train and prepare his workers for the more sophisticated workplace of the future. Eighth, the media positioned Feuerstein as a person who genuinely cared about his employees, community, and customers.

In addition, there were the tangibles that backed the media coverage such as the 800 number for providing aid, the Malden Mills training center for unemployed mill workers, 90-day benefit extension for mill workers, grants, and funding for training and retraining initiated by state and federal lawmakers. These tangibles gave witness to the words people were reading on a daily basis (Martins 1997).

Weaknesses

Several weaknesses could have severely hurt the organization. First, there was a lack of a concrete crisis communications plan at the time of the disaster (Slaboda 1998). Second, a spokesperson was not readily available at the fire. Third, there were suspicions about the fire origins and the pending investigations. Fourth, employee job security was at risk, and the holiday season was approaching. Fifth, financial support for rebuilding was slow and costly, and the fear of moving the mill to another location where overhead costs were cheaper always existed. Sixth, most of the objectives were not specified in measurable terms.

Objectives

Malden Mills public relations activities aimed at achieving impact and output objectives. There were three levels of impact objectives: informational, additudinal, and behavioural. One informational objective was to announce a plan to rebuild and maintain everyone's pay and medical benefits for up to 90 days.

Another informational objective was to reassure the general public and the customers that Malden Mills was not going to fold. Still another informational objective was to provide the media with details of each effort made to rebuild the mill, pay the workers, and obtain grant and assistance dollars from the government.

One attitudinal objective was to reinforce the employees' spirit toward Malden Mills. Another attitudinal objective was to ensure that the employees would support the plan to rebuild. The most noticeable attitudinal objective was to turn a negative situation into a positive one. Once Feuerstein made his announcement to keep the workers on the payroll, the positive spin on the situation took on a life of its own. Favourable news accounts began appearing at the national, not just local, level. Not only did Feuerstein immediately begin rebuilding, he gave each employee a $275 Christmas bonus and then paid the idle workers their full salary for December, February, and March. Many would have labeled that good public relations but poor business. Not so, Feuerstein told Paul Solman on the Public Broadcasting Service's *NewsHour*: "I consider our workers an asset, not an expense. . . . It would have been unconscionable to put 3,000 people on the streets. . . . You have a responsibility to the community" (Shields 2001; see also Ryan 1996: 4–5).

The media and local officials repeatedly praised the CEO for his handling of the Malden Mills incident (Coolidge 1996). Still another attitudinal objective was to improve the corporate image. Before the fire, the company was customer driven in promoting its products and developing its brands. Public relations strategists had always recognized that they had strong community ties, but only after the fire did they try to leverage those ties (Slaboda 1998).

The behavioural objective was to set an example for others. Feuerstein found himself learning that corporate America had become shortsighted and anti-worker. At a time when he could just sit back and enjoy the good media coverage about his company, he strove to change that shortsighted, anti-worker attitude in other companies by bluntly questioning those executives who were rumored to treat their employees unfairly.

The output objectives were to: respond immediately to the employees' concerns, make news releases available to local, regional, and national media, appoint people to respond to inquiries, and let the CEO be visible at events.

Programming

The main message of Malden Mills was in essence "We care about our employees, we will rebuild, and we will survive." The public relations strategists used the public information model. They disseminated information in a clear and concise manner without trying to twist the truth. The information went through various channels. The most common channel was the press, but word of mouth was also effective. Other times, the information traveled directly from the source to the intended receiver, such as the time Feuerstein announced his objectives to the employees.

Whether responding to the media, visiting burn victims, meeting with employees, recognizing the bravery of firefighters, appealing to legislators, or marking a milestone in the company's efforts to rebuild its facilities, Malden Mills successfully tied all of its special events by a single theme: corporate responsibility (Martins 1997).

Special events
Malden Mills undertook several activities to support its message. The following are some major events that took place after the fire.

- At a press conference held at Honeywell-Bull plant on January 11, 1996, Feuerstein announced a 30-day extension for compensation and benefits to his employees, and featured newly installed machinery at the mill (*Boston Globe*, January 12, 1996).
- At an honors breakfast on February 1, 1996, 8 firefighters were honored for putting out the Malden Mills fire. Also, the bravery of the 250 firefighters was recognized (*Boston Globe*, February 2, 1996).
- At another press conference held at Ann and Hope on February 9, 1996, Feuerstein announced again extended compensation and benefits (*Boston Globe*, February 10, 1996).
- Former Secretary of Labor Reich toured the mill on January 12, 1996, and presented the Corporate Citizen Award to Feuerstein. He praised the owner for paying workers and keeping his promise to rebuild. Reich also acknowledged Feuerstein as a rare example of corporate responsibility and promised to find funds for worker retraining (February 13, 1996).
- Feuerstein handed out certificates of training completion to his employees and, in return, was given an emotional standing ovation. He spoke of bringing back 100 percent of his employees and succeeding with the rebuilding efforts. Subsequently, the Malden Mills Communications Center, which was established to train workers idled by the fire, was shut down on April 8, 1997 (*Boston Globe*, April 9, 1997).
- A one-day ceremony was held on September 1, 1997 to dedicate the new mill complex. The American flag saved from the fire was raised at the end of the ceremony. The employees interviewed by the media again praised the owner for not moving the mill elsewhere and rebuilding (*Boston Globe*, September 2, 1997).

Media
Malden Mills used a wide variety of media but relied heavily on three local papers: the *Lawrence Eagle-Tribune*, *Boston Globe*, and *Boston Herald*. Also, the company's displays at the garment industry trade shows served as a vehicle for getting the word out that Malden Mills was rebuilding and providing support for its customers' needs. Lastly, Malden Mills created its own website to promote the diversity and strengths of the organization and its fabrics.

Short-term outcomes

Malden Mills' public relations efforts produced amazing results in a short period of time. The following is a summary of major results through late 1997.

- On January 3, 1996 at a White House briefing regarding a 19-day government shutdown, President Bill Clinton discussed the Labor Department's immediate assistance provided to Malden Mills workers (*Boston Globe*, January 4, 1996).
- On January 23, 1996, Feuerstein attended the State of the Union Address before Congress as a guest of President Clinton (*Boston Globe*, January 24, 1996).
- On March 7, 1996, Massachusetts lawmakers passed a Benefits Bill granting one-time financial support to mill employees (*Boston Globe*, March 8, 1996).
- On March 11, 1996, the American Jewish Historical Society presented Feuerstein with the Emma Lazarus Award for his dedication to his workers and his actions that "speak to the very best Jewish traditions" (*Boston Globe*, March 12, 1996).
- On June 5, 1996, the Department of Labor approved one million dollars for training in support of the advanced technology being brought into the rebuilt mill (*Boston Globe,* June 6, 1996).
- In December 1996, Aaron Feuerstein's new mill was praised as the center of the greatest textile revival in New England history (*Boston Globe*, December 8, 1996).
- In April 1997, Malden Mills closed its training center as most employees were able to return to work (*Boston Globe*, April 9, 1997).
- By Fall 1997, the rebirth of Malden Mills was widely celebrated (*Boston Globe*, September 2, 1997).
- Numerous letters to the editors, business feature articles, magazine stories, and radio and television programs focused on the heroic efforts of Feuerstein and his commitment to his employees. It was estimated that Malden Mills received over $55 million in free publicity (Gillett 1998).

The result: plant production pre-fire was 130,000 yards per week while post-fire it increased to 230,000 yards; overall productivity in the new facility rose by 25 percent and quality defects dropped by two-thirds (Daviss 2001: 209). In little over 12 months subsequent to the conflagration, "the insurance companies had paid about $180 million of the expected $302 million. In the months following, the fire investigation exonerated Malden Mills of any negligence [after a class action lawsuit was filed in December 1999 by 13 injured workers], and slowly the insurance companies began to pay the remaining millions due the company. His company was beginning to reach pre-fire revenues, and when asked about the experience, Feuerstein beamed with deep pride as he recalled what had become known as the 'Malden Miracle'" (Jha et al., nd, p. 2; see also *Boston Globe,* December 17, 1999; Klineman 2000).

In receiving this national attention, Feuerstein modestly admitted he was surprised at the kudos: "In my eyes, I did no more than just the simple right thing to do. . . . If we really believe man is created in the image of God, we've got to be sensitive to those creations who are made in that image. . . . You must recognize that labor is not merely an expense but also an asset" (The risks of keeping a promise 1996; Cavanagh and Bandsuch 2002: 113).

Subsequent developments
Feuerstein's heroic efforts also garnered praise from practitioners and scholars (see, for example, Boulay 1996; Borowski 1998; Kanso 2000; Seeger and Ulmer 2001; Ulmer 2001; Altman and DePalma 2003; Werhane and Watson 2003; Seeger et al. 2005). But Feuerstein faced a second leadership challenge when the final insurance installments failed to cover all his costs and he was forced to mortgage the company to creditors while also seeking contract negotiations with workers (*Boston Globe,* September 16, 2001, and November 17, 2001). To allow him time to maneuver, he took the firm into Chapter 11 bankruptcy in November 2001, a legal process that gave him continued control while he struggled to raise enough financing to pay creditors and lead the company out of bankruptcy (*Boston Globe,* November 30, 2001; 'The right thing' 2002).

In January 2003, the company reached an agreement with creditors, particularly a banking syndicate led by GE Capital, but Feuerstein was forced to step down as CEO until remaining debt could be eliminated (*Boston Globe,* January 29, 2003). By June, the streamlined 1,200-employee company had reduced its debt load from more than $170 million prior to the filing to less than $80 million. "This puts Malden Mills in a much more financially secure position and will support the continued growth of the company," said acting chief operating officer and chief financial officer David Orlofsky (*Boston Globe,* October 18, 2003).

Despite a heart operation and other setbacks, Feuerstein continued his hopes of buying the company back from the creditors. Those were dashed, however, when Michael Spillane, a former executive for Tommy Hilfiger U.S.A., was named the CEO in August 2004 by the new owners (Jewell 2004). The reinvigorated management team successfully avoided a threatened employee strike (*Boston Globe,* December 10, 2004), and restructured the firm to new profits in early 2005 (*Boston Globe,* February 17, 2005) to formally mark the end of nearly one hundred years of Malden Mills family ownership.

CASE VIGNETTE: Malden Mills

Based on your outstanding work at another business, you are the newly appointed director of public relations for an international consumer product firm based in your home city. The company has a generally good public image and you are happy about your appointment. However, you realize that the world is a more volatile place and the future is anything but certain. This corporate reputation case pointed to some plans and actions carried out correctly by the management. But in other actions the leaders were either ill prepared or made questionable decisions. After reading about the experiences at Malden Mills, what recommendations would you make to your management to better prepare your firm for future crises? How would you implement your recommendations, especially in terms of communications?

CONCLUSION

The Malden Mills public relations campaign was a test of survival, loyalty, faith, friendship, business relationships, commitment, and trust. Since it was more of a "trial by fire," Feuerstein should be commended for taking the appropriate steps. The company achieved its objectives of getting the message out. Malden Mills received a tremendous amount of free publicity simply by telling its story, making itself accessible to the media, and keeping everyone informed about its rebuilding and retraining efforts.

Looking back at the campaign now, company representatives recognize the importance of having a crisis communication system in place and maintaining solid employee and community relations. The campaign was an amazing testament to the will of the owner, the loyalty of his employees, and the support of the general public. The fire provided the mill with all the drama, emotion, and personal tragedy necessary for getting the public's attention. Yet, because the reaction to this crisis was so genuine, the response from around the nation was overwhelming.

Although the campaign was successful, the situation could have been less chaotic had the company had a contingent crisis communication plan. Such a plan would have allowed Malden Mills to resume production activities sooner. Also, it could have been more advantageous for Malden Mills had the company had a spokesperson on the scene to answer the flurry of questions the night of the fire. This could have quelled rumors that several employees died and reduced the panic of family members.

Three major lessons can be learned from the tragedy. A public relations campaign is bound to succeed if: (1) the boss is adamant about protecting his own people—the added value of genuine compassion speaks volumes for Malden Mills, (2) the company provides an immediate response to the situation and demonstrates honesty to all concerned publics, and (3) the relationship between the community and the organization is strongly based on mutual interdependence.

Corporate reputation stems from actions over time. It can be said that Feuerstein put responsibility to others ahead of his own interests, and in the end the cost was control of his family business. Excellent public relations and personal integrity were trumped by cold hard financial considerations. Yet from a corporate reputation perspective, his sacrifice ultimately ensured continued loyalty and respect to Malden Mills as a living entity—not just the expression of one individual.

ISSUES FOR FURTHER DISCUSSION

1   What does your company or institution say about its commitment to high values and reputation? How does it demonstrate this commitment?

2   Here is what Enron, the large energy reseller based in the US (later caught up in scandal), declared as its values in 1991:

- ■   *Communication:* We have an obligation to communicate. Here, we take the time to talk with one another . . . and to listen. We believe that information is meant to move and that information moves people.

- ■   *Respect:* We treat others as we would like to be treated ourselves. We do not tolerate abusive or disrespectful treatment.

- ■   *Integrity:* We work with customers and prospects openly, honestly and sincerely. When we say we will do something, we will do it; when we say we cannot or will not do something, then we won't do it.

- ■   *Excellence:* We are satisfied with nothing less than the very best in everything we do. We will continue to raise the bar for everyone. The great fun here will be for all of us to discover just how good we can really be.

Why do you think the company didn't keep its word? If you had worked at Enron during that time, do you think you would have been able to predict future developments?

APPENDIX 8.1

Selected Boston newspaper articles (listed chronologically):

Boston Globe:
Beyond Polartec: Malden Mills refashions its identity, February 17, 2005.

Malden Mills workers accept contract, December 10, 2004

New CEO named at Malden Mills, July 27, 2004.

Military spending shores up company, July 25, 2004.

Feuerstein undergoes heart operation, July 15, 2004.

Maneuvering for control of stronger Malden Mills, February 5, 2004.

Feuerstein gets loan package, January 9, 2004.

Lawmakers lobbying for Malden Mills, January 8, 2004.

Time for a miracle, December 3, 2003.

Another union OK'd in Malden Mills vote, October 25, 2003.

Malden Mills out of Chap. 11, October 18, 2003.

Feuerstein says buyback near, October 1, 2003.

Aaron Feuerstein's labor of love, September 14, 2003.

Creditors rap Feuerstein's bid to delay deal deadline, August 27, 2003.

Malden Mills gets March 7 deadline, February 19, 2003.

Malden Mills cuts deal with creditors: firm hopes to emerge from bankruptcy by June, January 29, 2003.

Bankrupt Lawrence, Mass.-based textile company nears agreement with creditors, January 28, 2003.

Malden Mills seen near accord in reorganization, Feuerstein may be left with less of firm, December 20, 2002.

Work for Pentagon boosts Lawrence, Mass., fleecemaker Malden Mills, November 21, 2002.

Malden Mills wins extension of key reorganization deadline, October 10, 2002.

Creditors hit Malden Mills recovery plan, October 3, 2002.

Malden Mills heroics overstated, September 29, 2002.

Worries at Malden Mills union voices fears on plan to move some work to China, August 30, 2002.

Malden Mills asks creditor to give it time, August 21, 2002.

Creditors question Lawrence, Mass., textile company's bankruptcy emergence, August 20, 2002.

Lawrence, Mass.-based textile maker plans to emerge from bankruptcy protection, August 6, 2002.

Textile firm Malden Mills to cut roughly 50 jobs in Lawrence, Mass., June 30, 2002.

Feuerstein may agree to give up stake in Malden Mills; proposal an option in reorganization, June 27, 2002.

Lawrence, Mass.-based textile company addresses role of owner, April 4, 2002.

Might Malden Mills Inc. lose it patriarch of fleece?, April 4, 2002.

Malden Mills will recall blankets; wiring flaws blamed; battered firm says it's hitting key sales goals, January 11, 2002.

Malden Mills's Feuerstein sees future beyond Chapter 11, December 2, 2001.

Malden Mills seeks Chapter 11 protection; textile maker to get $20M; Feuerstein to remain in control; Malden Mills files for Chapter 11, November 30, 2001.

Malden Mills "Optimistic" about funds but bankruptcy filing possible as Lawrence firm seeks $25M loan, November 27, 2001.

Malden Mills and the price of altruism, November 21, 2001.

State might help Malden Mills with insurance, November 20, 2001.

Malden Mills says Chapter 11 odds 50–50, November 19, 2001.

Malden Mills wrestles with debt woes, November 17, 2001.

Massachusetts' Malden Mills focuses on next hot product: fabrics that heat up, October 22, 2001.

Massachusetts defense contractors await military orders, October 4, 2001.

Malden Mills waits for contract talks, no date set yet for negotiations, September 16, 2001.

Fresh wound \ Malden Mills owner stung by negligence claims, December 17, 1999.

Cities turn to the future - Lawrence, Methuen celebrate Malden Mills rebirth, September 2, 1997, Metro Region Section, B1.

Malden Mills closes its training center - no longer needed as most return to work, April 9, 1997, Business Section, E2.

More than a factory Aaron Feuerstein's new mill is the center of the greatest textile revival in N.E. history, December 8, 1996.

What flames could not destroy, faith, loyalty inspire mill owner to rebuild from ashes and rubble, September 8, 1996, Metro Section, A1.

Feuerstein to receive Emma Lazarus Award, March 12, 1996, Business Section, 39.

$1M in retraining funds OK'd for Malden Mills, March 12, 1996, Business Section, 67.

Bill grants $300 to mill workers, March 8, 1996, Metro Section, 27.

Reich hails mill owner Feuerstein—hits other CEOs for abandoning workers, February 13, 1996, Business Section, 38.

Mill owner Feuerstein vows to pay idled workers for another 30 days, February 10, 1996, Business Section, 58.

Fire crews honored for bravery in Methuen, February 2, 1996, Metro Section, 62.

Malden Mills owner gets seat of honor, January 24, 1996, National/Foreign Section, 6.

Feuerstein extends pay offer to his workers, January 12, 1996, Business Section, 74.

Clinton talks of two local hardships, January 4, 1996, National foreign Section, 15.

Mill owner says he'll pay workers for month, December 15, 1995, B1, 50.

Explosion, fire destroy Methuen textile complex more than 30 injured, six critically; nearby residents evacuated, December 12, 1995.

Boston Herald:

Malden Mills want loan—fast; speedy lender charges higher interest rate, February 12, 2003.

Malden Mills deal: buy out or back away, January 29, 2003.

Malden Mills plan may be aired today, January 28, 2003.

Creditors: Malden Mills owner uses media for cover, December 21, 2002.

Malden Mills can't pay bills, November 30, 2001

REFERENCES

The authors acknowledge research assistance by Ariadne Magallanes in conducting this study.

Altman, J. W. and DePalma, M. C. (2003) *Polartec®* (B): Case Study. Boston Park, MA: Babson College, Arthur M. Blank Center for Entrepreneurship.

Argenti, P. A. and Druckenmiller, B. (2004) "Reputation and the corporate brand." *Corporate Reputation Review,* 6(4): 368–74.

Borowski, P. J. (1998) "Manager–employee relationships: guided by Kant's categorical imperative or by Dilbert's business principle." *Journal of Business Ethics,* 17(15): 1623–32.

Boulay, A. (1996) "Malden Mills: a study in leadership." *Quality Monitor Newsletter,* http://www.opi-inc.com/malden.htm, accessed October 16 2006.

Brokaw, T. (1996) *Dateline NBC.* Transcript, August 24. New York: NBC Television.

Cavanagh, G. F. and Bandsuch, M. R. (2002) "Virtue as a benchmark for spirituality in business." *Journal of Business Ethics,* 38(1/2): 109–17.

Christensen, L. T. and Askegaard, S. (2001) "Corporate identity and corporate image revisited: a semiotic perspective." *European Journal of Marketing,* 35(3/4): 292–315.

Coolidge, S. D. (1996) "Corporate decency prevails at Malden Mills." *Christian Science Monitor,* Business and money, March 28, 1, 30.

Cornelissen, J. P. and Elving, W. J. L. (2003) "Managing corporate identity: an integrative framework of dimensions and determinants." *Corporate Communications: an International Journal,* 8(2): 114–20.

Daviss, B. (2001) "Profits from principle," in J. E. Richardson (ed.), *Business Ethics 01/ 02.* Guilford, CT: Dushkin/McGraw-Hill, 207–12.

Fact Sheet (1998) Lawrence, MA: Malden Mills.

Fombrun, C. J. (1996) *Reputation: Realizing Value from Corporate Image.* Boston, MA: HBS Press.

Gillett, James (1998) Personal communication by an assistant to the authors, April 13.

Gotsi, M. and Wilson, A. M. (2001) "Corporate reputation: seeking a definition." *Corporate Communications: An International Journal,* 6(1): 24–30.

Gray, E. R. and Balmer, J. M. T. (1998) "Managing corporate image and corporate reputation." *Long Range Planning,* 31(5): 695–702.

Greyser, S. A. (1999) "Advancing and enhancing corporate reputation." *Corporate Communications: An International Journal,* 4(4): 177–81.

Helm, S. (2005) "Designing a formative measure for corporate reputation." *Corporate Reputation Review,* 8(2): 95–109.

Jewell, M. (2004) "Malden Mills CEO has tough act to follow." Wire story. New York: Associated Press, August 8.

Jha, L., Barrett, L., Parsons, J., and Hall, A. (n.d.) *Servant Leadership.* Participant manual, HEF 504. Lincoln, NE: University of Nebraska Cooperative Extension, 3 pp.

Kanso, A. (2000) "Malden Mills: how socially responsible public relations turned a tragedy into a triumph." *Business Research Yearbook: Global Business Perspectives,* 7: 857–61.

Klineman, J. (2000) "Malden Mills settles last victims' lawsuit." *Eagle-Tribune.* Lawrence, MA, December 7.

"Lawrence co-signs $3 million loan to help Feuerstein." (2003) Wire story. New York: Associated Press, February 26.

"Malden Mills workers OK strike." (2004) Wire story. New York: Associated Press, December 6.

Martins, Kathleen (1997) "Rising from the ashes: the Malden Mills fire. A case study presented to the Public Relations Theory and Practice class." Emerson College, Boston, December 7.

Marwick, N. and Fill, C. (1997) "Towards a framework for managing corporate identity." *European Journal of Marketing,* 31(5/6): 396–409.

Melewar, T. C. and Saunders, J. (2000) "Global visual corporate identity systems: using an extended marketing mix." *European Journal of Marketing,* 34(5/6): 538–50.

Podnar, K. (2004) "Is it all a question of reputation? The role of branch identity (the case of an oil company)." *Corporate Reputation Review,* 6(4): 376–87.

"The risks of keeping a promise." (1996) *New York Times,* C1, C3, July 4.

"The right thing; a boss saved them. Should they save him?" (2002) *New York Times,* Your business section, January 20.

Ryan, M. (1996) "They call their boss a hero." *Parade Magazine,* 4–5, 62, September 8.

Schultz, D. E. and Kitchen, P. J. (2004) "Managing the changes in corporate branding and communication: closing and re-opening the corporate umbrella." *Corporate Reputation Review,* 6(4): 347–66.

Schwaiger, M. (2004) "Components and parameters of corporate reputation—an empirical study." *Schmalenbach Business Review,* 56: 46–71.

Seeger, M. W. and Ulmer, R. R. (2001) "Virtuous responses to organizational crisis: Aaron Feuerstein and Milt Cole." *Journal of Business Ethics,* 31(4): 369–76.

Seeger, M. W., Ulmer, R. R., Novak, J. M., and Sellnow, T. (2005) "Post-crisis discourse and organizational change, failure and renewal." *Journal of Organizational Change Management,* 18(1): 78–95.

Siegbahn, C. and Öman, J. (2004) "Identity and image of a university." Master's thesis, #2004: 071SHU, ISSN: 1404–5508, Luleå, Sweden: Luleå University of Technology, Department of Business Administration and Social Sciences; http://epubl.luth.se/1404-5508/2004/071/LTU-SHU-EX-04071-SE.pdf, accessed March 18, 2007.

Shields, M. (2001) "Two extremes of corporate leadership." *Seattle Post-Intelligencer,* December 3.

Slaboda, Jen (1998) Personal communication by an assistant to the authors. April 13.

Stuart, H. (1999) "Towards a definitive model of the corporate identity management process." *Corporate Communications: An International Journal,* 4(4): 200–7.

Ulmer, R. R. (2001) "Effective crisis management through established stakeholder relationships: Malden Mills as a case study." *Management Communication Quarterly,* 14(4): 590–615.

Van Riel, C. B. M. and Balmer, J. M. T. (1997) "Corporate identity: the concept, its measurement and management." *European Journal of Marketing,* 31(5–6): 340–55.

Werhane, P. H. and Watson, O. W. (2003) Against the current: Malden Mills Inc. (B). Darden Case No.: UVA-E-0126-SSRN. Charlottesville, VA: University of

Virginia, Darden Graduate School of Business Administration, http: //ssrn.com/abstract=395483.

Westcott Alessandri, S. (2001) "Modeling corporate identity: a concept explication and theoretical explanation." *Corporate Communications: An International Journal,* 6(4): 173–82.

Yin, R. K. (2003) *Case Study Research: Design and Methods,* 3rd edn. Thousand Oaks, CA: Sage Publications.

Part III

Corporate reputation

Chapter 9

Projecting corporate character in the branding of business schools

Gary Davies and Rosa Chun

AT THE END OF THIS CHAPTER READERS SHOULD BE ABLE TO:

1   Understand how corporate reputation can be measured using a projective technique (brand as person) and using measures such as the Corporate Character Scale

2   Understand how to apply such thinking to develop a visual identity strategy and specifically a new corporate visual identity

KEY POINTS

- Managing an academic institution has its own unique challenges. On the one hand academic freedom is seen as central to an academic life; on the other, competing with other providers implies a need for a coherent and distinctive image

- A starting point for promoting a sound external image is having a clear view of what the organization stands for, in other words its mission, vision, and values. Here we discuss the visioning process at a leading business school and its relationship to reputation management

- Reputation should be measured for both employees and customers; to ensure what is promised through external communication is deliverable by the organization. By correlating reputation measures with stakeholder satisfaction it is possible to identify what is really valued about the organization

- Here the theme of innovation was identified as important and used to help define a brief for a new visual identity for competing design agencies. Agencies can differ markedly in their creative response to such a brief.

Qualitative market research can be used to select the most appropriate solution

■ A new corporate identity can form an important part of managing and changing the reputation of an organization

INTRODUCTION

Our chapter is concerned with the practicalities of implementing a new direction for the corporate reputation of an organization. It is an extended case study documenting a project we were both involved with for three years, the repositioning of Manchester Business School (MBS). Our intention is to illustrate the methodology that we and others have developed in Manchester over the past few years, specifically the use of the Corporate Character Scale to measure reputation, but in addition to that we intend to show how any organization can use visual identity as part of its reputation management. The reader will also be given insights into how a visioning process can work in tandem with the market research conducted on the reputation perceptions of internal and external stakeholders of MBS. First some general comments about the marketplace.

THE REPUTATION OF A BUSINESS SCHOOL

The business school industry is a large and still growing market. Revenues for the sector as a whole are close to US $6bn with a growth rate of close to 10 percent per annum (Argenti 2000). The amount of competition has increased and the boundaries of competition have been expanding. The technology of distance learning, centers being established overseas, and international partnerships with other business schools in other countries have made the industry more global. Reputed business schools are able to attract good applicants, good staff, and charge premium prices. Argenti (2000) suggests six factors that can lead to a stronger reputation for a business school: (1) an association with a reputable university, (2) a high-quality faculty, (3) high-quality students, (4) a strong image in the corporate sector, (5) strong alumni with high affiliation, and (6) good survey rankings.

There exist many different measures of reputation in higher education. In the United Kingdom teaching quality in higher education is assessed by regular inspection every five or more years. Research output is assessed in a research assessment exercise (RAE) with a similar frequency. Universities and their departments often include such quality indicators in their self-promotion. The RAE rating is used by academic job applicants and potential doctoral students to evaluate a university or a university department. The ratings have been often included in MBA guide books and published national and local newspapers including the *Financial Times*. However, the RAE is not uncontroversial as an exercise or as a measure. Should business schools in particular seek higher research ratings at the expense of other targets? (Piercy, 2000). There is concern on both sides of the Atlantic about the effects on faculty behavior and the management priorities within business schools that a focus on fundamental, rather than on applied research, might promote (Srinivasan et al. 2001). Questions are asked (and avoided) about the balance between the role of a university-based department's research and the applied nature of, in particular, MBA teaching (Triesmann et al. 2001); and with executive education (Prince and Stewart 2000) and about the resource allocation between these activities (Srinivasan et al. 2001).

Accreditation is a global source of reputation validity. The American based, but international, AACSB use the business school's mission and vision as a starting point for assessment (Bailey and Dangerfield 2000; Payne and Whitfield 1999; Jantzen 2000; Henninger 1998). Competitor bodies exist in Europe, such as AMBA and EQUIS, and schools will often seek to be accredited to a number of such bodies to demonstrate that they meet certain standards. Accreditation is the equivalent of a quality mark from an independent body.

While Business Schools may be concerned to acquire and promote such, objective, market signals of their quality and standing, external stakeholders will evaluate the reputation of a business school in a number of ways. One of the existing and still dominant methods is that from media rankings.

BUSINESS SCHOOL RANKINGS

The main product of the business school sector is the MBA. The MBA label is used to denote many quite different styles of course but most have a similar structure and aim. When potential and current stakeholders formally evaluate a business school's reputation as an MBA provider, their information sources may be divided into two, rankings from the media and their own perceptions gained through their own indirect and direct experiences of the school and its self-promotion. Rankings appear to offer impartial and objective data concerning standardized needs such as comparable average salary after graduation compared with previous salary and the fees charged, the number of faculty members holding a Ph.D., the number of international faculty members (those from different nationalities), the research output of the school, and many more.

The most prominent reputational rankings are those of *Business Week* and *US News & World Report* in the USA and the *Financial Times* in the UK. Interviews with the deans at 30 ranked US schools revealed that rankings have guided their schools' strategic action (Martins 1998). Even leading business schools believe that rankings have led to their losing control over the definition of their own success, that rankings stifle innovation and creativity and therefore contribute to standardizing business schools. Considering academic reputation as a composition of a set of specific qualities that differentiates one school from another (Fombrun 1996), ranking-led reputation management can, potentially, be quite detrimental. It can force business schools to play "a game of illusion" with very intangible results and even to choose to mispresent themselves (Corley and Gioia 2000). Playing the ranking game can threaten a school's identity (Elsbach and Kramer 1996) if they have to pretend to be what they are not or feel pressure to change to something they do not wish to be. Worse, should all schools play the ranking game, and do so more or less equally well, the same applicants would still be shared by the same providers in much the same way as before. There would be a general "blanding" rather than branding and thus differentiation of business schools as the MBA becomes commodified.

The ranking of a business school will be an important issue for both MBA applicants and alumni as the reputation of the school from which the qualification was obtained will influence the graduate's career opportunities. But applicants will also be concerned about the less tangible aspects of their choice of program and provider. Will they "fit in"? What is the style of teaching? The potential students might explore the school's website, receive word of mouth from an alumnus or guidance counselor, or have direct contact with a business school employee at a convention, fair, or during an interview. Although the perceptions of stakeholders are important in the reputation of any organization, little empirical work has been reported on the measurement of the perceptions of business schools compared with those of commercial organizations.

There has been a long argued link between the perception that stakeholders might have of an organization and its culture (Hatch and Schultz 1997). One of the linking factors is the organization mission and vision. Business schools have a distinctive style of culture, reflecting their being part of a University, rather than part of the business community that is their academic focus.

BUSINESS SCHOOL CULTURE

In a mainstream commercial business, decision-making and managerial responsibility for such things as external image can be addressed managerially. In a business school, or in any academic department, collectivism has a unique role. The role of dean has been disparagingly described as that of "herding cats" or "trying to raise the *Titanic* with one's bare hands" (Stevens 2000). Few decisions can be taken by such "managers," at least not without running the risk of a mauling at the next meeting of academic "colleagues." Decision-making in such an environment has to be collective at least in its spirit. Goffee and Jones (2000) describe the culture of one of the leading business schools as a "fragmented" organization, where both "sociability" and "solidarity" are lacking. Consequently the working environment is not particularly pleasant or friendly. The business schools should not worry about this, because such a culture attracts a self-selecting group of highly autonomous, egocentric individuals who are motivated, not alienated, by the freedom of the fragmented organization.

The main product of a business school, the MBA, is a high involvement product, just like an expensive car. But MBA students are seen as a different type of consumer due to the power producers have over them (Sturdy and Gabriel 2000: 995). It might be hard to see students as "customers" even though they have paid a high price for an MBA program. One logic is that students should be treated better than "just" the customers of a commercial organization. They are after all long-term stakeholders, as their own reputation and that of the school they attained their qualification from are intertwined. In reality, it seems customer satisfaction and loyalty in the business school context have been largely neglected as ideas (Henning-Thurau et al. 2001) or limited to the satisfaction with team members (e.g., Baldwin et al. 1997) rather than with the organization as a whole. The bargaining power of the student-customer is relatively low, especially that of full time students. While "repurchase rate" is one of the measures of customer loyalty in a commercial organization, it is largely irrelevant in the MBA market.

Uniquely if the student/customer fails to obtain the desired outcome, a qualification, there is little chance of a successful complaint. A second difference concerns the student-customer's involvement with the institution. Students, unlike commercial customers, are much more closely involved with their school, almost as close as internal stakeholders, the employees. Frequency of contact with staff and the use of school facilities are much higher than in most other service organizations. Unlike in a commercial organization, staff and students share many internal facilities, such as the library and restaurant. Therefore, student-customers will have a more direct and powerful influence on a school's culture and identity.

Given the highly unusual context offered by a typical business school and the amount of research conducted there, there is little published research into their corporate branding. Our objective is to fill the gap in the existing literature by measuring the image of a business school in the eyes of different stakeholders, and, having done so, to demonstrate how such insights can be used to provide the basis for a branding strategy. Our focus is one particular business school.

CASE VIGNETTE: The Manchester Business School (MBS) brand

Manchester Business School (MBS) was, with London, founded as one of the first two British business schools, in 1965. Although MBS has been consistently ranked within the top 10 in Europe and top 3 in the UK, competition has been intensifying in the business education market. The number of business schools has increased worldwide. The number of American business schools has reached 700. In the UK the duopoly of London and Manchester ended in the early 1970s. UK business schools now number some 109 from a mere 20 in the 1980s. Recently both Cambridge and Oxford universities have set up their own business schools. The new entrants have grown quickly and aggressively, threatening existing leading business schools such as MBS. Users of business school services have far more choice but they are unlikely to consider all possible options in detail. Logically they will construct a limited "consideration set" from which a more systematic choice can be made.

MBS has some tangible points of difference. It is well known for its "Manchester Method," a project-oriented "learning by doing" approach to education developed from its inception. For example, the International Business (IB) Project, introduced in the 1970s, allows students to work with companies interested in overseas markets for an 8-week period. The project approach differentiates American from British business schools (Wilson 1992: 48) but a similar approach is now used by many other European schools, thus reducing the potential for a claim of distinctiveness. Secondly, MBS is rated relatively highly in media ratings surveys for its international focus both in the nature of the curriculum, its faculty, and students.

In addition to the "country of origin" effect of being "European" and "British," the image of the city of Manchester, and of the parent brand the "University of Manchester" seems to affect the image of Manchester Business School. The identity of MBS is also influenced by its relationship with the University of Manchester and more recently with the Manchester Federal School (an alliance of the business related parts of the University, UMIST Management School, and MBS). This may have blurred the image of MBS somewhat. For example, Baden-Fuller et al. (2000), in their work on the reputation ranking of European MBA programs, interpreted the alliance as a "merger."

Vision and Mission

Recognizing the links between culture and reputation and the linking potential of Mission and Vision, MBS began a process of "Visioning." The visioning process began in 1998. It was led by the dean with the assistance of an external facilitator to establish the vision that faculty and support staff wanted to achieve for MBS by the year 2003. Groups of staff met to brainstorm and articulate a view of the future. The results were pooled in a draft mission and vision statement that was further refined by the staff groups debating and suggesting modifications to this and to successive re-drafts. Research into M&V statements has often focused on whether financial performance or employee motivation are linked to the existence or structure of an M&V statement (Chun and Davies 2001) and academic writers are still unclear about what vision and mission statements should include (Klemm et al., 1991). One model summarizes the main elements that are common to many, namely: purpose, strategy, values, and behaviour standards (Campbell and Tawaday, 1990). These headings were used to appraise the content of the evolving M&V statements. After a consultation process lasting nearly two years the mission and vision (Tables 9.1a and 9.1b) was published both internally and externally (for example on the corporate website).

Table 9.1a *Mission*

Our mission is to develop the business leaders of tomorrow, within a culture where undertaking original research and consultancy enriches and continually improves our teaching.

We aim to pursue our mission locally, nationally and internationally and primarily to the activities of post graduate and post experience education and training

---

Table 9.1b *Vision*

Manchester Business School is seen, globally, as an academic leader, one of the top business schools. We pride ourselves on our innovation, in "getting there first" to identify what senior managers will need to know and to do, not only today, but into the future.

Our work is guided by an inclusive stakeholder approach, which reflects the views of our employees, students, alumni, business partners, peer institutions and government and community organizations. Our key areas of activity are in designing programs which are valued and in delivering them how and when they are needed.

These programs are underpinned by the "Manchester Method," an approach to education which was developed at MBS. Since its early days the Manchester Method has been evolving but an emphasis on facilitated learning from real, practical example remains. One feature is that of a learning community, where a process of personal learning and development is undertaken through real-time experiences.

Commentators acknowledge that the School has an international reputation for research, an activity which is a crucial and distinguishing feature of our work. We aim to undertake research that provides our external stakeholders with new, often exciting and down to earth ideas and insights into business; ideas that are stimulating and relevant at local, regional, national, and international levels.

We aim to create a virtuous circle, one where research enhances and enlivens the experience of those we teach and their future prospects, such that we can command the necessary premium in the marketplace for our services.

Inside the School, we work in a lively, bustling atmosphere where ideas can be shared openly without the hindrance of internal boundaries. We strive to be honest and friendly in our dealings with each other. Our aim is that, right from day one, new arrivals feel supported and recognized and work as part of one large team to achieve the School's shared goals.

As a result, the spirit of Manchester Business School will be one of mutual support, confidence, trust and pride. We also value and rely upon those who have studied with us. We aim to remain helpful to them in their careers, supportive and concerned for their futures as they are for ours.

We recognize that our ambitions cannot be achieved alone. We continue to establish a range of strategic alliances and partnerships with carefully selected, equally prestigious individuals and organizations in both the public and private sectors. Such alliances enable Manchester Business School to broaden its scope and to become a single point of contact for education, training, research, recruitment, and consultancy services. These alliances complement the roles we have as part of the University of Manchester and the Manchester Federal School of Business and Management.   *Continued overleaf*

Table 9.1b —*continued*

We recognize the increasing role that technology will play in our work, both in our need to understand its effect on commercial activities, and also in supporting our own activities as an international business school.

We recognize and seek to serve a number of communities. These include:

- our local community (many of our employees have their roots there)
- the local, regional, national and international business and public sector communities (these are our clients, partners and the employers of those we teach)
- the academic community (we have a role to advance knowledge and to share these insights internationally).

Measuring the image and identity of business schools

Contemporary to the M&V process, the image (defined here as the perception held by students) and identity (defined here as the perception held by staff) of MBS were measured using the Corporate Reputation scale (Davies et al. 2003, 2004). The scale uses the personification metaphor to measure the image and identity of organizations. It contains seven dimensions (Table 9.2). The main dimensions, agreeableness, competence, chic, ruthlessness, and enterprise, can be subdivided into traits. The questionnaire was administered to a large sample of staff and students. Included in the questionnaire were four measures of satisfaction to allow a correlation between satisfaction and image/identity. In total 105 staff and 303 students (MBA, doctoral, executive, and undergraduates service taught by MBS faculty) responded, an estimated 70.3 percent response rate.

The relative scores on the 7 dimensions of corporate character for staff and students are shown in Figure 9.1 (see also Table 9.3). Students had a more positive view of the MBS persona than staff who rated it higher on ruthlessness (arrogance, controlling) and lower for enterprise (imaginative, innovative) and for agreeableness (open, concerned, sincere).

When the seven dimensions were correlated with "satisfaction" (Table 9.3), all but informality for staff correlated with respondent satisfaction significantly. Student satisfaction correlated with informality with a significance level only at 0.05. All other correlations were significant at 0.01 or better.

Stepwise regression of satisfaction against the seven dimensions showed that staff and student satisfaction could be explained mainly by agreeableness. Staff satisfaction was further explained by machismo and (negatively) by informality and ruthlessness. Student satisfaction was also explained by competence.

Of the various correlations and scores, those for enterprise became a focus of comment by those seeing the results of the surveys. As a research-driven organization, MBS as other (but by no means all) business schools is inherently innovative. The culture was also one that supported constant change in the design and delivery of the curriculum. Yet staff in particular did not perceive themselves as enterprising. There was clearly a need to address internal as well as external

Table 9.2 The seven dimensions of corporate character

Agreeableness	Enterprise	Competence	Ruthlessness	Chic	Informality
Cheerful	Cool	Reliable	Arrogant	Charming	Casual
Pleasant	Trendy	Secure	Aggressive	Stylish	Simple
Open	Young	Hardworking	Selfish	Elegant	Easy Going
Straightforward	Imaginative	Ambitious	Inward Looking	Prestigious	
Concerned	Up to date	Achievement Oriented	Authoritarian	Exclusive	**Machismo**
Reassuring	Exciting	Leading	Controlling	Refined	Masculine
Supportive	Innovative	Technical		Snobby	Tough
Agreeable	Extrovert	Corporate		Elitist	Rugged
Honest	Daring				
Sincere					
Trustworthy					
Socially Responsible					

Table 9.3 Correlations of the seven dimensions of corporate character with respondent satisfaction

Dimension	Agreeableness	Enterprise	Ruthlessness	Chic	Competence	Informality	Machismo
Staff	0.703	0.424	−0.432	0.279	0.635	0.034	0.445
Students	0.623	0.357	−0.256	0.224	0.565	0.096	0.305

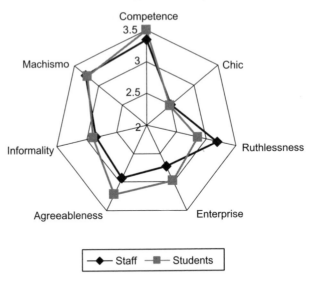

MBS image and identity

Figure 9.1 The image and identity of MBS as seen in 1998

perceptions. "Innovation," one of the items assessing enterprise, was also allied with competence in the context of a business school, and this became the word that was used to encapsulate the new communications strategy. It was valued by both staff and students as an aspect of the MBS character. MBS was inherently innovative as a research centre and able therefore to provide tangible evidence in support of the brand claim. The first focus would be a new visual identity.

Changing visual identity

Olins (1989) likened the use of corporate symbols to that of the need of a new country or a new regime to establish symbols and rituals. The confederacy developed their own flag (their logo) and established a capital city (corporate headquarters). It had its own currency and army, which had its own distinctive uniform. Each of these has its own functional purpose but each has its own symbolic meaning. Olins invites us to think of France after its revolution against its monarchy, a new flag the tricolor, the Marseillaise, the metric system, a new calendar, and the new title of Emperor for Napoleon, the Eiffel Tower, the Arc de Triomphe and the celebration of Bastille day. As he notes, countries "celebrate their reality with pageants and national monuments whose symbolic value is infinitely more significant than their economic value." His point is that organizations do the same.

Aldersey-Williams (1994) defines visual identity as an "expression—visual but also attitudinal—of a company's character." Munari (1999) explains that a trademark can "express force or delicacy, development, durability, flexibility, richness, stability, drive—each of these qualities has a suitable sign and color." He explains how simple shapes such as squares, triangles, and circles can be used to symbolize different attributes and, if they are modified, by for example stretching the basic shape, how they can be made to add different aspects to the character implied by the logo or trademark. The logo encapsulates and evokes the associations that we make with an organization. They can be extremely powerful in evoking the company or brand they are associated with and the associations we then make with the brand itself.

In recent years MBS had used their full name in a distinctive typeface instead of a logo. Other schools tended to use logos, often containing heraldic shields and other icons denoting tradition. A brief was prepared to send to a number of design agencies to solicit their reactions and to select from these an agency to work with MBS to evolve a new visual identity.

The agency responses

In 2000, six design agencies were asked to "pitch" for the work to create a new corporate logo for MBS that would reflect its new mission and vision and the platform of "innovation" that the marketing department used to encapsulate the essence of both the visioning process and the reputation research.

Two were shortlisted from their initial presentations. One had chosen a relatively traditional design playing on the letter "M" and the idea of "opening doors." The vertical lines in the letter "M" were each drawn to represent a door, "opening to the future" as the agency explained. The second agency's approach was far more radical. Their logo was a simple green-colored box shape with the words "Manchester Business School" written underneath. They explained that each group of stakeholders or even each part of MBS would be asked to superimpose its own thinking onto the box. They illustrated their thinking with some drawings, for example of a knife and fork either side of the box to represent the restaurant and a handle on one side of the box with steam rising from the top to represent the coffee bar.

Group discussions were held among staff and students where respondents were asked to suggest adjectives that came to mind to describe a business school with the two short-listed treatments for the logo. The adjectives used for the opening door logo included: clear, professional, traditional, corporate and academic, but also: boring, rigid, not unique, too industrial, uninspiring. Those for the green box included: different, simple, modern, imaginative, easy going, adaptable, young, friendly, but also: unprofessional, cute, simplistic, too trendy, not prestigious, and childish.

In summarizing the group discussions the coordinators wrote, "There was no strong link between the opening door logo and the direction chosen from last year's market research for our identity (trust, innovation, excitement, not arrogant). Some respondents did not spot the symbolism of the opening door. The green box approach created an immediate reaction during the group discussions. Of the two treatments the green box is clearly closer to the direction MBS wish to pursue. But it needs further development as an idea to make it appear more professional and less childish."

The agency who had offered the green box, a small company, "Design Associates," were asked to rework their design in the light of the research. After a number of attempts and further discussion, the color of the box was changed to purple, (because the color was in most cultures a sign of being up-market) and the design made less linear and more complex.   A strap line was added, "Forward Thinking." The result was a less childish, more professional look, and one which was certainly different (Figure 9.2).

Over the coming months various parts of MBS developed their own sub-logos, Figures 9.3 and 9.4. Business cards and letter headings were changed. The corporate website was redesigned to embrace the new logo. The new corporate branding created considerable interest in the media, with articles about it in the *Financial Times*, *Design Week*, the *Marketeer*, and *Time Magazine*. Research is currently

Manchester Business School
forward thinking

Figure 9.2 *Final version of the MBS logo.*

Figure 9.3 *Example of sub-logo signage*

Figure 9.4 *Example of sub-branding: the Center for Business Research logo*

being undertaken to assess any change in the perception of the MBS character that might be associated with the new approach.

CONCLUSIONS

The creation of visual identity is not at first sight something that can be driven by an analytical process. While brands may rely on both the tangible and intangible, logos and other forms of visual identity are essentially representational. Whether they have any inherent symbolic value is debatable, but the logos often used to represent business schools use the traditional symbolism of heraldry (coats of arms, mottoes) imagery that is derived from their university associations. There are no rules that imply that such an approach is mandatory. Indeed recent logos imply that the idea of an inherent meaning in the logo design itself may be misleading. For example the Orange logo has no obvious links to telecommunications nor to corporate character. The obvious links from the Virgin name and logo are far from intended.

The logo derived for MBS is not traditional nor is it symbolic in the sense that it represents a "square" business school. By being different it does imply that something different is supposed to be associated with the organization behind the logo. While the reality of what is delivered by an organization is important in corporate branding, symbolism and imagery will also be important as part of any attempt to emphasize differences in markets that could otherwise become commodified.

The new corporate brand strategy was devised by considering the factors that satisfied the main groups of stakeholders in a systematic way. Implementing a new marketing strategy is unlikely to be easy in the fragmented and individualistic culture represented by a business school. Having hard data as the basis for the strategy appeared to facilitate the process, particularly data derived from a rigorous process of research and a research approach that was being developed within the school itself. In the coming years application numbers to the Manchester MBA rose for the first time in many years. The new look was only a part of a number of changes that could have created this greater interest but was seen as an important part of the school's repositioning. In October 2004 the University of

Manchester merged with its sister University UMIST. The decision was taken to implement a unified corporate visual identity and, as a consequence, the Manchester Business School adopted the University logo with the addition of the business school name. The square box logo was quietly dropped.

ISSUES FOR FURTHER DISCUSSION

1 As a practical exercise take the basic box logo and try to imagine you are running a research group at MBS and you want to develop your own version of the logo to express some aspect of the group's personality or character.

2 Compare the approach to logo management at MBS with that in your own company or one you have worked in. Most companies are very proscriptive about the use of their logo, with little or no deviation allowed. Could the approach at MBS be used more widely? What advantages and disadvantages might there be?

3 Choose a selection of company logos. Using the words in the Corporate Character Scale describe the company behind the logo. Compare what you decide with examples of corporate advertising from the company.

REFERENCES

Aldersey-Williams, H. (1994) *Corporate identity*. London: Lund, Humphries.

Argenti, P. (2000) "Branding B-schools: reputation management for MBA programs." *Corporate Reputation Review*, 3(2): 171–8.

Baden-Fuller, C., Ravazzolo, F., and Schweizer, T. (2000) "Making and measuring reputation: the research ranking of European business schools." *Long Range Planning*, 33: 621–50.

Bailey, J. B. and Dangerfield, B. (2000) "Applying the distinction between market-oriented and customer-led strategic perspectives to business school strategy." *Journal of Education for Business*, 75(3): 183–7.

Baldwin, T. T., Bedell, M. D., and Johnson, J. L. (1997) "The social fabric of a team-based M.B.A. program: network effects on student satisfaction and performance." *Academy of Management Journal*, 40 (6): 1369–97.

Campbell, A. and Tawaday, K. (1990) *Mission and Business Philosophy*, Oxford: Heinemann.

Chun, R. and Davies, G. (2001) "E-reputation: the role of mission and vision statement in positioning strategy." *Journal of Brand Management*, 8(4): 315–33.

Corley, K. and Gioia, D. (2000) "The reputation game: managing business school reputation." *Corporate Reputation Review*, 3(4): 319–33.

Davies, G., Chun, R., da Silva, R., and Roper, S. (2004) "A corporate character scale to assess employee and customer views of organization reputation." *Corporate Reputation Review*, 7(2): 125–46.

Davies, G., Chun, R., da Silva, R., and Roper, S. (2003) *Corporate reputation and competitiveness.* London: Routledge.

Elsbach, K. D. and Kramer, R. M. (1996) "Members' responses to organizational identity treats: encountering and countering the business week rankings." *Administrative Science Quarterly,* 41: 442–76.

Fombrun, C. J. (1996) *Reputation: Realizing Value from the Corporate Image.* Boston, MA: Harvard Business School Press.

Goffee, R. and Jones, G. (2000) "What holds the modern company together?" *Harvard Business Review* (November/December): 133–48.

Hatch, M. J. and Schultz, M. (1997) "Relations between organizational culture, identity and image." *European Journal of Marketing,* 31(5–6): 356–65.

Henninger, E. A. (1998) "Perceptions of the impact of the new AACSB standards on faculty qualifications." *Journal of Organizational Change Management,* 11(5): 407–24.

Henning-Thurau, T., Langer, M. F., and Hansen, U. (2001) "Modeling and managing student loyalty: an approach based on the concept of relationship quality." *Journal of Service Research,* 3(4): 331–44.

Jantzen, R. H. (2000) "AACSB mission-linked standards: effects on the accreditation process." *Journal of Education for Business,* 75(6): 343–9.

Klemm, M., Sanderson, S., and Luffman, G. (1991) "Mission statements: selling corporate values to employees." *Long Range Planning,* 24(3): 73–8.

Martins, L. L. (1998) "The very visible hand of reputational rankings in US business schools." *Corporate Reputation Review,* 1(3): 293–8.

Munari, B. (1999) *Made in Italia.* Milan: Instituto Nazionale Editoriale Italiano.

Olins, W. (1989) *Corporate Identity.* London: Thames and Hudson.

Payne, S. L. and Whitfield, J. M. (1999) "Benchmarking for business schools/colleges: implementing an alternative; partnership approach." *Journal of Education for Business,* 75(1): 5–9.

Piercy, N. (2000) "Why it is fundamentally stupid for business school to try to improve its research assessment exercise score." *European Journal of Marketing,* 34(1/2): 27–35.

Prince, C. and Stewart, J. (2000) "The dynamics of the corporate education market and the role of business schools." *Journal of Management Development,* 9(3): 207–19.

Srinivasan, S., Kemelgor, B., and Johnson, S. D. (2000) "The future of business school scholarship: an empirical assessment of the boyer framework by US deans." *Journal of Education for Business,* 75(3): 75–80.

Stevens, G. E. (2000) "The art of running a business school in the new millennium: a dean's perspective." *SAM Advanced Management Journal,* summer: 12–28.

Sturdy, A. and Gabriel, Y. (2000) "Missionaries, mercenaries or car salesman? MBA teaching in Malaysia." *Journal of Management Studies,* 37(7): 979–1002.

Trieschmann, J. S., Dennis, A. R., Northcraft, G. B., and Niemi, A. W. (2001) "Serving multiple constituencies in business schools: MBA program versus research performance." *Academy of Management Journal,* 43(6): 1130–41.

Wilson, John F. (1992) *The Manchester Experiment: A History of Manchester Business School 1965–1990.* London: Paul Chapman.

Chapter 10

Creating better corporate reputations

An Australian perspective

Grahame Dowling

AT THE END OF THIS CHAPTER READERS SHOULD BE ABLE TO:

1   Understand the relationship between terms such as corporate—brand, image, identity, and reputation in Figure 10.1
2   Draw a customized diagram identifying the major factors that shape their company's various corporate images based on Figure10. 2
3   Identify many of the prime sources of risk to a company's images and reputations

---

KEY POINTS

■   A company does not have *a* corporate image or reputation—it has many of them. These are both stakeholder-based constructs
■   Different sets of factors in Figure 10.2 combine to create the images that each stakeholder group has of a company
■   Corporate reputations are formed when a person compares their image of a company with their values and expectations about its appropriate behavior
■   Companies are judged against the performance of their peers
■   The management imperative is to build a company that creates social, emotional, and economic value for its key stakeholders
■   Boards of directors can play a key role in enhancing or destroying their company's images and reputations

---

INTRODUCTION

In recent years Australia like most other western countries has suffered its share of major corporate crises. They have included the complete collapse of companies (e.g., Ansett Airlines and HIH Insurance), the implosion of one of Australia's most respected boards of directors (viz., NAB bank), a poorly handled case of product contamination (Pan Pharmaceuticals), and numerous cases of poor strategic judgments by CEOs. These disasters have been in addition to the usual number of minor crises arising from the everyday operations of companies, such as: union disputes, accidents, breakdowns, and the backlash from competitive excess. These corporate crises have tarnished the reputation of Corporate Australia and this has resulted in a loss of trust and support by many of its constituents. For example, in 2004 the advertising agency Grey Worldwide conducted a survey of Australians (consumers and employees) who gave companies a grade of C— (quoted in Lloyd 2004). They were considered to be greedy, selfish, untrustworthy, and lacked leadership and innovation.

In fact, Corporate Australia, like its corporate counterparts, America, Argentina, Brazil, Britain, Canada, et al., have a big job to do to restore their tarnished reputations. One consequence is that many companies now have to "sell" their corporate reputations to their stakeholders in order to secure their social and commercial licenses to operate. For example, the sales pitch to some of these key groups is:

- *employees*—we are a good, safe place to work;
- *customers*—we stand behind our products and services;
- *society*—we are a good corporate citizen;
- *investors*—our reports and forecasts are reliable;
- *insurers*—we are a sensible risk;
- *government*—because of our economic and social contribution, support us;
- *regulators*—trust our interpretation of, and compliance with, the law.

A good corporate reputation will actively support these sales messages.

This chapter looks at how companies can build and in some cases restore their good names. It does so from an Australian perspective. While Australia is similar to "the west," it is also the product of a mixture of cultures that provides a unique business environment. The next section briefly highlights some of the aspects of the Australian business culture that affect the creation of corporate reputations. Following this, I outline a blueprint for corporate reputation development. The chapter concludes with a discussion of some of the challenges and issues facing the managers tasked with enhancing their company's desired reputation.

AUSTRALIA

Because of the heritage of Australia, its businesses adopt a unique perspective on the creation, role, and usefulness of corporate reputations. The country is essentially a British (then later European) enclave sitting at the bottom of Asia that is fascinated by many of the exploits of the United States. Thus we draw from each sphere of influence. For example, the British heritage has endowed the country with a very strong institutional structure, namely, its laws, judicial system, regulators, stock exchange, accounting bodies, etc. (Carson et al. 1999). These structural elements define the "rules of the game" in which business is conducted. Here contracts are enforceable without undue reliance on the social relationships that are often found in Asia. Thus, while the reputations of the commercial parties to a transaction are important in helping to secure business, contracts take precedence over these as a means of ensuring compliance (as opposed to posting one's reputation as a "security bond" in a transaction). This is seen by the fact that very few companies use the courts to claim damages for the loss of reputation due to the actions of others.

The US influence is felt in many ways. For example, Australia's business education, thinking, and practice tend to follow US trends. Thus, there is a tendency for the share market to (heavily) influence the board and executive management behavior of public companies. And like the US, this has led to some corporate malpractice and to what many in society regard as corporate greed. However there are some interesting points of difference with the US business practice. For example:

- The overt brashness of a celebrity-style CEO is not broadly welcomed.
- There is little "rah, rah" adulation for internal statements of intent like vision and ethics—while these statements may exist, they are often ignored by many employees.
- There is only limited corporate support for public ratings of the reputations of companies—they are more often than not regarded as "beauty contests" by many senior managers.
- The use of corporate advertising and videos to tell the "story" of the company is not as widespread.

Thus, some of the "tools" used in the US to create a better corporate reputation are less evident in Australia.

The Asian influence on business is the new emerging force. While Australia has long been an exporter of raw materials (coal, iron ore, and more recently natural gas) to the region, this has been a specialized operation practiced by a few big companies (Dowling 1987). Recently, the rise in imported manufactured goods and the export of specialist foods (like seafood) and services (like education, engineering, law, and accountancy) combined with increased levels of immigration from Asia has created an interest in Corporate Asia (Crombie 2005). One issue that is emerging from our business dealings with various Asian countries is an increased sensitivity to the concept of "face," that is, a person's image or credibility in the eyes of his or her peers. For example, in a business context a person's title and business card signal status and the way these identities are handled by another party shows cultural understanding and sensitivity.

A crucial factor in any country that affects the reputations of its business enterprises is the expectations of the society about the roles of companies. These are shaped by general social trends and the good and bad behavior of companies. For example, some of Australia's biggest companies (its big banks, post office, major airline, railways, and largest telecommunications provider) still have a quasi-government-endorsed community service obligation (CSO). While they can compete vigorously in their chosen markets, the government and public commentators note any attempt to disenfranchise segments of the community because these are unprofitable. While this CSO is an aftermath of the time when these organizations were either government owned or highly regulated, it does establish an informal social benchmark for "big business." And it is the behavior of these big businesses that sets the moral tone by which many other companies are judged.

The expected morality of Australian business is often revealed in the comments of (business) journalists. Consider the following quote:

> Australia's retail shareholders have jump-started a new wave of investor activism, sparked into action by months of reading about sky-high remuneration, poor corporate governance and executive excess.
>
> (Nicholas 2003: 13)

What an observation like this reflects is a rise in anti-business sentiment. And within two years of this statement the Australian Corporations Act required that the remuneration of public company top executives be voted on at the annual general meeting. While the vote is non-binding, it does send a strong signal to the board of directors about perceptions of executive management's value for money. An "against" vote is also ammunition for others to criticize the company involved (Sykes 2005).

Like many other countries, Australian companies have been under the spotlight for their transparency and corporate governance performance (e.g., Uren 2003). And some unexpected outcomes have emerged. For example, in 2004 the board of directors of one of the country's most respected companies (the NAB bank) imploded. After the big financial loss of an overseas subsidiary and a large foreign currency trading loss, tensions among directors surfaced in the press. The result was the sacking of the CEO and later the resignation of the chairman of the board. Soon after this, 70 percent of the board and the executive management team left the company. The new CEO expects the bank's reputation will take years to rebuild. One final case provides insight into the nature of corporate Australia and the reputations of its companies.

CASE VIGNETTE: James Hardie

James Hardie is a company founded in Australia over a hundred years ago. In its earlier years it made a range of building products that contained asbestos. These were subsequently found to be very dangerous to the people who made them and used them in construction activities. As these people became sick and started to sue the company, it (and the government) realized that this was a "long-tail" crisis with serious public health ramifications. As the full extent of the potential financial compensation for victims emerged, James Hardie engaged in an interesting corporate restructure. In December 2001, shareholders (90 percent of whom were Australian) voted to accept a unanimous board of directors' recommendation to establish a new parent company in the Netherlands. Having moved offshore, the company then put money into a statutory fund to compensate its Australian asbestos victims.

Now the official story for the corporate restructure was to (1) facilitate international growth—85 percent of earnings were from outside Australia, and (2) to minimize corporate taxes—it was estimated that about $30 million would be saved annually (statement by the CEO accessed from www.jameshardie.com, 8/13/2004). However, as the amount of funding for the victims of asbestosis came into dispute, it was realized that the parent company had limited its liability to its two Australian-domiciled subsidiary companies. Also, the company had no legal obligation to provide top-up funding over that which it had previously committed.[1] Thus, this "regulatory arbitrage" strategy as it is sometimes called (Partnoy 2004: 48), had two economic outcomes. One was that it saved tax—the Australian taxation department was not impressed. The second was that it capped the liability of the asbestos claimants—they, their unions, the Australian government, and many journalists were not happy! (Gettler 2005a). Thus James Hardie's actions clearly signaled a "shareholder" (as opposed to a social entity) view of the company. And its record share price in August 2005 suggested that investors appreciated the company's off-shore strategy.

The James Hardie case highlights some of the key issues facing boards of directors, CEOs, and Chief Reputation Officers who set out to create a better reputation for their company. The next part of this chapter discuss three of these issues, namely:

■ *The stakeholder dilemma*: who is first among equals.
■ *Organizational drivers of corporate reputations*: what factors need to be put in place.
■ *Crises*: and other ways to damage a good reputation.

CREATING GOOD CORPORATE REPUTATIONS

Any discussion of a blueprint for corporate reputation change can quickly get bogged down in some confusing terminology. Hence, the first stage in this endeavor is to establish a set of terms that will be used throughout this chapter. With this terminology established, the focus shifts to identifying the different types of people who form a reputation of a company, and then the different sets of factors that combine to shape the evaluations of these company stakeholders.

TERMINOLOGY

To date, writers have struggled to reach consensus about definitions of the various terms used to describe the reputations of a company (e.g., Abratt 1989; Melewar and Jenkins 2002). One reason for this is that each of the terms below is variously used in the disciplines of economics, strategy, organizational theory, and marketing. Hence, to provide a common language for the rest of this chapter, corporate reputation and its related constructs are given the following formal and working definitions (Dowling 2004):

- *Corporate identity*: the attributes, symbols, nomenclature, and behaviors used by the company to express and identify itself. The role of corporate identity is to answer the question—*Who are you?*
- *Corporate brand*: the promise made by the company. The corporate brand answers the question—*What is your offer?* (It also largely determines if people *like you*.)
- *Corporate image*: the beliefs and impressions held by stakeholders about the company. The corporate image answers the question—*What do people think about you?*
- *Corporate reputation*: the overall evaluation (often expressed as admiration, respect, and esteem) in which a company is held. Corporate reputation answers the question—*Are you good or bad?* (It also determines if people *trust* the company.)
- *Reputation capital*: the stock of trust and goodwill signified by the company name. Reputation capital answers the questions—*Are you strong or weak? Are you valuable?*

As the definitions imply, a company's corporate identity and its corporate brand are the drivers of the corporate images and corporate reputations held by stakeholders.[2] And reputation capital is the strength and value attached to the name of the company by internal managers and the investment community. This set of definitions captures the ideals of the company (its identity and brand), the

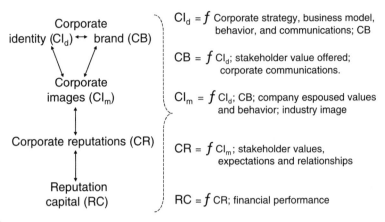

Figure 10.1 *The family of corporate reputation constructs*

perceptions of stakeholders (image and reputation), and the outcomes of interest to the company (such as trust and reputation capital). Thus they are an "active" set of definitions in the sense that they describe how stakeholders think, feel, and might behave towards the company if they think it is essentially "good" or "bad" (Goldsmith 2004–5).

The left side of Figure 10.1 shows that the definitions above form a family of related constructs. For example, a company's identity and brand (CI_d and CB) shape people's beliefs (CI_m), and these in turn shape their evaluations (CR). The right side of Figure 10.1 shows some of the main factors that previous research has identified that drive each construct (Fombrun 1996; Fombrun and van Riel 2004; Dowling 2001; Larkin 2003). The next section continues with the "family" theme and introduces the idea that companies have a family of stakeholders to whom they must appeal. Following this I illustrate how companies can use these constructs to form better reputations.

STAKEHOLDERS

Stakeholders are people and organizations who can affect, or who are affected by, the achievement of the company's objectives (Freeman 1984). Dominique ten Berge has noted that most companies have four broad groups of stakeholders (1988):

- *Normative groups*—provide the authority for an organization to function. They may also set the rules and regulations by which activities are carried out. These groups exist within and outside the organization. Examples of outside groups are regulatory agencies and trade associations. Examples of inside groups are the board of directors and various high-level management committees who set policy.

- *Functional groups*—directly affect the operations of the organization. The most important of these groups is employees—especially those who "carry" the organization's core capabilities with them and who deal directly with the stakeholders who really matter to the enterprise. Other groups include suppliers, business partners, and professional service providers such as law firms, market research firms, and advertising agencies.
- *Customers*—provide the long-term survival for private-sector companies, or the raison d'être for public-sector organizations. Because their needs are so diffuse, customers are usually segmented into a set of sub-groups (Dowling 2004).
- *Diffused groups*—have an interest in the company or have (given themselves) a mandate to protect the rights of other stakeholders. Journalists, unions, and special interest groups are examples. When active, these groups often drive publicity about the organization and may also directly affect its operations. (See for example, the anti-McDonald's website: www.mcspotlight.org.)

The current Anglo-American model of corporate governance and the legal framework in Australia both suggest that companies should adopt a broad circle of concern, be it with specific consideration given to shareholders. For example, just after being judged by its peers as Australia's most admired company with the most admired board, the CEO of Westfarmers said that "the role of the board is to look after shareholders"—with the caveat that company behavior "is totally in accordance with what society and the regulators expect of us" (James 2005). Thus, for Westfarmers, and the James Hardie company mentioned earlier, shareholders are "the first among equals" as the saying goes.

However, whenever a company has distinct groups of stakeholders with different needs, there will exist the potential for conflict among these groups regarding what they want managers to do. This can be thought of as different self-interested stakeholder groups competing in a "market" to influence a company. One company that has effectively managed such a "market for influence" for more than thirty years is Southwest Airlines. Herb Kelleher, the legendary founder of the US airline, had a clearly focused business model that delivered good value customers and created substantial shareholder value. He also had a clearly articulated rank ordering of his stakeholders. When asked the question

Which do you put first, your employees, your customers, or your shareholders?

his answer was clear.

> You put your employees first. If you truly treat your employees that way, they will treat your customers well, your customers will come back, and that's what makes your shareholders happy.
>
> (Lucier 2004)

Employees love hearing this. And in a service-based industry this logic makes intuitive sense. In Australia, the small Bendigo Bank has a similar approach. Its business model is built around supporting employees to understand and meet the local community's banking needs. As measured by the annual corporate reputation quotient (RQ) administered by AMR Interactive, the bank rated more highly than its bigger, national counterparts in 2003, 2004, 2005, and 2006.

At the heart of stakeholder management is the simple idea that listening to, and engaging with, key stakeholders should be the first step in trying to avoid potential conflict. Consider the case of the Westpac bank.[3] In 1991 it suffered a crisis of confidence with its employees, customers, shareholders, the regulators, and the government. Some of the bank's business practices were found to be grossly deficient, and it posted the biggest loss in Australian corporate history at that point in time. The bank was castigated in the popular and financial press for months. This was so bad, that customer service employees were reluctant to wear their uniforms on the way to work. And many senior managers in the bank "moved on" as the saying goes.

At this stage, senior management in Westpac thought that the way to regain public confidence was to adopt a classic, old-fashioned, message-driven public relations strategy—take control of the communications agenda and pound home their story. However, this strategy created a problem for the newly appointed corporate affairs team. They soon realized that a "we have the answers" approach was wrong. They set out to educate senior managers that a "they have the answers" approach was the better strategy. What followed over the next ten years was a program whereby the bank systematically listened to, and engaged with, its key stakeholder groups. This "more engagement—two-way communication" strategy was underpinned by formalized listening posts in the form of a number of advisory groups (employees, suppliers, environmentalists, and community leaders) feeding their ideas and concerns to a subcommittee of the board of directors tasked with improving the bank's social responsibility. By 2004, Westpac was rated as Australia's best example of a socially responsible company (Gettler 2005a).

HOW COMPANIES CREATE THEIR REPUTATIONS

The previous section really poses a dilemma for managers wanting to improve their company's various reputations. The dilemma is that because different stakeholders have different relationships with a company, they will hold a variety of images and reputations of the same company. A corollary of this fact is that a different configuration of factors will drive the images of each stakeholder group. To handle this complexity, a generalized framework is introduced in Figure 10.2 that can be adapted for use with any particular group of stakeholders. (For examples of this see my earlier book, Dowling 2001.)

One thing that is important about the framework presented below is the notion that the good corporate images and reputations held by stakeholders come from deep inside the company. While many companies will proclaim that they are "good," it seems that this proclamation resonates best when the company is transparent enough that people understand what it does and how it creates value for its various stakeholders. This transparency then needs to be supported by good deeds. It is a lot like putting your money into different forms of investments. Those that you understand create a greater feeling of confidence than those that are mysterious.

Figure 10.2 shows the main factors that influence the desired image a company wishes to project to its stakeholders. The symbolism here is as follows—factors in boxes are things that managers can more easily change; factors in dashed circles are co-produced by stakeholders and the company, and images in shaded circles are the key outputs of the image forming factors. Managers can look at each set of factors to see where they can engineer change.

Another way to think about the factors in Figure 10.2 is that they are the sources of information that a person uses to shape his or her image of a company. For example, the images of employees are determined by what they think about

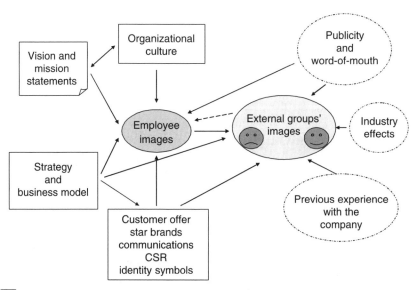

Figure 10.2 *Creating a desired corporate image*

their company's key identifying attributes, and their feelings about other people's evaluation of their company. Employees buy-in to the factors in the four boxes at the left of the figure, and a feeling that other people favorably evaluate the company should result in the employees having a good corporate image. And a good image often fosters greater self-confidence, cooperation with company policies, and internal corporate citizenship behaviors. This self-reinforcing amalgam has become known as "employee engagement."

Figure 10.2 also suggests a number of managerial guidelines. For example, it is unlikely that simply changing the company's corporate identity symbols (such as the company logo) will have a major impact on the images held by most people. To achieve significant change in the way that people think about a company will often involve making changes to some very basic activities—things like the culture of the organization and the offer it makes to employees and customers. Quick-fix solutions are seldom effective by themselves. However, if they are used to "signal" some fundamental changes in other activities they are more likely to have an image and reputation payoff.

In the model of corporate reputation formation laid out in this chapter, managers use their best endeavors to make changes to the factors in Figure 10.2 that improve stakeholders' beliefs and impressions (corporate image) of their company. This (desired) image will then be filtered through each stakeholder's value system such that they will then form their reputation of the company. The periodic surveys of community attitudes towards companies provide insight into these values.

To illustrate this effect consider the findings of the Australian researcher Don Porritt (2005). From his extensive analysis of the Australian reputation quotient studies he found that a company's reputation for financial success may adversely affect the company's overall reputation. For example, when a company is perceived to be making above-average profits at the expense of its service to the community and/or by increasing the workload of its employees, then there is a backlash against this company by everyone except the shareholders. This backlash is more pronounced for those companies where consumers believe that there is little real choice among competitors. It occurs in part because there is a widespread cultural value in Australia of giving everybody a "fair go."

As noted in the introduction to this chapter, in the court of public opinion, much of Corporate Australia has been convicted of being an unsavory character. The belief that companies put profits before people (their employees, customers, and the community) sits uneasily with basic Australian values like fairness, tolerance, equality, aspiration, and respect (Atkin 2006). Australian companies were also accused of being boring and unoriginal. Hence it was of little surprise that when Richard Branson's Virgin companies commenced operations in Australia with flair and their "take on the big boys" stance, the company went straight to the top of many corporate polls (Lloyd 2004).

In summary, the desired image that a company wishes its stakeholders to have of it is built on the basic foundations of the company—its strategy, business model, statements of intent, organizational culture, corporate social responsibility (CSR), and the products and services offered. In the eyes of stakeholders these factors create, as the marketers say, a value proposition for each stakeholder group. Good strong value propositions that sit easily with the expectations of stakeholders, when backed by consistent and good corporate communications and behavior, ultimately create good corporate reputations. There are no short-cuts to being well respected. However, there are some quick ways to damage a good corporate reputation.

CRISES AND OTHER WAYS TO DAMAGE A GOOD CORPORATE REPUTATION

A crisis nearly always exposes the underbelly of a company (i.e., those factors in boxes on the left side of Figure 10.2). And it may also reveal the communication skills and crisis-handling capabilities of the company's senior managers. Together these can be a pleasant or unpleasant sight. When a crisis reveals an inherently good company, the reputation capital that has been built up can be drawn down to provide it with a second chance. However, unlike the US where the game of baseball (and some criminal laws) suggests that it is "three strikes before you are out," Australians are less forgiving.

In recent years Australians have loved to hate their banks. As reflected in the annual RQ studies, the big four commercial banks (that serve the vast majority of Australia's retail and business customers) have consistently been positioned towards the bottom of the list of Australia's most respected high-profile com-panies. In times (long) passed, they formed a cosy club of not very different, nor very innovative, financial institutions. They had an extensive branch network that gave them a broad footprint throughout the community. Banking was a private and personal service, one that was largely respected by the people who worked in the industry and by its customers.

As government regulations were relaxed each bank set out to be more com-petitive, to grow, and to produce higher returns for their shareholders. Like many other companies that were involved in newly deregulated industries (such as airlines, postal, electricity, and telecommunications) mistakes were made as they learnt how to compete. Often these mistakes went largely unnoticed by the general public until a journalist decided to frame one as a human-interest story. The 1991 famous Westpac Letters Affair being a case in point where some foreign currency loans made to farmers and small businesspeople led to their bankruptcy (Carew 1997). This episode badly damaged the bank's reputation because it exposed what happens when smart bankers sell complex financial products to naive customers. (This was one of the events that precipitated the Westpac stakeholder initiative noted earlier.)

A side-effect of deregulation was that the mistakes and crises plus the new attitude towards all consumers as a source of profit, combined to degrade the once-good reputations of these companies—in the general community, among many customers, and of particular concern among many of the bank's own employees. Also, each subsequent wave of cost-cutting, or downsizing, or restructuring, or whatever term was fashionable at the time, reinforced the feeling among employees that their job security was tenuous. And as more and more companies carried out a similar practice, it started to erode the belief that stable employment until retirement was likely (Lloyd 2004). When employees start to lose confidence and trust in their own companies, the internal culture starts to erode. Because the fundamental building blocks of good corporate images and reputations reside on the inside of a company, then any loss of employee commitment and loyalty can signal impending trouble.

Another source of reputation risk in many companies is their board of directors (Dowling 2006). As the various corporate train wrecks around the world amply demonstrated, the directors were not able to identify the early warning signals of impending disaster (Deloitte 2004). And in many cases as the corporate autopsies revealed, the board played a contributing part in the disaster (Gettler 2005a). For example, in some cases the audit and risk committees placed too much reliance on the reports provided to them by executive management. In other cases the selection process of a new CEO failed to identify flaws in the character or the skill set of the chosen candidate. Sometimes the board signed off on a strategy (such as a takeover) or a new venture (such as a big Internet play) that was inappropriate for the company. And in some spectacular cases, the board encouraged unrealistic growth targets, which when not met were punished by firing the CEO with a huge termination bonus (*Fortune* 2005). The old Chinese saying that "the fish rots from the head" was seen to apply in many companies (Garratt 2003). And the response from the government and the corporate regulators was to introduce Sarbanes–Oxley style regulation to make directors more accountable for their actions.

CORPORATE REPUTATION DILEMMAS AND CHALLENGES

Australian companies, like many of their overseas counterparts, are facing some troubling dilemmas and significant challenges regarding the creation, protection, and enhancement of their corporate reputations. At the top of the list of these is the role and influence of the share market.

In the 1980s the primary role of the share market was to support companies (e.g., through capital raisings) with secondary roles to act as a scorecard of performance and a vehicle for investors. Today, however, the roles are often reversed. Many public companies seem to exist for the "pleasure" of the market. Boards and CEOs are at the mercy of their growth predictions and the expectations of institutional investors. While senior company executives are often heard to complain about this situation, they have helped to design their own frustration. They make bold predictions about their company's future performance and they directly tie their often considerable remuneration (e.g., through options packages) to these predictions. An industry of professional investors has grown up to scrutinize corporate performance and to trade on the "mistakes" of senior managers—lionizing better than expected performance, praising the meeting of expectations, and castigating under-performance. Managing the market's expectations and the potential reputation damage from unrealistic public benchmarks of performance is a key challenge for senior managers and their boards of directors.

Related to the share-market challenge is the issue of perceived corporate greed. Many companies now face the dilemma of how to state a huge and sometimes a record profit result while not being perceived as greedy. And for some types of companies, this issue is highly visible.

Consider the case of Australia's most prominent investment bank—Macquarie Bank. This company is one of Australia's emerging global corporate brands. Having started as a private investment bank, Macquarie became a public company and has been very successful in Australia, continually being rated as excellent in industry polls. The dominant internal culture of Macquarie, like many other such banks, is one characterized by deal-making, hard work, competitiveness, and (visible) success. Macquarie is often described in the business press as "the millionaires' factory" due to the payment of high bonuses to senior staff. While employees dislike this description being used in the public domain, it does signify an interesting attribute of investment banks. While the blandishments of company websites and annual reports extol the importance of shareholders and customers, in reality senior executives are often the most important group of stakeholders. They set both the principles and the amount of their own remuneration packages (Partnoy 2005).

A variation on this corporate reputation dilemma is often highlighted by the CEO's termination package. For example, in the US where the "numbers" can be staggering—for example, Carly Fiorina was paid $42 million from Hewlett Packard and James Kilts $100 million for his departure from Gillette—this issue is particularly acute. Both left because of poor performance. But this was of little concern to them as their employment contract, negotiated at the time of their first employment, stipulated that "poor performance" was not a sufficient "cause" for their termination (Colvin 2005). What boards of directors don't seem to realize is the signal that this type of contract sends about greed and excess to employees, the business press, and the general community.

Another issue facing Australian companies is how to manage the perceptions and expectations of stakeholders about their role in society. Often surveys about Corporate Australia (like the one noted in the introduction) reveal that Australian citizens do not understand or appreciate the role companies play in the economic development and prosperity of the country. And when employees and outsiders lose confidence in their companies, there is potential for the reputation of Corporate Australia to be simultaneously eroded from the inside and the outside.

To reflect on the role of Corporate Australia, the Australian Government tasked a Corporations and Markets Advisory Committee with compiling a report titled "The Social Responsibility of Corporations" (Australian Government 2006). It provided encouragement and frustration for both sides of the argument that Australian companies need to be more socially responsive. While the report reaffirmed that CSR is important, it also recommended no change to the current reporting requirements or legislative policy settings. Many managers and board members were relieved that no new compliance procedures were forthcoming. (Any significant changes would have also signaled that the past CSR efforts of many companies had been unacceptable.) Many CSR advocates welcomed reassurance that CSR was important, but were frustrated not to receive more potential direct government support for their cause. (The cause-related marketing insert at the end of the chapter highlights some of the issues facing managers who try to use CSR to enhance the reputations of their company.)

A final challenge facing Australian and many overseas companies is *growth*. And when the favored path to growth is via innovation, then this challenge is both big and dangerous. Consider what is involved here. Companies establish their reputations on the back of their continuously good past performance. And a company's good reputation with a stakeholder is both a predictor of its future behavior, and in many cases a type of security bond that it offers for the delivery of its corporate promise. Now innovation (mostly) and growth (very often) involve *change* and *risk*—things that immediately put a good company reputation at risk. The "offer" to stakeholders is essentially that "because we have been good at doing XYZ in the past, will you now trust us to do something quite different in the future." Some companies are prepared to use their good reputations to back their new endeavors while others prefer to create a separate company brand name to pursue growth and innovation. While the work by David Aaker and Kevin Keller on brand extensions provides some guidance about which type of strategy to use, this is an area that needs more research (Aaker 1991, 1996; Keller 2003).

CAUSE-RELATED MARKETING: BECOMING GOOD BY DOING GOOD

From 1991 to 1993 the big Australian supermarket chain Coles got together with Apple Computer and 12 of its major suppliers (like Pepsi and Nestlé) to run an "Apples for Students" program. The idea was for shoppers to collect their supermarket dockets and give these to schools so that they could trade them in for computers. ($100,000 worth of shopping got one PC.) Each year over $10 million worth of computer equipment and accessories were given to schools. And over the course of the program 70 percent of Australia's schools and kindergartens participated.

This was a program that aligned the financial incentives of its corporate sponsors with the needs of the broader community in which they operated. We could assume that the corporate images and reputations of the sponsors were enhanced, especially among parents, teachers, and school children.

In Australia as elsewhere, many such cause-related marketing programs have been launched. However these, and other types of CSR initiatives, have their critics. Some of the arguments against targeted CSR are: (1) It is the more marketable, charitable causes that will attract most corporate support, and this will undercut the "no strings attached" pure philanthropy that companies have traditionally given to a wider range of causes. (2) Many such programs are reactionary in the sense that their motives are really to stave off possible criticism rather than "do good." (3) These programs don't produce a direct financial return to the company and thus lower profits and the share price. (4) It is the role of elected governments to shape social welfare not faceless, unelected corporate managers with their own private agendas. From P. Kotler, et al., *Marketing* (Sydney: Prentice Hall, 1998), 127–8.

CONCLUSIONS

Many years ago Australia was known around the world as "the land of the long weekend." This image was not completely unfounded, and was fueled by the Australian Tourist Commission's advertising of the country using the local's love of sport, beer, barbecues, sun, and surf. It was also perpetuated by Paul Hogan's classic advertisements for Foster's beer in the UK and his movie *Crocodile Dundee*. This image was great for attracting tourists and for those companies that exported products that fit this image—such as surf wear (Billabong) and beer (Foster's). But it didn't help the majority of Australian companies wanting to export manufactured goods or services.[4] And then the country won the 2000 Olympic Games. Sydney put on such a good event that the world took notice and the President of the IOC called them the "best games ever." The success of these Games had two effects on Corporate Australia. One was that every Australian company stood a few inches taller. The other was that now the image of Australia became more of an asset for our exporters and global companies.

Against this backdrop some Australian companies made more of this good image than others. For example, the medical products companies Cochlear (hearing devices), CSL (blood), ResMed (sleep apnoea devices), and Sonic

193 ■

Healthcare (pathology) all consolidated their good reputations, both in Australia and overseas. Others like AMP (financial services in the UK), NAB (financial services in the US), and Telstra (telecommunications in Hong Kong) badly managed their overseas forays. These mistakes damaged their corporate reputations (because poor performance came from a company that was expected to be good). It then made it more difficult for these companies to use this intangible resource for competitive advantage with companies in their supply chain and across various segments of target customers.

A good corporate reputation has operational value—it helps to consolidate and enhance the relationship a company has with its important stakeholders. In contrast, a poor corporate reputation can be a lead weight and increase the friction in these relationships.

ISSUES FOR FURTHER DISCUSSION

Stakeholders

Figure 10.2 is a generalized framework to help managers identify the most important factors that drive the creation of the corporate images of stakeholders. Pick a company that you know well (maybe your own), and draw three customized versions of this diagram—one for employees, one for customers, and the other for shareholders. Which factors are common in each diagram and which are different? Which factors are more and less important in creating a good image for these different groups of stakeholders? Which factors should the company continuously monitor and what type(s) of information would be best suited for this task? In order to see how the corporate images of each group of stakeholders get transformed into their corporate reputations, what other information would the company need to monitor?

James Hardie: A Lost Cause?

There is little doubt that James Hardie is a company with a very poor public reputation in Australia. One suggestion that has been put to Meridth Hellicar, the chair of the board of directors, is for the company to adopt a social cause and to "do some social good" in order to help repair the company's poor standing in the Australian community. Should the company pursue such a course of action?

You might like to start thinking about this issue by first visiting the company's website to discover what sort of a company this is (i.e., its products, the geographic markets where most of these are sold, customers, branding strategy, etc.).

See www.jameshardie.com.au

NOTES

1   However, the board did state that it had a moral obligation to help these asbestos victims as much as possible and in December 2005 the State Government of New South Wales finally forced the company to commit sufficient money to a Medical Research and Compensation Fund to cover the expected total liability.

2   The plural of corporate images and corporate reputations is used because different groups of corporate stakeholders generally have different perceptions and emotions about the same organization.

3   This case was presented by Tim Williams, senior Advisor, Corporate Responsibility and Sustainability, of Westpac, at the Factiva Forum in Sydney on July 21, 2005.

4   Raw materials like coal, iron ore, wool, and wheat have always been strong exports.

REFERENCES

Aaker, D. (1991) *Managing Brand Equity*. New York: Free Press.

Aaker, D. (1996) *Building Strong Brands*. New York: Free Press.

Abratt, R. (1989) "A new approach to the corporate image management process." *Journal of Marketing Management*, 5(1): 63–76.

Atkin, D. (2006) "Setting a values compass." *Australian Financial Review*, March 6, 32.

Australian Government, Corporations and Markets Advisory Committee (2006) *The Social Responsibility of Corporations*, www.camac.gov.au

Carew, E. (1997) *Westpac: The Bank that Broke the Bank*. Sydney: Doubleday.

Carson, S. J., Devinney, T. M., Dowling, G. R., and John, G. (1999) "Understanding institutional designs within marketing value systems." *Journal of Marketing*, 63, special issue: 115–130.

Colvin, G. (2005) "Outraged over CEO exit packages? You're too late." *Fortune*, March 7, 34.

Crombie, G. (2005) *The Way of the Dragon*. Milton, Qld: Wrightbooks/John Wiley.

Deloitte (2004) *In the Dark: What Boards and Executives Don't Know about the Health of Their Businesses*. Sydney.

Dowling, G. R. (1987) "Buying is marketing too: Japan's influence in the Australian coal business." *Long Range Planning*, 20(1): 35–43.

Dowling, G. R. (2001) *Creating Corporate Reputations*. Oxford: Oxford University Press.

Dowling, G. R. (2004) "Corporate reputations: should you compete on yours." *California Management Review*, 46(3): 19–36.

Dowling, G. R. (2004) *The Art & Science of Marketing*. Oxford: Oxford University Press, ch. 6.

Dowling, G. R. (2006) "Reputation risk: it's the board's ultimate responsibility." *Journal of Business Strategy*, 27(2): 59–68.

Fombrun, C. J. (1996) *Reputation*. Boston: Harvard Business School Press.

Fombrun, C. J. and van Riel, C. (2004) *Fame & Fortune*. Upper Saddle River, NJ: Financial Times/Prentice Hall.

Fortune (2005) "How the HP board KO'd Carly." *Fortune*, March 7, 65–7.

Freeman, E. R. (1984) *Strategic Management: A Stakeholder Perspective*. Boston: Pitman, 84.

Garratt, B. (2003) *The Fish Rots from the Head*. London: Profile Books.

Gettler, L. (2005a) "Taking care of business." *Sydney Morning Herald,* Special CRI Report, April 4, 1–4.

Gettler, L. (2005b), *Organizations Behaving Badly*. Sydney: Wiley, 38–42.

Goldsmith, P. (2004–2005) "Corporate reputation management." *Critical Eye* (December–February): 46–9.

James, D. (2005) "Strong, silent types." *BRW*, August 25–31, 58.

Keller, K. L. (2003) *Strategic Brand Management*. Upper Saddle River, NJ: Prentice Hall.

Larkin, J. (2003) *Strategic Reputation Risk Management*. New York: Palgrave-Macmillan.

Lloyd, S. (2004) "Greedy, dishonest, boring, faceless." *Business Review Weekly*, April 22–8, 32–9.

Lucier, C. (2004) "Herb Keheller." *Strategy + Business*, 35, summer, 119–25.

Melewar, T. C. and Jenkins, E. (2002) "Defining the corporate identity construct." *Corporate Reputation Review*, 5(1): 76–89.

Nicholas, K. (2003) "Boards beware of stroppy shareholders." *Australian Financial Review*, December 1, 13.

Partnoy, F. (2004), *Infectious Greed*. London: Profile Books.

Partnoy, F. (2005) "A serious question for all the overpaid bankers." *Financial Times*, August 4, 11.

Porritt, D. (2005) "The reputational failure of financial success: the 'bottom line backlash' effect". *Corporate Reputation Review*, 8(4): 198–213.

Sykes, T. (2005) "Who's on the executive pay hit-list?" *Australian Financial Review*, September 28, 25–6.

ten Berge, D. (1988) *The First 24 Hours*. Oxford: Basil Blackwell.

Uren, D. (2003) *The Transparent Corporation*. Sydney: Allen & Unwin.

Chapter 11

An attitudinal measure of corporate reputation

Albert Caruana

AT THE END OF THIS CHAPTER READERS SHOULD BE ABLE TO:

1 Recognize that different stakeholders consider different aspects of corporate reputation
2 Consider utilizing an attitudinal conceptualization of corporate reputation
3 Follow the outlined procedure for the operationalization of corporate reputation from a chosen stakeholder's perspective

---

KEY POINTS

■ There is often considerable confusion in distinguishing among corporate identity, image, and reputation. In corporate reputation the focus is on differences among the various stakeholders of the firm

■ The prevalent definition of corporate reputation is critically considered and the various attempts at developing questionnaires to measure it are evaluated. An alternative attitudinal measure of corporate reputation is put forward that is developed in the context of the theory of planned behavior

■ A procedure that enables the development of questionnaires can provide a direct evaluation of corporate reputation. This also provides a diagnostic procedure tailored to provide management with insights as to how corporate reputation can be improved

■ The robust questionnaire development procedure outlined opens the way to future research that can provide a more meaningful examination and understanding of the variables that influence corporate reputation and the effect this in turn has on other concepts

INTRODUCTION

Corporate reputation has received increasing attention in recent years. Its importance is highlighted in the literature, primarily because of the various beneficial outcomes that have been suggested that it is capable of providing. These include: the intention to purchase a service; a positive outlook of buyers towards salespersons and products; attracting investors, lowering the cost of capital and enhancing the competitive ability of the firm; and the ability to attract good employees.

The area of corporate reputation suffers from an absence of sufficient clarity, particularly in its theoretical underpinning. At times the theoretical issue is not considered at all. At other times either a stakeholder's "perception" is put forward as its basis or a firm's perspective that emphasizes signaling theory. Signaling theory suggests that a firm will provide signals through its actions and communications. The company adopts these signals to reveal hidden attributes to its stakeholders. Signaling theory shows that "high signaling costs" ensure that it is in both parties' interest to send honest signals despite prima facie incentives to deceive. Therefore, a rational stakeholder expects a sensible company to honor the implicit commitment transmitted by a signal. Failing to honor the commitment is perceived by the consumer to be economically unwise. The signals emitted form the basis of the company's corporate reputation.

The literature exhibits a number of attempts that have been made to measure corporate reputation. These attempts are rendered all the more challenging due to an absence of clarity among the use of the terms corporate identity, corporate image, and corporate reputation that have at times also been used interchangeably. Berens and Van Riel (2004) group the various measures developed under three main headings, namely those relating to: (1) social expectations; (2) corporate personality traits; and (3) trust. The result is a plethora of measures with myriad dimensions that are meant to capture the corporate reputation construct with little agreement on an acceptable measure with the necessary measurement rigor able to help develop and deepen the theory related to corporate reputation.

This chapter takes an attitudinal perspective of corporate reputation within the context of the theory of planned behavior (Ajzen 1991). Although the approach presented here represents a fundamental departure from current methods it is in no way intended to muddy the water further. Rather, it seeks to latch on to an established theory with established questionnaire-building procedures that provides an opportunity for rapid advances in better understanding of the role of corporate reputation in relation to other concepts. In this chapter, corporate identity, corporate image, and corporate reputation are first reviewed and the main ways in which corporate reputation is currently measured are considered. It proceeds to argue for an alternative attitudinal measure within the theory of planned behavior and maps out an application of the theory to the development of questionnaires to measure corporate reputation. The potential advantages and implications are highlighted and possible limitations are indicated.

CORPORATE IDENTITY, CORPORATE IMAGE, AND CORPORATE REPUTATION

The terms corporate reputation, corporate identity, and image create a certain degree of confusion that requires clarification. Unfortunately, despite significant contributions in the last few years towards understanding and identifying corporate identity, a definitive definition of this concept and its measurement does not yet exist. Moingeon (1999) holds that organizational identity is a conceptual advance over organizational culture because it permits researchers to explain in more depth the dynamics of organizations. The author also argues that a diagnosis of organizational identity is both an analysis of the visible part of the organization (the symbolic products) and an analysis of the hidden part of the organization (the organizational *imaginaire*), which is a much harder task. Yet again corporate identity has been defined in terms of an organization's ethos, aims, and values that create a sense of individuality and differentiation. Following a review of the literature, Melewar and Jenkins (2002) examine the definitions, models, and specific elements of corporate identity and propose a holistic model for corporate identity, based on four dimensions—communication and visual identity, behavior, corporate culture, and market conditions. Interestingly, Bromley (2000) who argues that corporate identity is the way members conceptualize their organization, restricts it therefore to the view of internal stakeholders, be they employees, managers, and others.

Stuart (1999) looks at corporate image claims that if corporate identity is well managed, then the resulting corporate image will accurately reflect the values, beliefs, and strategic direction of the company. Much of the research on corporate image is about the way an organization presents itself to its publics, especially visually (Bromley 2000). Gotsi and Wilson (2001) review different viewpoints in the marketing literature in an attempt to clearly define the concept of corporate reputation and identify its relationship with corporate image. The authors differentiate between the "analogous" school of thought, which views corporate reputation as synonymous with corporate image, and the "differentiated" school of thought, which considers the terms to be different but according to the majority of the authors, interrelated. They argue that, on balance, the weight of literature suggests that there is a dynamic, bilateral relationship between a firm's corporate reputation and its projected corporate image.

On the basis of the above, corporate identity primarily arises from internal stakeholders and the important formative aspects are primarily functional, non-media dimensions that include the strategy and stances adopted by the organization. Visual enhancements, like logos and branding, play an important but secondary role. On the other hand, it is corporate image with its emphasis on external stakeholders and its stronger emphasis on branding and media dimensions that sustains a firm's desired positioning. Notwithstanding, it would not be possible to achieve a tenable corporate image in the absence of a relevant corporate identity as it is the latter that sustains it. Therefore, while short-term success in building a positive corporate image may be possible (e.g. for a new company, or in an image repositioning exercise through extensive use of media advertising), long-run success is not sustainable in the absence of congruence provided by a meaningful corporate identity. Without the sustenance that corporate identity can provide, corporate image success is at best fleeting. Figure 11.1 seeks to capture the above in diagrammatic form.

Fombrun (1996: 72) defines corporate reputation as (*italics added*) "a *perceptual* representation of a company's *past actions and future* prospects that describes the firm's *overall appeal to all* of its key constituents when *compared* with other leading rivals." This definition emphasizes the process of how corporate reputation comes about. It makes four main points: it establishes perception as the basis for reputation formation; it recognizes the existence of various stakeholders but suggests the aggregation of these perceptions across stakeholders; it puts forward the relative nature of the perception process in relation to competitors; and it holds that reputation is cumulative, being the result not only of a company's latest actions but also of its past actions. Gotsi and Wilson (2001) argue that reputations embody two fundamental dimensions of firms' effectiveness: an appraisal of firms' economic performance, and an evaluation of firms' success in fulfilling social responsibilities. It has been said that in today's world, the emotional viewpoint of the media and public opinion predominate and they influence changes in corporate reputation. Critical news reports and specific negative incidents have an ability to diminish the reputation of a firm. In this context the media, especially

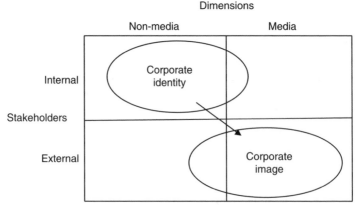

Figure 11.1 *Matrix indicating domains of corporate identity and corporate image*

print media, plays a crucial role since most stakeholders rely on print and visual media to obtain and disseminate information about a firm.

Fombrun's definition has been very influential and has conditioned much of what has come later. Moreover, the idea that corporate reputation is an aggregation of the perception of different stakeholders has received wide acceptance. For example, Dalton (2003: 27) defines corporate reputation as the sum of all the values that stakeholders attribute to a company based on their perception and the interpretation of the image that it communicates and its behavior over time. This position is supported by other writers who assert that reputation is the sum total of stakeholders' perceptions and a direct function of the perceptions of the public involved with a company or its brands. Yet this notion of corporate reputation as an aggregation of all stakeholders' salient perceptions probably owes its origin to the position adopted by the first questionnaire on corporate reputation used by *Fortune* in its Most Admired Companies measure since 1983. One can appreciate its "practical" summary benefits for communication purposes in such a publication; however such an aggregation does not exist in the perception of any stakeholder group and is a complete fiction. Wartick (2002: 376–8) provides a practical example to show how this process of aggregation can be very misleading. In line with this position this chapter argues that any aggregation should be of *single* stakeholder's perception and there is not one but a number of corporate reputations for a firm that necessarily vary by stakeholder group. Therefore, in considering corporate reputation the emphasis is on differences among the various stakeholders of the firm while in the case of corporate identity and corporate image the emphasis is on differences among firms, which differences enable the firm to achieve a desired positioning.

CURRENT QUESTIONNAIRES USED TO MEASURE CORPORATE REPUTATION

The area of corporate reputation will develop more holistically and be able to provide management with worthwhile findings only if researchers are able to ensure more rigor in the measures that are meant to capture corporate reputation. Following a review of the literature, Berens and Van Riel (2004) identify three main types of perceptions to discuss and/or measure corporate reputation, namely those relating to: (1) social expectations; (2) corporate personality traits and (3) trust. Each is reflected in fairly well-established questionnaires such as (1) the annual *Fortune's* (latest 2006) Most Admired Companies and the *Reputation Quotient* (Fombrun, Gardberg and Sever 2000) (2) *Corporate Personality* scale (Davies, Chun, da Silva, and Roper 2001) and (3) *Corporate Credibility* scale (Newell and Goldsmith 2001), respectively. The result is myriad dimensions that are meant to capture the corporate reputation concept. Moreover, examination of these measures often indicates poor or dubious questionnaire development procedures that stall real progress in better understanding corporate reputation. These questionnaires will be considered in more detail.

The *Fortune* Most Admired Companies and the Reputation Quotient (RQ) questionnaires represent the two principal social expectation type of measures that have been used. Possibly because it was the first of its kind, *Fortune* magazine's annual list of America's most admired companies enjoys high visibility and recognition. Since 1983 *Fortune* has asked top executives, directors, and financial analysts to rate companies within their industries on eight or nine attributes depending on whether American or global companies are being assessed. The attributes are: (1) long-term investment value; (2) financial soundness; (3) wise use of corporate assets; (4) quality of management; (5) quality of products or service; (6) innovativeness; (7) ability to attract and retain talented people; (8) social responsibility to the community and the environment; and in the case of global firms (9) effectiveness in doing business globally. Fryxell and Wang (1994) criticize the *Fortune* index in that out of the eight attributes used for American firms the first four attributes listed above relate to performance, while constructs like innovation, corporate social responsibility, and management quality and human resources issues are being captured by single-item measures. Indeed, confirmatory factor analysis indicates that with the exception of the question dealing with "Social responsibility to the community and the environment," the reply to the rest of the questions are being influenced by the perceptions that respondents have of the financial potential of the particular firm (Fryxell and Wang 1994: 11). This, therefore, suggests that the *Fortune* index measures little beyond the firm's reputation for financial performance.

In measuring corporate reputation via the Reputation Quotient (RQ), Fombrun, Gardberg, and Sever (2000: 243) use the following "integrative" definition that holds that corporate reputation "is a collective representation of a firm's behaviour and outcomes that describes the firm's ability to render valued results to multiple stakeholders." This perspective, which has also been used in other subsequent research, indicates a signaling perspective as against the earlier definition of Fombrun (1996: 72) that had a stronger emphasis on stakeholder perception of corporate reputation. Indeed, the original RQ consisted of 32 questions grouped into 8 categories subsequently reduced to a 20-question version to make up an aggregate measure that scores an organization on six categories. These are reported to be: (1) emotional appeal (good feeling about the company/admire and respect the company/trust the company); (2) products and services (stands behind products–services/offers high-quality products–services/develops innovative products–services/offers products–services that are good value); (3) vision and leadership (has excellent leadership/has a clear vision for the future/recognizes and takes advantage of market opportunities); (4) workplace environment (is well managed/looks like a good company to work for/looks like it has good employees); (5) financial performance (record of profitability/looks like a low-risk investment/strong prospects for future growth/tends to outperform its competitors); (6) social responsibility (supports good causes/environmentally responsible/treats people well). As part of the validation testing the authors report the removal of the 3 emotional appeal questions and report that the remaining 17 questions load onto a single Rational Appeal factor. They therefore suggest that corporate reputation combines two factors: Emotional Appeal and Rational Appeal. In addition, work-in-progress has been reported involving cross-nationality validity and equivalence testing to develop a "global" RQ. However, given the nature of the instrument this is likely to be no easy task.

The operationalization of the RQ instrument is inadequately grounded in theory and it is hard to see how the definition used has guided instrument development. Moreover, the process of aggregation pursued that involves obtaining an overall score that purports to provide the aggregate reputation of all stakeholders appears to be driven by commercial rather than sound measurement considerations. The resultant aggregate score is too approximate to meaningfully capture and communicate the perception of anyone and can be quite misleading. In addition, insufficient support is provided to arrive at a balanced view of the rigor underlying the development of the RQ instrument, including its dimensionality, reliability of individual factors, and thorough testing for validity.

A second stream of measures of corporate reputation has focused on personality. The idea of corporate personality comes from the existence of a five-factor structure identified in human personality research which Aaker (1997) extended and applied to develop her brand personality instrument. Inspired by this work, Davies et al. (2001) make use of the "personality metaphor" to look at organizations. They in turn seek to extend the measure of brand personality to capture both external corporate image and also internal corporate identity. Utilizing this approach the authors identify seven rather than the five factors in Aaker's original instrument. Some commonality is reported among the two sets of factors. More recently, Slaughter, Zickar, Highhouse, and Mohr (2004) have developed an organizational personality instrument whose items share many commonalities with the instrument proposed by Aaker. This is an interesting stream of research that could benefit from further theoretical development and measurement testing. A deeper explication of the theoretical basis for the use of personality or its metaphor in relation to organizations as against perceptions would also be beneficial. It might be best to treat external corporate image and internal corporate identity as part of organizational personality which makes it possible for management to clearly position the firm by consciously emphasizing one or a set of possible organizational personality dimensions. Therefore, while organizational personality seeks to emphasize differences among brands, corporate reputation needs to recognize differences among the many stakeholders of the same brand.

The third stream of measures of corporate reputation has focused on corporate credibility and owes its inspiration to the important role that source credibility plays in communications and advertising. Corporate credibility is defined by Newell and Goldsmith (2001: 238) as the perceived expertise, reliability, trustworthiness, and truthfulness of a company. Using established questionnaire development procedures corporate credibility is captured via eight questions consisting of the two dimensions of expertise and trustworthiness. These dimensions appear to be important in building corporate reputation but are likely to be more appropriately envisaged as variables that result in corporate reputation but are not a direct and integral part of the concept.

In all the measures that have been considered there is an underlying assumption that corporate reputation should be a "net" aggregation of the perceptions of all the different stakeholders. It is here argued that any attempt at identifying an overall corporate reputation among all stakeholders is a measurement fiction that is not reflective of any constituent stakeholder's reality. Each stakeholder may have knowledge about issues concerning the company that extend beyond narrow stakeholders' interest but the weighting attributed to these issues cannot be as high as the weighting given to those issues that directly impact the stakeholder group. This aspect of aggregation across stakeholders has clouded the concept's measurement and requires revision.

AN ALTERNATIVE ATTITUDE-BASED MEASURE

Corporate reputation is rooted in perceptions that give rise to beliefs. It can be argued that the point of departure is that stakeholders initially continue to accept current beliefs concerning the corporate reputation of the firm. Such beliefs have privileged status and do not require justification. However, new perceptions resulting from additional or changing information that is processed requires justification and may result in a change of belief and an adjustment in corporate reputation. With such a perspective it is possible to consider beliefs as the mechanism that allows the formation of a corporate reputation.

A look at the literature indicates that an attitudinal basis offers a useful foundation for advancement in developing a sound corporate reputation measure. Indeed, Fombrun (1996: 37) at one point does in effect put forward such an attitudinal perspective describing corporate reputation as the overall estimation in which a company is held by its constituents. The author further argues that a corporate reputation represents the "net" affective or emotional reaction—good or bad, weak or strong—of customers, investors, employees, and the general public to the company's name. This position reflects early work by Levitt (1965) who describes perceived company reputation as the perception of the extent to which a particular vendor company is well known, good or bad, reliable, trustworthy, reputable, and believable. Using the attitudinal approach of Levitt, Brown (1995: 175) measures corporate reputation using 6, 7-point, bipolar questions that ask respondents to compare the firm under consideration to all companies in the industry and to rate the firm on a set of items as follows: the very best—the very worst; the least reliable—the most reliable; the least reputable—the most reputable; the least believable—the most believable; not at all known—the best known; and the least trustworthy—the most trustworthy. On the basis of the above it appears that an attitudinal measure of corporate reputation is able to offer a useful way forward.

ATTITUDES AND THE THEORY OF PLANNED BEHAVIOR

The view of attitudes held by most contemporary social psychologists suggests that the main attribute of an attitude is its evaluative nature, and consists of a disposition to respond favorably or unfavorably to an object, person, institution, or event (Ajzen 1988: 4). An attitude comprises three main components: behavioral beliefs, affect, and behavioral intentions, that ultimately result in action. Beliefs consist of knowledge, ideas, and opinions about an attitude object. For most attitude objects (the firm or organization in our case), people may have a set of beliefs. Beliefs about the possible consequences of the behavior and the value the person gives to these outcomes result in behavioral beliefs. The more positive beliefs are associated with the company and the more positive each belief is evaluated, the more favorable the overall behavioral beliefs component will be. Of course the beliefs comprising the behavioral beliefs need not be true or correct; they need only to exist in the person's mind. The outcome of an attitude is behavioral intentions that consist of a tendency to act or react in a certain way with respect to the attitude object (Ajzen 1988). It includes intentions, commitments, and actions which have to do with the attitude object. It consists of what people say they do or would do under particular conditions. For instance, investing persons who hold a positive attitude towards a company may express the intention to buy the company's shares and vice versa.

The theory of planned behavior (TpB) argues that human behavior is influenced by attitudes toward a specific behavior, rather than by general attitudes. These attitudes are the result of beliefs about the possible consequences of the behavior and the value the person gives to these outcomes. Thus, individuals form certain beliefs about an object and these beliefs, in turn, lead to the formation of attitudes that are consistent with them. Since beliefs already have a positive or negative connotation, persons inevitably acquire a favorable or unfavorable attitude toward an attitude object. TpB offers a framework-linking attitude towards an object together with Subjective Norms (SN) and Perceived Behavioral Control (PBC) to behavior intention and actual action. Behavioral intentions reflect the willingness of the individuals to try to perform the particular behavior. Generally, the stronger the individual's intention to engage in a particular behavior the more likely the individual is to actually perform that behavior.

APPLYING THE QUESTIONNAIRE DEVELOPMENT PROCESS IN THE TpB TO CORPORATE REPUTATION

It is possible for individuals to have multiple attitudes and corporate reputation can be treated as one such attitude. On the basis of the TpB, it is possible to utilize both an indirect belief-based measure of corporate reputation as well as a direct attitude-based measure of corporate reputation. Both belief-based and attitude-based measures of corporate reputation need to be developed from the perspective of *one* of the many possible stakeholder perspectives. However, in capturing the attitude-based measure of corporate reputation it is possible to have the *same* instrument across the different stakeholders groups by using the semantic scale format for a six-question measure as described by Brown (1995). It would take the following form:

Compared to all companies in the industry how would you rate XYZ Company:

■ the very worst	: __: __:: __: __:: __: __:: __:	■ the very best
■ the least reliable	: __: __:: __: __:: __: __:: __:	■ the most reliable
■ the least reputable	: __: __:: __: __:: __: __:: __:	■ the most reputable
■ the least believable	: __: __:: __: __:: __: __:: __:	■ the most believable
■ not at all known	: __: __:: __: __:: __: __:: __:	■ the best known
■ the least trustworthy	: __: __:: __: __:: __: __:: __:	■ the most trustworthy

This questionnaire is known to be unidimensional, exhibits high item-total correlations and provides good levels of reliability in terms of Cronbach alpha (Brown 1995). The scale consists of a mix of adjectives together with the least reliable/most reliable item that helps capture the overall evaluation.

Indirect belief-based items provide an alternative way of measuring corporate reputation. These must necessarily be developed for *each* stakeholder group and the questions used are unlikely to be common across the different stakeholders' groups. Indeed where any commonality in beliefs may exist the particular belief may be subject to a different weighting for evaluation purposes. The set of beliefs identified together with their "explanation" of corporate reputation allows for depth and enhanced understanding. In essence the set of identified beliefs and their subsequent evaluation are similar to dimensions of a concept. They provide a diagnostic capability that can make for meaningful corporate reputation management action. Ajzen (2002: 8–11) provides a procedure for building the belief-based questionnaire. The author starts by pointing out that: (1) in identifying beliefs it is necessary to identify beliefs that are readily accessible in memory (salient); (2) unlike in the case of the attitude-based measure of corporate reputation, the belief-based questions need not exhibit internal consistency as it is the single aggregation resulting from the beliefs that is the measure, and (3) testing of reliability should be via test-retest procedures. A first step involves piloting. In the case of the corporate reputation of a particular stakeholder group the researcher will be looking at a list of the most commonly held beliefs (modal accessible beliefs) among the group. The first step is to ask about advantages followed by the disadvantages and finally probing for further issues. The advantage question for a service firm could be framed along the following lines:

- Compared to all companies in the industry, what do you believe are the advantages of using the services provided by XYZ Company?

If a long list of beliefs results it is possible to group these into categories and a subset included in a questionnaire to capture the concept. Each of the beliefs identified need to be suitably worded and accompanied by a 7-point scale described by extremely unlikely (= 1) and extremely likely (= 7) at either end. In addition, the same issue also needs to be evaluated with a 7-point scale suitably described at either end. This procedure for building the questions that make up the measure needs to be repeated for each advantage/disadvantage identified.

CASE VIGNETTE: Virgin

We like to think that corporate names mean something. By selecting products from certain firms we are not just buying a product. We may be reducing perceived risk, saving time to spend it doing other more important things in life or simply using our purchase to make a statement about our lifestyle choices. Of course we often pay a premium for the privilege—often without even batting an eyelid. Take the Virgin group, with the quirky, innovative, and fun positioning that sets it apart from the other large, faceless corporations. The company is epitomized by its founder Richard Branson who has built the Virgin empire that encompasses unrelated businesses that include, trains, cars, finance, soft drinks, music, mobile phones, holidays, wines, publishing, bridal wear, and cosmetics. The Virgin name is an effective source of differentiation in the market for the different businesses under this umbrella brand. However, the Virgin name does not stand for the same values among investors as among customers.

Yet in today's increasingly global marketplace, large multinational corporations adopt more than one stance. Take the likes of Procter & Gamble and Unilever. Between them, they own almost every consumer product you could think of. They differentiate primarily at the individual product brand level rather than at the corporate level. It is probably correct to say that consumers do not care much as to who owns which brand. In all likelihood the average shopper may not know or care that Max Factor belongs to Procter & Gamble and that Flora margarine belongs to Unilever, as long as the product is able to meet his or her needs. But other stakeholders often do. There are those for whom this knowledge is relevant. It is pertinent to management and staff; it is important to investors, shareholders, regulators, and many others. Yet what is relevant is unlikely to be the same or equally relevant to all.

CONCLUSION

This chapter commenced by considering the issue of corporate identity, corporate image, and corporate reputation. It recognizes the internal stakeholder focus of corporate identity and its effect on corporate image. The latter effect is among external stakeholders and is enhanced via strong media inputs. It further argues that the present aggregation of all stakeholders to arrive at a "net" corporate reputation is erroneous. Any aggregation of corporate reputation should be of a *single* stakeholder's perception and there is not one but a number of corporate reputations for a firm that necessarily vary by stakeholder group. Examination of some of the principal questionnaires currently in use to capture corporate reputation indicates various shortcomings that include both measure deficiencies and an absence of a clear theoretical base. Without development in this area it will be difficult to foster further understanding and theory testing and development.

In line with various indications provided by other authors, this chapter argues for an attitude-based measure of corporate reputation and proposes the adoption of the theory of planned behavior as an underpinning theory. In this context it suggests adopting the questionnaire development methodology of this theory, arguing that it is possible to measure corporate reputation either as a belief-based and/or attitude-based concept. The decision as to which measure to opt for depends much on the use that it will be put to. If the objective of the organization is to understand the corporate reputation held by one of its stakeholder group, it can utilize both methods. The firm would use the attitude-based measure as an aggregate summary score of corporate reputation among the particular stakeholder group while it would use the belief-based measure to allow for deeper diagnostics and understanding. The results from both measures should be highly correlated as the same concept is being captured. On the other hand, if the organization wishes to measure its corporate reputation among different stakeholder groups it can use the attitude-based measure that provides a summary measure for each stakeholder group. Moreover, since the measure will have the same questions, a direct comparison of scores is possible. However, it should not be aggregated to arrive at some supposed overall measure of corporate reputation. Beliefs and their evaluation will necessarily vary by stakeholder group so a comparison among stakeholders is not possible with a belief-based measure of corporate reputation. For the purpose of theory development either belief-based or attitude-based measure of corporate reputation can be used but an attitude-based measure would appear to be more appropriate. This questionnaire development process allows for the systematic investigation of variables that have a direct effect on corporate reputation as well as the incorporation of SN and PBC and their effect on intentions. It opens the way for deeper understanding of the role of corporate reputation.

Like any other theory, the theory of planned behavior is not without its critics. Thus, other theorists have proposed that the attitude's accessibility in memory is what influences the attitude–behavior link. Therefore, it is in cases when the individual has direct contact with the attitude object, has a particular vested interest in the behavior, or is significantly confident about the attitude, that the attitude–behavior link is most likely to predict behavior. Notwithstanding these observations, the operationalization of corporate reputation via TpB as has been discussed can potentially open the way to building a useful understanding of the role of corporate reputation, enabling empirical investigation of the effect of such variables as trust, service quality, and satisfaction on corporate reputation and in turn its effect on various outcomes.

ISSUES FOR FURTHER DISCUSSION

1 Is a focus on the concepts of brand and organizational personality likely to be more useful than an emphasis on corporate image and corporate identity?
2 What are the principal variables that are likely to have a direct effect on corporate reputation? What are some of the likely outcomes of corporate reputation?
3 Is corporate reputation more relevant to service firms rather than to industrial or consumer product firms?
4 Compared to other companies in one of the industries the firm competes in, identify the key advantages and disadvantages you associate with using the product offerings of Virgin taking a (a) customers', (b) shareholders', and (c) employees' perspective.
5 Repeat the exercise for Unilever to identify the key advantages and disadvantages you associate, taking a (a) customers', (b) shareholders', (c) employees' perspective. Contrast your findings for Virgin and Unilever.
6 To what extent can one speak of one overall corporate reputation?

REFERENCES

Aaker, J. L. (1997) "Dimensions of brand personality." *Journal of Marketing Research*, 34(August): 347–56.

Ajzen, I. (1988) *Attitudes, Personality and Behaviour.* Buckingham: Open University Press.

Ajzen, I. (1991) "The theory of planned behaviour." *Organizational Behavior and Human Decision Processes*, 50: 179–211.

Ajzen, I. (2002) *Constructing a TpB Questionnaire: Conceptual and Methodological Considerations*, http://www-unix.oit.umass.edu/~aizen/

Berens, G., and Van Riel, C. B. M. (2004) "Corporate associations in the academic literature: three main streams of thought in the reputation measurement literature." *Corporate Reputation Review*, 7(2): 161–78.

Bromley, D. B. (2000) "Psychological aspects of corporate identity, image and reputation." *Corporate Reputation Review*, 3(1): 31–42.

Bromley D. B. (2002). "Comparing corporate reputations: League tables, quotients, benchmarks, or case studies?" *Corporate Reputation Review*, 5(1): 35–50.

Brown, S. P. (1995) "The moderating effects of insuppliers/outsuppliers status on organizational buyer attitudes." *Journal of the Academy of Marketing Science*, 23(3): 170–81.

Dalton, J. (2003) *LSPR Ethics and Reputation*, http://slo.spem.si/press/priloge/novica31_PR_and_Ethics.ppt

Davies, G., Chun, R., da Silva, R., and Roper, S. (2001) "The personification metaphor as a measurement approach for corporate performance." *Corporate Reputation Review*, 4(1): 113–27.

Fombrun, C. J. (1996) *Reputation: Realizing Value from the Corporate Image.* Boston: MA: Harvard Business School Press.

Fombrun, C. J., Gardberg, N. A., and Server, J. M. (2000). "The reputation quotient: a multi-stake holder measure of corporate reputation." *Journal of Brand Management*, 7(4): 4–13.

Fryxell, G. E. and Wang, J. (1994) "The fortune corporate 'reputation' index: reputation for what?" *Journal of Management*, 20(1): 1–14.

Gotsi, M. and Wilson, A. M. (2001) "Corporate reputation: seeking a definition." *Corporate Communications: An International Journal*, 6(1): 24–30.

Levitt, T. (1965) *Industrial Purchasing Behavior: A Study of Communications Effects.* Boston: Harvard Business School.

Melewar, T. C. and Jenkins, E. (2002) "Defining the corporate identity construct." *Corporate Reputation Review*, 5(1): 76–90.

Moingeon, B. (1999) "From corporate culture to corporate identity." *Corporate Reputation Review*, 2(4): 352–60.

Newell, S. J. and Goldsmith, R. E. (2001) "The development of a scale to measure perceived corporate credibility." *Journal of Business Research*, 52(3), 235–47.

Slaughter J. E., Zickar, M. J., Highhouse, S., and Mohr, D. C. (2004) "Personality trait inferences about organizations: development of a measure and assessment of construct validity." *Journal of Applied Psychology*, 89(1): 85–103.

Stuart, H. (1999) "The effect of organizational structure on corporate identity management." *Corporate Reputation Review*, 2(2): 151–64.

Wartick, S. L. (2002) "Measuring corporate reputation." *Business & Society*, 41(4): 371–92.

Chapter 12

Corporate reputation building
An Asian perspective

Nopporn Srivoravilai and T. C. Melewar

AT THE END OF THIS CHAPTER READERS SHOULD BE ABLE TO:

1   Understand the economic and non-economic determinants of corporate reputation
2   Appreciate the cultural complexities that exist in the understanding of a generic research concept
3   Realize the importance of long-term corporate reputation in the Asian context

KEY POINTS

- Reputation is a term that is difficult to verbalize and is usually used interchangeably with other related words such as image, identity, or brand
- Few studies have discussed in great detail about the risk of not having an acceptable reputation. Nowadays, practitioners are well aware of reputation risk and regard it as one of the most critical threats to corporations
- Different stakeholders usually focus on different aspects of reputation. Investors, for instance, would generally pay stronger attention to financial performance of a company than would its consumers
- Reputation can be influenced by many factors. However, to date, there has been no clear idea about the comparative impacts of economic and non-economic factors on corporate reputation building

INTRODUCTION

Since the 1990s, business communities have observed an increasing trend of globalization, fierce market competition, and a rapid development of technology such as wireless communication and the Internet. Companies around the world search for and exploit sources of competitive advantage to survive and beat their rivals. Not only do they have to deal with their competitors but also the scrutiny from other demanding and knowledgeable stakeholders such as consumer, regulator, and media. Constituents such as regulators and broader communities have shown their strong concerns about recent corporate crimes connected to large and profitable companies. Three following cases exemplify this issue:

- *American International Group (AIG)*, a financial conglomerate whose operations are in more than 130 countries and jurisdictions, is the world's leading international insurance and financial services entity. Its affiliates and subsidiaries provided services such as commercial and industrial insurance, life insurance, asset management, and financial products trading. In 2003, it was accused of accounting fraud and had to pay a fine of more than 10 million US dollars to settle a case with the US Securities and Exchange Commission. In 2004 and 2005, it was charged for conspiracy to violate securities laws and accounting fraud. Hank Greenberg, the former CEO, resigned in March, 2005. Until now, he and the company have still been under heavy scrutiny.
- *Enron*, a US-based energy company, was one of the world's leading electricity, natural gas, and communications companies, with claimed revenues as high as 100 billion US dollars in 2000 (approximately equal to the GDP of New Zealand in 2005). It was also rated as America's most innovative company by *Fortune* magazine for six consecutive years. At the end of 2001, however, the company suddenly collapsed as it was revealed that Enron's executives had committed systematic and well-planned accounting fraud. Its European offices filed for bankruptcy in November, 2001, whereas the head office sought Chapter 11 protection in the US at about the same time. Even though the company still exists, there is no longer any business operation except the management of its property and the handling of legal challenges.
- *Livedoor Co., Ltd.*, found in 1995 and listed in the Tokyo Stock Exchange in 2000, is a Japanese Internet service provider which runs a web portal and several other businesses. Employing more than 1,000 people, the company has become one of the country's biggest Internet companies via a series of acquisitions and stock-swap mergers. In the third week of January, 2006, news about its scandal broke as Tokyo prosecutors started to investigate possible violations of securities laws by its executives. Its founder and CEO, Takafumi Horie, and other executives were arrested for securities and accounting fraud. The share price of the company slumped very quickly.

These examples suggest that the maximization of profit and shareholders' wealth may not be the only objects for companies. Companies also have to show that they are socially responsible, otherwise their reputation may be damaged. The repercussion of illegitimate actions and impaired reputation can be so acute that companies cannot completely recover. The above examples and other cases (e.g. Arthur Anderson and WorldCom) point to the importance of conforming to relevant regulations and maintaining corporate reputation.

The significance of corporate reputation is generally not conspicuous to practitioners unless a crisis happens. In reality, possessing good corporate reputation may render several benefits. Past research has shown that it has significant and positive relationships with operating outcomes; benefit in forms such as customer satisfaction, purchase intention, and joint venture performance (e.g. Davies et al. 2003; Saxton and Dollinger 2004).

Despite the apparent importance of corporate reputation, it is still imperfectly understood as to how corporate reputation is built and maintained, especially in the cases of companies outside the US and Europe (Fombrun and Van Riel 1997). Existing findings deem to have limited generalizability and further studies are required. To help fill such a gap, this study used qualitative research techniques (i.e. semi-structured interview and focus group) to investigate the determinants of corporate reputation of companies in Asia. This chapter will review extant literature on reputation building from three main disciplines (i.e. strategic management, marketing, and sociology) and subsequently describe data collection and analysis procedure. Findings will then be discussed and relevant examples given.

LITERATURE REVIEW

A survey of literature suggests that a company should be able to build its reputation by managing both economic and non-economic factors which may be either internal or external to the company. This section briefly reviews articles about reputation building and points out other potential determinants.

Economic determinants of corporate reputation

Product and service quality
One of the factors that has a strong impact on a company's reputation is its product and service quality. Economists and marketers argued that, given other things equal, companies that deliver high-quality products and services tend to get higher regard from their customers (e.g. Weigelt and Camerer 1988). Consistently high-quality products and services make customers feel that their manufacturers or service providers are dependable.

According to Fombrun (1996: 62), service quality is specifically important in the service sector because of the lack of tangible measures of service performance. Professional service providers, such as law firms and investment banks, usually rely on word-of-mouth communications among current and potential customers in gaining new business. They, therefore, must provide the high quality of service that they promise to customers in order to build and retain their reputation. Companies must also ensure that their products and services appear reliable to its customers and other public audiences. Failure to do so can result in eroded profitability and damaged reputation. In practice, the string of lawsuits which service companies (e.g. Arthur Andersen, AIG, Livedoor, etc.) faced in the 1990s is a good example of this claim.

Several empirical studies have confirmed that the quality of products and services can affect corporate reputation. According to the interviews with business executives in various industries (e.g. retailing, utility, and banking), Davies et al. (2003) found that the quality of product and service is classified as a component of firms' core values which shapes reputation. Previous studies also point out that the association between corporate reputation and product and service quality may not be simple and direct. For example, the relationship between product and service quality and corporate reputation can be mediated by customer satisfaction (Carmeli and Tishler 2005). High product and service quality is an important determinant of corporate reputation but it alone is not sufficient for effective reputation building. The product and service quality must also meet customers' expectations in other aspects (e.g. physical appearance) and render customer satisfaction to be able to effectively influence the impressions formed in customers' minds. However, this does not necessarily imply that a customer will be able to assess a company's reputation only when he/she already purchased its products and services. In addition to direct experience with companies, customers can evaluate the reputation of a company via some forms of communication with the company and its environments instead.

Capabilities and competences

In strategic management research, these two concepts have been found to affect corporate reputation. Capability refers to a combination of *competence* and *strategic processes* (e.g. physical resources deployment and development, etc.) which a company uses to deliver its special knowledge in the form of products, services, and other results that create value for customers and other stakeholders. Competence refers to skill, knowledge, technological expertise, and specific culture which are possessed by a firm.

Capabilities and competences can influence a company's reputation in many ways. For instance, relational competence (i.e. corporate character, social sensitivity, and social utility) can drive corporate reputation and indirectly enhance firm performance (Long-Tolbert 2000). Corporate character is referred to as the qualities of a company that are socially desirable and that contribute to social harmony in organizational relationships. Social sensitivity is defined as a construct that exemplifies a company's socially responsible activities and caring practices directed toward stakeholders, the general public, and the environment.

Social utility is described as the extent to which a company's activities contribute to the fulfillment of personal life goals and higher-order needs that enhance the overall quality of life for consumers. These aspects were found to be positively associated with corporate reputation, with social utility being the most influential factor among the three domains. This is because consumers are primarily motivated to find ways to cope with the daily pressures of life and devote time to more personally rewarding goals (Long-Tolbert 2000). A company that can deliver appropriate values to consumers and whose activities help fulfill consumers' life goals is more favorably regarded than those who cannot.

Other corporate capabilities (e.g. innovation, management skill, and strong leadership) also have significant and positive association with corporate reputation. For example, learning capability was found to be positively correlated with the reputation of banks, which in essence means that it can be implied that financial service companies can foster their names through the continuous acquisition of new information, information dissemination, and shared interpretation of information obtained (Blazevic and Lievens 2004).

Economic and financial performance

Since the late 1990s, economic and financial performance has probably been the most widely studied source of corporate reputation. The prevalence of the studies about firm performance is understandable because firm performance has a strong impact on the decision-making of virtually all constituents. Investors, for example, purchase stocks or financial securities based on the current and historical earnings of companies and generally favor companies with better and more stable incomes. Customers, especially those of banks and insurance companies, usually purchase services from winning firms because it is more likely that successful companies can continuously provide high-quality services and products and always be there to satisfy any guarantees made. In addition, given that no negative issue is involved, the public usually welcome successful companies setting up new plants or branches in their areas because it is hoped that the arrivals of these firms will boost domestic employment and economy.

Among prevailing empirical studies, those in strategic management have provided the largest amount of evidence about the effect of economic performance on reputation. For instance, both market performance (represented by the market to book value ratio) and accounting performance (represented by the return on invested capital ratio) have been found to be positively correlated with the reputation of companies across industries (Fombrun and Shanley 1990). Dividend yield is also negatively associated with corporate reputation, suggesting that firms with high growth prospects[1] (lower dividend yields) have a better reputation in the long term.

Likewise, the return on asset ratio (income before extraordinary items deflated by total assets), the market to book value ratio (market value of common equity deflated by book value of common equity), and the sales growth have been found to be positively associated with the corporate reputation of companies listed in *Fortune*'s most admired companies annual survey (Black et al. 2000). Similarly, Dunbar and Schwalbach (2000) discovered that accounting performance (e.g. the return of capital ratio, the liquidity ratio, and the amount of equity capital) and market performance (e.g. the stock return and the growth in stock values) of German companies have positive effects on their reputations.

According to past articles, the impact of economic performance on corporate reputation is assumed to be static and instantaneous. Only a few researchers investigated the dynamic nature of the effect. Roberts and Dowling (2002), for example, found that a company's reputation is positively and significantly influenced by its return on assets in each of the four preceding years. Technically, they ran a fourth-order autoregressive model to investigate the impact of lagged financial performance outcomes on the reputation of companies in *Fortune* 1000 database. Approximately 15 percent of the variance in reputation is explained by prior financial performance. This has two implications. First, under the condition of uncertainty, strong financial performance results in good corporate reputation. Second, a financial halo exists (Brown and Perry 1994; Capraro and Srivastava 1997). Respondents of the *Fortune* survey may be influenced by historical financial performance and merely give a financial reputation score, rather than an overall one.

In spite of consistent findings about the positive impact of performance on corporate reputation, the relationship between them is, in reality, complex. The causal direction between these two concepts is not conclusive and several studies have found that corporate reputation can also drive firm performance. More studies on the causal issue are therefore required to help resolve this current puzzle.

Finally, the size of a company has consistently been found to be positively associated with corporate reputation even though its operationalizations are different from one study to another. For instance, size is computed as a logarithmic transformation of total sales (Fombrun and Shanley 1990), the number of employees (Shrum and Wuthnow 1988), or the logarithm of the market value of common equity (Black et al. 2000).

Non-economic determinants of corporate reputation

The evaluation of a company's reputation is not based only on the economic dimension. Nowadays, stakeholders of companies also have concerns about social issues such as environmental damage and management transparency. Non-economic factors have also been evidenced to drive corporate reputation in both for-profit and not-for-profit organizations. In this sub-section, non-economic antecedents of corporate reputation will be discussed.

Corporate social responsibility and governance

There is a general belief about the reason for the existence of a company: to maximize wealth for its shareholders. Whilst this idea may still be true, it does not portray a complete picture in this area. Not only do companies vie for profits and try to satisfy their stockholders but they also compete for respect from several groups of constituents such as regulators, environmentalists, and larger communities. The positive relationship between corporate social performance and firm performance found in many studies (e.g. Hammond and Slocum, 1996; Orlitzky et al., 2003; Sen and Bhattacharya, 2001) also strengthens this trend.

In the reputational landscape, corporate social responsibility (CSR) and governance have been evinced as being linked with corporate reputation. The contributions of companies to social welfare (e.g. charitable contributions and foundations) are found to be positively linked with corporate reputation (Fombrun and Shanley 1990). In Dowling's (2004) study, social accountability (e.g. ethical activities, fairness, honesty, etc.) is significantly and positively associated with companies' reputation. Rated by leading business journalists, the social accountability scores have the highest beta (standardized) coefficient in the regression analysis. It can be implied that, from the journalist's viewpoint, corporate social accountability is of more concern than other factors (e.g. corporate competences, corporate personality, etc.). It also indicates that the most important agenda for a group of stakeholders may not be the same as those of other groups, given their roles and duties in the business societies. Unlike journalists, investors, for instance, tend to place more weight on the profitability and market performance of a company rather than its social performance.

Additional evidence can be found in the studies of Padanyi and Gainer (2003), Radbourne (2003), and Turban and Greening (1997). The first two articles investigated the impact of several factors on the reputation of not-for-profit organizations. It was found that good and effective governance is one of the most important drivers. The last article studied the effect of corporate social performance on corporate reputation from the perspective of a potential employee (business student). According to Padanyi and Gainer (2003), the relationship between the growth in effective governance and the growth in peer reputation is statistically significant and positive, suggesting that an organization's effective governance, such as a transparent and well-functioning board of directors, can lead to a positive impression being formed by its constituents.

Radbourne (2003) also obtained similar conclusions although a different research method was employed. According to general managers of performing arts companies, corporate reputation is acknowledged as an important asset and found to stem from stable and sound management. Good governance such as open communication with the government, the quality of board directors, transparent decision-making, and strict financial reporting were suggested to help maintain a company's reputation. However, the research showed no differentiation between the need for a positive reputation and company's size, structure, budget, and mission.

Lastly, based on the opinions of business students as future employees, Turban and Greening (1997) showed that corporate reputation is positively associated with employee relations, community relations, and the treatment of the environment. According to the social identity theory, future employees regard companies with positive social performance as more favorable and more attractive employers since employees expect to have more positive self-concepts when becoming their workers.

Media presence and media relations

Whilst most antecedents of corporate reputation are internal to the company, there are also salient external factors. Media presence and relations, for instance, have been considered important to the reputation building of companies. Media presence and relations refer to the exposure and connection that a company has with the press or other forms of mass media. The media themselves act not only as a vehicle for advertising or as the reflection of reality about a company's activities, but also as an agent who actively influences audiences' impression and information consumption.

In the past, the role of media presence and relations was found to be mixed. Media relations is positively correlated with corporate reputation (Dowling, 2004). Similarly, positive media presence such as favorable comments in newspapers has a positive impact on the impression formed in the mind of customers and employees of an organization. However, the extent of the impact may depend on other factors such as personal experiences or personal interest in the organization. That is, those factors can moderate the relationship between media presence and corporate reputation.

In contrast, Fombrun and Shanley's (1990) finding suggested that the higher the profile of a company and hence the greater the scrutiny of the company by the media, the worse its reputation. The negative effect of media exposure was unexpected and may be explained as follows: First, media reporters are only interested in the events that impugn corporate management. Second, the external public react negatively to all forms of publicity. Finally, only negatively predisposed evaluators rely on media accounts of firms.

In conclusion, the antecedent of corporate reputation in past research is multiple but only some dimensions have been empirically investigated. Economic determinants have been widely studied. However, researchers have tended to pay more attention to non-economic factors in recent years. Before ending this section, two observations can be made as follows. First, a company whose reputation is measured must be substantially known to its stakeholders to make the reputational assessment as clear as possible. Personal experience or individual contact with the company can effectively influence the impression which an audience ascribes to the company. Second, the communication channel or the way in which corporate audiences learn about the past actions of a company is assumed to be substantially effective (e.g. no significant noises or seriously false information) to allow the audiences to estimate its reputation as precisely as possible.

DATA COLLECTION AND ANALYSIS

Qualitative methods were employed to collect and analyze data for this research since the corporate reputation concept has been argued to be socially constructed and as a relevant phenomenon is still relatively poorly understood. Besides, qualitative studies could enrich existing numerical findings and help answer certain questions which could not be resolved solely on the basis of statistical calculation. An example is why many profitable companies are not as reputable or admired as some less profitable or even loss-making peers.

In the study, semi-structured interviews were conducted with ten experts including public-relations consultants and business executives; and a focus group was carried out with a group of six consumers. Thailand was chosen as the setting for this study because its business sectors share oriental values with those of countries in the same region (e.g. Singapore and Hong Kong) and the country has been recorded as being culturally different from western countries (Hofstede 1980; Powpaka 1998). Whilst by no means perfect, studying corporate reputation building in Thailand is expected to help enhance the generalizability of reputation theories and add insights into extant findings.

Respondents were asked to indicate their opinion on the definition of corporate reputation construct and its determinants. Each interview was tape-recorded and lasted for approximately 90 minutes. The interviews were transcribed and analyzed following Miles and Huberman's (1994: 10–11) suggestion. A coding scheme was designed based on literature and transcripts. Data were grouped according to relevant codes. Antecedents of corporate reputation were subsequently identified based on organized data and were compared with those obtained from literature.

FINDINGS AND DISCUSSION

Findings in this study simultaneously confirm and add more insight into existing research. In general, respondents were found to be hesitant when they had been asked about the meaning of corporate reputation. Most interviewees could not clearly verbalize the concept, but rather, describe its possible determinants. This is in line with several studies (e.g. Groenland 2002; MacMillan et al. 2002). According to Groenland (2002), for instance, Dutch respondents (consumers and business executives) could not provide a clear definition of the construct and rather describe the cause of corporate reputation than the abstract concept itself.

When asked about possible determinants of corporate reputation, Thai respondents pointed out many factors. Most respondents suggested that economic factors (e.g. performance, size, and corporate capabilities) are dominant drivers of corporate reputation, yet simultaneously accepted that non-economic factors are increasingly important as well. All of the determinants extracted from interviews are summarized in Table 12.1 and briefly discussed as follows.

In line with extant research, members of the focus group representing customers argued that service quality is one of the primary features they determine when they assess a company's reputation. Speed, in particular, is an attribute which firms must attempt to improve but they should not compromise it with critical factors such as accuracy and reliability. Focus group members discussed about these as presented below:

Member 1:   services . . . the services should be good.
Interviewer: What do you mean by "good"? How good is good?
Member 2:   Hmm . . . speed . . . the response of companies should be quick . . .
Member 3:   It should be as if some people are there all the time to serve us. Give us a free number to call or . . . call us back within 5 minutes after we leave our message. Something like these.
Member 2:   Don't make customers be irritated . . . don't let them wait and wait for answers.
Member 4:   I think we have to consider the accuracy and reliability of companies as well. For example, for consultancy firms, we expect them to complete their works quickly and accurately.

Moreover, a respondent also shared her working experience about the impact of product and service quality on customer expectation, which in turn affects corporate reputation:

I strongly agree . . . like our own company, we emphasize product and service quality. It's a matter of product and service excellence, whether

Table 12.1 *Drivers of corporate reputation suggested by respondents*

Drivers of corporate reputation	Explanation by respondents
1 Products and services quality	For a company (especially those in professional services), products and services quality (e.g. speed, convenience, accuracy, etc.) can affect customer satisfaction, which in turn can influence customer's impression about that company.
2 Firm performance (financial and non-financial)	A mixed opinion about the effect of financial performance on corporate reputation. Only certain stakeholders (e.g. investors and shareholders) may take into account financial performance in assessing a company's reputation. For non-financial performance, reputable companies usually are the ones that succeed in implementing branding strategies and other public relations policy.
3 Size	In certain cases, smaller companies (e.g. having fewer employees, small size of asset, etc.) may be perceived as less reliable or less credible companies (e.g. hospitals).
4 Corporate capabilities	If a company excels in something, its stakeholders will learn about this and spread by word-of-mouth.
5 Individual reputation (employee or customer reputation)	For a company, individual reputation of employees, executives, and customers can help enhance the overall reputation of that company (i.e. borrowing someone else's reputation). For instance, a company identifies itself with a celebrity customer in order to gain as much fame and respect as possible from outsiders.
6 Visual identity (uniforms, premises, etc.)	Beautiful premises and uniforms can enhance the reputation of the company especially those in the aesthetic businesses.
7 Environmental responsibility	Ensuring that the business operation reflects the company's responsibility about its environment.
8 Security	Corporate reputation can be enhanced when a company makes customers feel secure about purchasing products and services from the company.
9 Legitimacy (regulative and normative legitimacy)	Avoiding conflict of interest in any business deals and not breaching relevant regulations (i.e. attempting to attain regulative legitimacy). Additionally, certain practices such as quality assurance can help improve customer confidence in a company, which in turn can help boost its corporate reputation, especially those in the service industry.

your employees are really good at their jobs. Hi-end customers don't mind paying us premium prices yet they care about our services. They want to make sure that we treat them as special customers . . . provide them with quick assistance and give them any convenient choices . . . The product and service quality issue is important for reputation management

(Manager, a middle-sized hospital)

According to the interviews, two issues should be noted. First, the effect of product and service quality on reputation is complicated as it may directly and indirectly influence (via other factors such as customer satisfaction) the impression formed by customers. Second, the quality of product and service seems to mostly affect the customers, rather than other types of stakeholders.

Like product and service quality, firm performance was frequently mentioned by respondents to be a driver of corporate reputation. However, the extent to which it affects reputation may differ according to types of performance and stakeholders. For instance, the effect of financial performance on reputation assessment should be strong, particularly for groups of investors and corporate analysts, even though customers in certain industries (e.g. investment banking, insurance, hotel, etc.) also appraise the financial outcomes of their dealers when evaluating dealers' prestige. In addition, non-financial performance indicators (e.g. innovativeness, productivity, customer satisfaction) can directly affect financial performance and concurrently influence the impression of relevant stakeholders. In other words, there may be a mediating relationship between non-financial performance, financial performance, and corporate reputation. The following dialogues show the general comments of respondents about the impact of firm performance on reputation.

> Ok . . . in most basic, basic things . . . it reflects in sales and reflects in market shares compared to competitors' . . . it reflects in . . . umm . . . market capitalization relative to market valuation of competitors.
>
> (Vice President, a public relations consulting firm)

> Yes, I think being the market leader shows that we are a reputable company.
>
> (Office Manager, a public relations consulting firm)

> I guess it must have effects on reputation assessment . . . especially for shareholders since they actually care about dividend and earning per share. For investors, I think it's the same especially when they want to make a new investment. They usually have their eyes on profitable companies . . . I think that should be it.
>
> (Research Manager, a middle-sized hospital)

According to interviewees, corporate capability is another economic factor which can help shape corporate reputation. This is certainly true for service companies (e.g. hospitals, engineering consultants, management consultants, etc.) as they do not sell tangible products, but rather their intangible quality (e.g. credibility, reliability, and consistency) usually derived from various types of capabilities. Again, the relationship between a company's capabilities and reputation can be complex. A number of extant studies have shown that capabilities are positively associated with firm performance, which also can affect corporate reputation. Two experts gave their opinion about the effect of corporate capabilities on corporate reputation as follows:

> For our industry, I think the things that determine corporate reputation are . . . the degree of globalization, advanced technology, know-how . . . hmmm . . . and also the asset size.
>
> > (First Vice President, an international investment bank,
> > Thailand office)

> Well . . . this definitely has effects on corporate reputation. If we are competent about the things we do, then there should be an impact.
>
> > (Second Vice President, an international investment bank,
> > Thailand office)

Apart from economic factors, respondents suggested that non-economic factors (e.g. visual identity, social responsibility, legitimacy, and the reputation of individuals) can help shape positive corporate reputation. A respondent, for example, pointed out that a company can borrow its CEO or director's reputation to help improve corporate reputation. Another interviewee contended that even little things such as the color of employees' uniform, the sentences recorded in the answering machine, and the template of corporate emails, can affect corporate reputation. The third respondent also added that:

> When we talk about corporate reputation building . . . According to my research experience, it will first start from the fact that a company attempts to build its own identity. Then, customers or other stake-holders form the image about the company by looking at its corporate identity. As time goes by, the image earlier formed in the mind of stakeholders will be judged to be corporate reputation of that particular entity. From the viewpoint of marketing communication and advertising, I think we should get back to how stakeholders receive and interpret signals.
>
> > (Associate Professor, the school of journalism of a
> > public university)

In addition to corporate identity, corporate social responsibility and legitimate corporate actions were proposed to be potential drivers of corporate reputation. Interviewees emphasized that these issues have become crucial for the construction of reputation and gave comments as follows:

> Sure, it's a part of reputation building . . . as I told you about our global policy, if we want to make loans for any projects that have environmental impacts, we have to ensure that the projects pass all of our criteria.
>
> (CEO, an international investment bank, Thailand office)

> Umm . . . it's possible. It may be another factor that helps enhance reputation and brand for our local office.
>
> (Office Manager, a public relations consulting firm)

> I agree. Overall, I think it's now essential since it plays a part in reputation building. For us, we already got ISO9002 and started to prepare ourselves to apply for HA.
>
> (Vice President, a small hospital)

The fact that respondents pointed out the effects of legitimate actions and social responsibility on reputation is consistent with the tightened control by regulators after several rounds of corporate scandals. Besides, even though profit maximization is one main reason for the existence of companies, this reason alone is currently not justifiable since stakeholders are now more knowledgeable than before and tend to demand both good money and good governance from the companies.

In summary, the field data suggest that the drivers of corporate reputation are diverse. In line with existing research, economic factors such as firm performance and capabilities were suggested to be major determinants; whereas soft factors (e.g. identity, corporate social responsibility) were also noted to be as important as economic factors in this area. Business executives should attempt to manage both types of determinants to ensure the best outcome of reputation building and to avoid unnecessary crises as corporate audiences keep a closer watch on companies.

CASE VIGNETTE: Bangkok Nursing Home Hospital

The Bangkok Nursing Home Hospital, one of the first private hospitals in Thailand, was established by a small group of expatriates in 1898 under a Royal Charter from King Rama V. It has the primary aim of providing the best of modern medical care for patients from over seventy different countries. Today, BNH Hospital has been widely accepted throughout Asia as an excellent international medical facility, with some of the most complete and up-to-date facilities in the country. Its 110 years or so of serving both Thai and expatriate communities are further enhanced by its reputation and durable tradition of providing genuine service to all people.

From 1997 to 2001, the hospital encountered a financial problem which was mainly caused by the 1997 Asian Economic Crisis. Apart from undertaking a financial restructuring program, it devised a new strategic plan and implemented various marketing and operation strategies. Of all these, the strategy of reputation building was one which received serious attention from the hospital. BNH employed several marketing communication tools (e.g. promotional campaigns, advertising, and event marketing) to help project a positive image to its stakeholders. Quality of products and services, customer relationship management, and the reliability of the business process were among the most emphasized strategies of the hospital. Besides, a corporate visual identity program (e.g. redesigning its logo, refurbishing its premises, etc.) was implemented to further improve the hospital's reputation. In 2006, it was expected that these programs would contribute to the achievement by the hospital of an overall margin of 72,200 million bahth, up almost 250 percent on the 2002 figure.

ISSUES FOR FURTHER DISCUSSION

Mainstream research on corporate reputation has focused on the positive consequences of corporate reputation. Very few studies have explored the downside of possessing good corporate reputation. Discuss the potential disadvantages of a company having good corporate reputation. In what circumstances and to what extent could these disadvantages exceed the advantages of corporate reputation?

NOTES

1   In financial research, it can be argued that a company paying high dividend is the one which is profitable but, for a long-term investor, a company which has higher dividend yield simultaneously signals that its managers cannot find attractive investment opportunities capable of ensuring future cash flows. In other words, the potential for growth is diminished.

REFERENCES

Black, E., Carnes, T., and Richardson, V. (2000) "The market valuation of corporate reputation." *Corporate Reputation Review,* 3(1): 31–42.

Blazevic, V. and Lievens, A. (2004) "Learning during the new financial service innovation process antecedents and performance effects." *Journal of Business Research*, 57(4): 374–91.

Brown, B. and Perry, S. (1994) "Removing the financial performance halo from *Fortune*'s 'Most Admired' Companies." *Academy of Management Journal*, 37(5): 1347–59.

Capraro, A. and Srivastava, R. (1997) "Has the influence of financial performance on reputation measures been overstated?" *Corporate Reputation Review*, 1(1–2): 86–92.

Carmeli, A. and Tishler, A. (2005) "Perceived organizational reputation and organizational performance: an empirical investigation of industrial enterprises." *Corporate Reputation Review*, 8(1): 13–30.

Davies, G., Chun, R., Silva, R., and Roper, S. (2003) *Corporate Reputation and Competitiveness*. Routledge: London.

Dowling, G. (2004) "Journalists' evaluation of corporate reputations." *Corporate Reputation Review*, 7(2): 196–205.

Dunbar, R. and Schwalbach, J. (2000) "Corporate reputation and performance in Germany." *Corporate Reputation Review*, 3(2): 115–23.

Fombrun, C. (1996) *Reputation: Realizing Value from Corporate Image*. Boston: Harvard Business School Press.

Fombrun, C. and Shanley, M. (1990) "What's in a name? Reputation building and corporate strategy." *Academy of Management Journal*, 33(2): 233–58.

Fombrun, C. and Van Riel, C. (1997) "The reputational landscape." *Corporate Reputation Review*, 1(1–2): 5–13.

Groenland, E. (2002) "Qualitative research to validate the RQ dimensions." *Corporate Reputation Review*, 4(4): 308–15.

Hammond, S. and Slocum, J. (1996) "The impact of prior firm financial performance on subsequent corporate reputation." *Journal of Business Ethics*, 15(2): 159–65.

Hofstede, G. (1980) *Culture's Consequences: International Differences in Work-Related Values*. Beverly Hills, CA: Sage.

Long-Tolbert, S. (2000) "A conceptual framework and empirical tests of the antecedents and consequences of corporate reputation: a study of consumer markets." Ph.D. thesis, Ohio State University.

MacMillan, K., Money, K., and Downing, S. (2002) "Best and worst corporate reputations: nominations by the general public." *Corporate Reputation Review*, 4(4): 374–84.

Miles, M. and A. Huberman (1994) *Qualitative Data Analysis*, 2nd edn. Thousand Oaks, CA: Sage.

Orlitzky, M., Schmidt, F., and Rynes, S. (2003) "Corporate social and financial performance: a meta-analysis." *Organization Studies*, 24(3): 403–41.

Padanyi, P. and Gainer, B. (2003) "Peer reputation in the nonprofit sector: its role in nonprofit sector management." *Corporate Reputation Review*, 6(3): 252–65.

Powpaka, S. (1998) "Factors affecting the adoption of market orientation: the case of Thailand." *Journal of International Marketing*, 6(1): 33–55.

Radbourne, J. (2003) "Performing on boards: the link between governance and corporate reputation in nonprofit arts boards." *Corporate Reputation Review*, 6(3): 212–22.

Roberts, P. and Dowling, G. (2002) "Corporate reputation and sustained superior financial performance." *Strategic Management Journal*, 23(12): 1077–93.

Saxton, T. and Dollinger, M. (2004) "Target reputation and appropriability: picking and deploying resources in acquisitions." *Journal of Management*, 30(1): 123–47.

Sen, S. and Bhattacharya, C. (2001) "Does doing good always lead to doing better?: consumer reactions to corporate social responsibility." *Journal of Marketing Research*, 38(2): 225–43.

Shrum, W. and Wuthnow, R. (1988) "Reputational status of organizations in technical systems." *American Journal of Sociology*, 93(4): 882–912.

Turban, D. and Greening, D. (1997) "Corporate social performance and organizational attractiveness to prospective employees." *Academy of Management Journal*, 40(3): 658–72.

Weigelt, K. and Camerer, C. (1988) "Reputation and corporate strategy: a review of recent theory and applications." *Strategic Management Journal*, 9(5): 443–54.

Index

Page numbers in *Italics* represent Tables and page numbers in **Bold** represent Figures

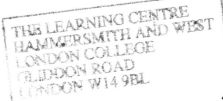